World of the Right

The contemporary radical Right is not merely a series of nationalist projects but a global phenomenon. This book shows how radical conservative thinkers have developed long-term counter-hegemonic strategies that challenge prevailing social and political orders both nationally and internationally. At the heart of this ideological project is a critique of liberal globalisation that seeks to mobilise transversal alliances against a common enemy: the 'New Class' of global managerial elites who are accused of undermining national sovereignty, traditional values, and cultures. *World of the Right* argues that while the radical Right is far from a unified political movement, its calls for sovereignty, civilisational orders, and multipolarity enable complex, strategic convergences with illiberal states such as China and Russia, as well as states and people in the Global South. The potential consequences for the future of the liberal world order are profound and wide-ranging.

RITA ABRAHAMSEN is Professor in the Graduate School of Public and International Affairs at the University of Ottawa.

JEAN-FRANÇOIS DROLET is Professor in the School of Politics and International Relations at Queen Mary University of London.

MICHAEL C. WILLIAMS is University Research Professor in the Graduate School of Public and International Affairs at the University of Ottawa and Global Professorial Fellow at the Institute for Humanities and Social Sciences at Queen Mary University of London.

SRDJAN VUCETIC is Professor in the Graduate School of Public and International Affairs at the University of Ottawa.

KARIN NARITA is Research Associate in Japanese Politics and International Relations in the School of East Asian Studies at the University of Sheffield.

ALEXANDRA GHECIU is Professor in the Graduate School of Public and International Affairs and Director of the Centre for International Policy Studies at the University of Ottawa.

World of the Right
Radical Conservatism and Global Order

RITA ABRAHAMSEN
University of Ottawa

JEAN-FRANÇOIS DROLET
Queen Mary University of London

MICHAEL C. WILLIAMS
University of Ottawa

SRDJAN VUCETIC
University of Ottawa

KARIN NARITA
University of Sheffield

ALEXANDRA GHECIU
University of Ottawa

Shaftesbury Road, Cambridge CB2 8EA, United Kingdom

One Liberty Plaza, 20th Floor, New York, NY 10006, USA

477 Williamstown Road, Port Melbourne, VIC 3207, Australia

314–321, 3rd Floor, Plot 3, Splendor Forum, Jasola District Centre, New Delhi – 110025, India

103 Penang Road, #05–06/07, Visioncrest Commercial, Singapore 238467

Cambridge University Press is part of Cambridge University Press & Assessment, a department of the University of Cambridge.

We share the University's mission to contribute to society through the pursuit of education, learning and research at the highest international levels of excellence.

www.cambridge.org
Information on this title: www.cambridge.org/9781009516105

DOI: 10.1017/9781009516075

© Rita Abrahamsen, Jean-François Drolet, Michael C. Williams, Srdjan Vucetic, Karin Narita and Alexandra Gheciu 2024

This publication is in copyright. Subject to statutory exception and to the provisions of relevant collective licensing agreements, no reproduction of any part may take place without the written permission of Cambridge University Press & Assessment.

When citing this work, please include a reference to the DOI 10.1017/9781009516075

First published 2024

A catalogue record for this publication is available from the British Library

A Cataloging-in-Publication data record for this book is available from the Library of Congress

ISBN 978-1-009-51610-5 Hardback
ISBN 978-1-009-51608-2 Paperback

Cambridge University Press & Assessment has no responsibility for the persistence or accuracy of URLs for external or third-party internet websites referred to in this publication and does not guarantee that any content on such websites is, or will remain, accurate or appropriate.

Contents

	Acknowledgements	*page* vi
1	A Diverse and Global Right	1
2	The Gramscian Right, or Turning Gramsci on His Head	34
3	Deconstructing the Global Administrative State	67
4	The War of Position: Towards a Right Common Sense	108
5	The Right World	144
	Bibliography	183
	Index	208

Acknowledgements

This book was made possible by the grant 'World of the Right: Radical Conservatism and International Order', awarded by the Social Sciences and Humanities Research Council of Canada (SSHRC, grant #435-2017-1311) in 2017. Our first thanks therefore go to the SSHRC for their generous support and for making the research possible. We have also benefitted from financial and logistical support from the Centre for International Policy Studies (CIPS) at the University of Ottawa, whose funding helped us bring the authors together for an intensive week of research and writing in May 2022. Special thanks are due to Anna Bogic, the CIPS coordinator, for her efficient and friendly organisation and facilitation. Our respective institutions, the Graduate School of Public and International Affairs at the University of Ottawa and the School of Politics and International Relations at Queen Mary University of London, have provided supportive and collegial working conditions. The final revisions to the manuscript were completed in the privileged setting of the Stellenbosch Institute for Advanced Study (STIAS).

Throughout the duration of the project, we have benefitted from the enthusiastic help of numerous research assistants. Charles Takvorian, Maxime Touchette, and Sébastien White joined us for an intensive week of research and writing in May 2022 and played a crucial role in getting the process off the ground. Their research and language skills, their detailed literature reviews, not to mention their energy and good humour, helped shape the book as a collaborative effort. Mateus R. Ramos joined us in Ottawa from the Federal University of Goiás in Brazil during the winter semester of 2023, and we are grateful to Global Affairs Canada who made the visit possible by awarding Mateus a grant from the prestigious Emerging Leaders in the Americas Program. Mateus helped deepen our understanding of

Brazilian politics and the country's place in radical Right networks, and we truly appreciate his dedication and insights, as well as his joy in experiencing snow for the first time. In the early stages of the project, Tulin Sehzar Ilayda Coruk and Sara Zaidi provided a comprehensive review of the literature on the transnational attack on liberal family values, abortion, and LGBTQ+ rights, which proved tremendously useful for Chapter 5. The same chapter was enriched by Oliwia Wasik's invaluable research assistance on the geopolitics of the radical Right, while Jocelyn Kane and Colin Kaduck joined us in the final sprint to complete the index in record time.

In the course of the project, we have tested our ideas at numerous conferences, seminars, and departmental talks, sometimes together, other times separately. The list of these events is long, and since we have endeavoured to write a relatively short book, we hope it suffices simply to express our deep gratitude to everyone who attended or participated in these sessions, whether in Canada, the UK, the US, Brazil, India, Italy, France, Germany, or South Africa. Every probing question helped us sharpen our argument and analysis. The ISA Roundtable in Montreal in 2023 where we presented the draft manuscript to a packed and engaged audience merits special mention. Thanks to everyone who attended and pushed for clarifications, and especially to our discussants Robert Vitalis and Dan Nexon, whose supportive and incisive comments significantly helped us adjust and finetune the argument. We are also grateful to the reviewers at Cambridge University Press for their insightful reports, to John Haslam for his interest, encouragement, and support, and to everyone at the Press for their work in bringing the book to publication.

Writing a book always incurs a lot of personal debts of gratitude. When six authors write a book, these debts multiply by at least a factor of six and risk becoming exponential. In the interest of brevity, then: friends, family, partners, parents, sons and daughters, cats and dogs, thank you all so much for your support and understanding, for keeping us sane, for making us laugh, and for still being there at the end of the project. We could not have done it without you.

1 A Diverse and Global Right

This is a book about the global politics of the radical Right. We started working on the Right in 2015, when the election victory of President Donald Trump was a vague possibility, an unlikely worst-case scenario. We had a sense that there was a 'World of the Right', a commonality to the various nationalist, right-wing parties and movements that were gaining prominence in country after country – that around the globe, the Right was not only ascendant but also interlinked. After the Brexit referendum and the election of Trump, the more radical parts of the Right gained yet further strength, in Brazil, the Philippines, France, Germany, Hungary, and Poland – to mention only a few. The formal political connections between parties, movements, and individuals were relatively easy to trace. They met at international gatherings such as the Conservative Political Action Conference (CPAC) – once a rather small gathering of American conservatives – organised summits, and bilateral meetings, and formed coordinated groups in the European Parliament. For all their emphasis on national identity, on 'America First' and 'Taking Back Control', there was an unmistakable international dimension to their nationalist, populist agendas. We concluded that despite the Right's diverse, dispersed, and divided articulations, it was increasingly necessary to speak of a globally interconnected Right.[1]

In the COVID winter of 2022, the less formal linkages, discursive resonances, and populist dimensions of this interconnectedness played out in the city where many of us live, when a convoy of trucks occupied Parliament Hill and the streets of downtown Ottawa. In

---

[1] Rita Abrahamsen, Jean-François Drolet, Alexandra Gheciu, Karin Narita, Srdjan Vucetic, and Michael C. Williams, 'Confronting the International Political Sociology of the New Right', *International Political Sociology* 14:1 (2020), 94–107.

freezing temperatures, the protesters condemned the Canadian government for its alleged abuse of power during the pandemic – and they did so in a language that echoed the critiques that the intellectual vanguard of the radical Right had carefully developed over the previous decades. As the so-called Freedom Convoy set up their noisy camp in the centre of a city not often the focus of international attention, they gained worldwide notoriety on social and mainstream media. Soon copy-cat demonstrations were organised in cities around the world, in Brussels, Canberra, Wellington, Oslo, Paris, and countless US cities. While the protests and the participants were diverse, the demands often incoherent, and the accusations frequently conspiratorial, they had one unifying factor: they all shared a deep disdain for the experts and the technocratic elites that had mandated vaccines and lockdowns. It was this managerial elite that was to blame not only for the pandemic restrictions but also for so much of what was wrong with the world. These views were repeated at 'Rolling Thunder Ottawa', a follow-up rally at the capital's National War Memorial in April 2022. One of the speakers at the protest was a man identified only as Daryl, a Canadian veteran who had served in Bosnia, Afghanistan, and Iraq:

> At my lowest, I began searching for answers to why I had to go do what I did in all those different countries, and in doing so I discovered who the real enemy of this world is: the elites, the ones who are controlling what we hear, what we see, what we read, our education system, our monetary system.[2]

This book seeks to explain how this recognisably populist vision of the world has become so widespread. Rather than a conventional political ideology, this is a form of thinking and speaking that promotes right-wing politics on a scale that is global rather than

---

[2] Matthew Lapierre, 'Police Outnumber Bikers at "Rolling Thunder" Ceremony as Speakers Evoke Memory of "Freedom Convoy" Protests', *Ottawa Citizen* (30 April 2022). 'Rolling Thunder' was also the codename for a US bombing campaign during the Vietnam War.

geographically confined and that is radical in both methods and tactics. To fight liberalism, it has turned the left-wing hero Antonio Gramsci on his head and engaged in a carefully crafted counter-hegemonic struggle. This is no mere posturing or the ephemeral operation of a thin ideology; it reflects a relatively novel and revolutionary intellectual orientation. This 'radical Right', as we call it, has developed an international political sociology with the power both to identify a common enemy – the New Class of international 'managerial elites' – and to mobilise 'the people' against it. These movements are not just national: in fact, the global is a crucial part of the radical Right's intellectual foundations and political strategies.

The political strategy of the radical Right is multifaceted, targeting diverse audiences via old and new media, through multiple channels and techniques of communication, at many different venues. Nationalist and populist in character, this strategy is also international because its populism seeks to unify socially and geographically disparate groups through specific understandings of their marginalisation by liberalism and globalisation. In Marxian terms, the radical Right strategy is to try to bring its existing and potential supporters to self-consciousness, turning them from analytically identifiable but political inchoate classes (or in the case of the Right, diverse social groups) *in* themselves to politically aware and active classes *for* themselves. A key to understanding the novelty and relevance of the radical Right is thus to appreciate both its transnational revolutionary impulse and its foundational precepts concerning the so-called liberal international order (LIO).

Grounded in the study of politics and International Relations, this book also draws on insights from other fields, including sociology and political and intellectual history. This multi-faceted approach provides a broad conceptual and empirical understanding of what otherwise often appears as a disjointed series of kneejerk right-wing attacks on the advances of civil rights, immigration, and other targets in the global culture wars. Like all scholarly approaches to these themes, ours is not without risks. Our intention is neither to over-intellectualise, nor legitimise, the actors under study, or to bestow them with an academic or scientific credibility that they often do not deserve. As scholars of right-wing politics, we always face the danger of being accused of normalising even the most fringe elements of those movements. Such risks aside, we firmly believe that to counter the rise of the radical Right and to achieve a less destructively polarised politics, we need to understand their ideas and their attractions for large sections of the population. This book is an effort towards that understanding.

AN ILLIBERAL INTERNATIONAL? MAPPING A GLOBAL RIGHT

The near worldwide rise of radical right-wing parties and movements has transformed not only domestic politics but also international relations. Increasingly, the threat to the LIO is seen as stemming not only from illiberal powers such as China and Russia but also from *within*, due to the rise of right-wing nationalist and populist governments and their domestic constituencies.[3] While the various nationalist personalities and parties – from Trump in the US to Jair Bolsonaro in Brazil and Narendra Modi in India, to Georgia Meloni's Brothers of Italy, Marine Le Pen's Rassemblement National, and Viktor Orbán's Fidesz – are far from unified in their ideas and policies, a globally connected Right is emerging.

One way to trace this interconnectedness is through the activities of CPAC. Established in 1974 by the American Conservative Union (ACU) as an annual meeting for US conservatives, CPAC has evolved into a series of global festivals for the Right, increasingly including the more radical parts of the movement. The first European CPAC was held in Budapest in 2022 and featured an opening address by Prime Minister Viktor Orbán, who declared that under his leadership Hungary was 'the laboratory where we managed to come up

---

[3] Alexander Cooley and Daniel Nexon, *Exit from Hegemony: The Unravelling of the American Global Order* (New York: Oxford University Press, 2020); Rebecca Adler-Nissen and Ayşe Zarakol, 'Struggles for Recognition: The Liberal International Order and the Merger of Its Discontents', *International Organization* 75:2 (2021), 611–634.

with the antidote for progressive dominance'. To replicate this success elsewhere, Orbán argued, conservatives must 'make friends'. According to him, their opponents, 'the progressive liberals and the neo-Marxists have unlimited unity', whereas conservatives squabble over the smallest issues. In order to counter the progressives' threat to 'the whole of Western civilization', conservatives must 'coordinate the movement of our troops, because we face a great challenge'.[4] The focus on international unity was even more overt at the second Budapest CPAC in May 2023, which met under the slogan 'United We Stand' and was billed as 'creating the liberals' nightmare: the international convergence of national forces'.[5]

Seeking to construct a unique platform for 'joining with our allies in North and South America, in Europe, Japan, Israel, and Australia', the two Budapest conferences did indeed bring together a large number of conservative friends, including congressman Eduardo Bolsonaro, a prominent figure on the Brazilian Right and son of the then president, who addressed the conference via video link. The Bolsonaros were no strangers to CPAC: Brazil has hosted its own annual meeting since 2019. The 2021 event was presided over by President Jair Bolsonaro and the highlight was a virtual speech by President Trump. Anticipating the defeat of Bolsonaro at the polls, the 2022 edition was a more subdued affair. It was nevertheless dubbed a 'conservative Lollapalooza', featuring former Trump spokesperson Jason Miller and several protégés of Steve Bannon, Trump's one-time political strategist. It also brought together right-wing personalities and politicians from across Latin America, including Argentina's Javier Milei, then congressman and now president, and former Chilean presidential candidate José Antonio Kast. In the words of Kast, 'For us it is very important to meet, to discuss and to get to know what the radical left is doing in different countries in Latin America.'[6]

---

[4] Victor Orbán, 'Speech at the CPAC on 19 May 2022', *Viségrad Post* (19 May 2022).
[5] The phrase is from the website of CPAC Hungary 2023, www.cpachungary.com.
[6] Nick Burns, 'Latin America's "CPAC Right" Still Has Big Ambitions', *Americas Quarterly* (15 November 2022).

The Latin American Right met again at the first Mexico CPAC in 2022. Bannon addressed the conference via video link, while Matt Schlapp, the chairman of CPAC's parent group the ACU, used his opening remarks to express his fear that Latin America's 'godless communism' would spread to the US.[7] Schlapp made a subsequent appearance at Israel's first CPAC in 2022, alongside prominent US conservatives such as the Ohio senator J. D. Vance and the media personality Ben Shapiro.[8] CPACs have also spread to Australia, Japan, and South Korea, with CPAC organisers in Japan pledging support for strengthening conservative cooperation within the so-called Quad (the strategic dialogue comprising Japan, India, Australia, and the US) and across the Indo-Pacific through the establishment of an Asia-Pacific Conservative Union, or APCU.

CPAC promoters are therefore not exaggerating: their events have become an important international stage for leading conservatives and provide opportunities to build bridges and cultivate alliances between right-wing individuals, groups, and political parties. The traffic in radical conservative ideas, policies, and personalities at these events is geographically multi-directional rather than uni-directional from the Euro-Atlantic to the rest of the world. Certainly, there was a great deal of fanfare about Bannon going to CPAC Japan in 2017, and about ex-United Kingdom Independence Party (UKIP) leader Nigel Farage and Breitbart News Network editor-in-chief Raheem Kassam appearing at CPAC Australia in 2019. But Jair Bolsonaro figured prominently on the 2023 CPAC programme in Washington DC, and the leader of the Japan Conservative Union (JCU) and founder of CPAC Japan, Hiroaki 'Jay' Aeba, also known as Jikido Aeba, has been a regular speaker at CPACs for more than a decade.[9]

---

[7] Brendon O'Boyle, 'At CPAC Mexico, "Orphaned" Right Tries to Build Home as Region Tacks Left', *Reuters* (19 November 2022).

[8] Zac Beauchamp, 'CPAC Goes to Israel', *Vox* (23 July 2022).

[9] Aeba has close ties to the religious organisation Happy Science. Graig Graziosi, 'Japanese Cult Representative Is Speaking for the 10th Year in a Row at CPAC', *The Independent* (9 April 2021). He flaunts his association with figures on the American Right on the JCU website; the JCU has likewise made hay out of Aeba's attendance of CPAC Hungary.

Attendance at CPAC meetings also serves to bestow legitimacy and an appearance of importance to right-wing groups that may be relatively marginal in their home countries. A case in point is AfriForum, an organisation that seeks to represent the white Afrikaner minority in South Africa. In post-apartheid South Africa, Afrikaner nationalists have struggled to establish a domestic political platform that is not tainted by their historical association with white supremacist power. But recognition abroad helps with recognition at home. When AfriForum's deputy CEO Ernst Roets spoke at the 2022 CPAC in Budapest, it was not only an opportunity to tell the world about alleged discrimination against Afrikaners in South Africa but also a way of strengthening the organisation's domestic visibility and legitimacy.

CPAC internationalisation is but one indicator of a globally interconnected Right. There are numerous other conferences, summits, and more or less formal networks and forms of collaboration. The Madrid Forum is of particular importance. Spearheaded by the Spanish radical Right party Vox and its leader Santiago Abascal, the Forum describes itself as a 'coordinated effort between different actors, from different ideological spheres, who share their determination to face the threat posed by the growth of communism on both sides of the Atlantic'.[10] The centrepiece of this transatlantic front is the *Madrid Charter: In Defence of Democracy and Freedom in the Iberosphere*, which has been signed by more than 150 politicians and activists in Europe, the US, and Latin America – including Italy's Meloni and Brazil's Eduardo Bolsonaro – and over 10,000 people worldwide. Through the Charter, Vox promotes the concept of the *Iberosphere* – in effect, a new type of 'imagined political community' that would bring together over 700 million people who 'share a deep-rooted heritage and possess a significant economic and geopolitical potential' based on a pan-Hispanic identity and

---

[10] Nathalia Urban, 'The Global Far Right Is Betting the House on Bolsonaro', *Jacobin* (19 October 2021).

Catholic faith.¹¹ Abascal and other Vox delegates have toured Latin America to promote and recruit signatories to the Madrid Charter, meeting with senior politicians in Colombia, Ecuador, Mexico, and Peru. In 2022, the Madrid Forum organised its first regional meeting in Bogotá, with delegates from the Vox party and right-wing groups from Colombia, Peru, Cuba, Venezuela, and Chile forming a transatlantic right-wing alliance.

Further indicators of a globally interconnected Right can be found in the National Conservatism (NatCon) Conferences, run by the Edmund Burke Foundation and its chair Yoram Hazony, author of *The Virtues of Nationalism*. Thus far, NatCon meetings have been held in London, Washington, Rome, Brussels, and Orlando, among other cities, bringing together hundreds of delegates from around the world. NatCon has attracted ever more high-profile politicians from the right of mainstream conservatism and has become a meeting place for a diverse collection of '"dissidents", "neo-reactionaries", "post-lefties", or the "heterodox" fringe – though they're all often grouped for convenience under the heading of America's New Right'.[12]

Countless right-wing leaders and personalities circulate within these other networks too. The US media superstar Tucker Carlson appeared at the NatCon in Washington in 2019, and with great fanfare took his FOX TV show to Hungary for a week in 2021. Marion Maréchal, the granddaughter of Jean-Marie Le Pen and prominent French politician, was a big hit at the 2018 CPAC in Washington, while Viktor Orbán is a regular star guest at important right-wing summits. Texas senator Ted Cruz addressed delegates at the VOX party in Madrid, stressing their 'shared values',[13] and numerous

---

[11] See Richard Sanders, 'Spain's Vox Sets Its Sights on Latin America', *World Politics Review* (14 December 2021). Robert Semonsen, 'Vox's Abascal Meets Bolsonaro to Promote Transatlantic Alliance', *The European Conservative* (15 December 2021).

[12] James Pogue, 'Inside the New Right: Where Peter Theil Is Placing His Biggest Bets', *Vanity Fair* (20 April 2022).

[13] Ishaan Tharoor, 'The GOP Alliance with Europe's Far-Right Deepens', *The Washington Post* (12 October 2021).

parties and individuals are strengthening their ties with the Likud party of Benjamin Netanyahu in Israel. These include the Hindu nationalist government of India's Prime Minister Narendra Modi, as well as Orbán and others from the Visegrad group of countries.[14]

National political leaders on the radical Right revel in demonstrating friendships in public and via public diplomacy. Modi has a long history of cultivating shared camaraderie not only with Israel's prime minister but also with Bolsonaro and Trump. In September 2019, Modi famously went to Houston, Texas, where he clasped hands with Trump in front of 50,000 people.[15] The same year he visited Bolsonaro in Brasilia, who in turn was guest of honour at India's Republic Day parade in 2020. Bolsonaro's Minister of Foreign Affairs, Ernesto Araujo, showered praise on India, suggesting that the country 'is modernising itself without giving up its traditions and values, and is being built from its roots and essence and not from the dogmas of those who form the post-nationalist or anti-nationalist world ... Only nations that recognize themselves as nations can aspire to be something in the world. That is the lesson of India and also the one that Brazil is trying to give to the world.'[16] More recently, Prime Minister Modi's attention has turned to Italy's Meloni, who was welcomed by Modi as the main guest and keynote speaker at the 2023 Raisina Dialogue, India's premier world affairs conference.

We must avoid the temptation to exaggerate the unity of the Right. At the same time, it is crucial not to fall prey to a search for national differences that effaces the international dimensions, and thus retreat into a methodological nationalism that sees claims of globality as sensationalist and even tending towards conspiracy

---

[14] Dani Filc and Sharon Pardo, 'Israel's Right-Wing Populists: The European Connection', *Survival* 63:3 (2021), 99–122. The relationship with Israel helps insulate leaders and parties from criticisms that they are pursuing anti-Semitic discourses and policies.

[15] Weeks after the 'Howdy, Modi' rally in Texas, a group of mostly right-wing members of the European Parliament visited Indian-administered Kashmir, whose 'special status' the Modi government had revoked earlier that year.

[16] Ricardo Senra, 'O encontro entre o "mito" e o "messias": o que Bolsonaro traz na volta da Índia para Brasil', *BBC Brazil* (28 January 2020). Our translation.

theories, denying that the global dimensions have any real significance.[17] The global activities and interconnections we have described certainly do not represent a unified 'right-wing international'.[18] They are often diffuse and diverse; divergences and conflicts are as common as convergences.[19] But they are not purely ad hoc. They represent strategic attempts to build transnational links, to spread and exchange ideas, and, perhaps above all, to gain exposure and generate energy and commitment. The highly mediatised spectacles of CPAC, NatCon, and other right-wing meetings serve not only to generate connections but also to perform unity and thus solidify the image of the radical Right as a movement with power, purpose, and momentum – a performative politics that can itself be symbolically powerful. They constitute a crucial aspect of what we call the radical Right's counter-hegemonic strategy, a performative politics of global radical Right networks. As the brief illustrations above suggest, simply dismissing the radical Right's global dimensions is increasingly unconvincing. Analyses that move beyond the national/international divide and its methodological entailments are essential.

GLOBALITY AND THE GLOBAL RIGHT

A core puzzle of this book is the extent to which it makes sense to speak of the international prominence of the radical Right as a *global Right*, as opposed to simply a simultaneous upsurge of a variety of national right-wing parties or movements that are primarily the

---

[17] See, for instance, the position of one of the most influential of these analysts, Cas Mudde, *The Far Right Today* (Cambridge: John Wiley & Sons, 2019); and the discussion in Mihai Varga and Aron Buzogány, 'The Two Faces of the "Global Right": Revolutionary Conservatives and National-Conservatives', *Critical Sociology* 48:6 (2022), 1089–1107.

[18] Logically, 'right-wing internationalism' can seem an oxymoron because the right is nationalist in nature but compare with Mussolini's attempts in the early 1930s to set up a 'Fascist International'. Jens Steffek, 'Fascist Internationalism', *Millennium* 44:1 (2015), 3–22; Kye J. Allen, 'An Anarchical Society (of Fascist States): Theorizing Illiberal Solidarism', *Review of International Studies* 48:3 (2022), 583–603.

[19] Clifford Bob, *The Global Right Wing and the Clash of World Politics* (Cambridge: Cambridge University Press, 2012), 5.

products of economic dislocation and inequality.[20] At the thinnest analytic level, the globalised Right seems a typical network phenomenon – a group of 'actors working internationally on an issue, who are bound together by shared values, a common discourse, and dense exchanges of information and services'.[21] Clearly this captures key dimensions of a globally interconnected Right. However, we suggest that the conditions of today's global Right require a wider rethinking of its relationship to the global in two ways. First, it is constituted by transnational interactions operating at multiple scales. Second, it defines itself and is co-constituted by its relation to the global, not just to the national.

Regarding the first, studies of globalisation have argued for decades that the domestic and the international are entwined in novel structures and power relations with crucial impacts on the relationship between the global, the national, and the local. These relationships go beyond the rise of networks or of digital media, important as these often are.[22] Contemporary global politics is not just a matter of connectivity between discrete actors who remain largely within national/international, state/society divides, nor are the local, the national, and the international neatly stacked on top of each other in the manner of conventional levels of analyses. Indeed,

---

[20] Numerous studies have stressed economic factors as the key explanation for the rise of right-wing populism within individual countries. While we recognise the importance of the economic, our analysis emphasises how disadvantaged groups have to be politically mobilised and how a particular conceptualisation of the global is a key part of the radical Right's ability to do so. On economic factors, see Dani Rodrik, 'Why Does Globalization Fuel Populism? Economics, Culture, and the Rise of Right-Wing Populism', *Annual Review of Economics* 13:1 (2021), 133–170; Eric Protzer and Paul Summerville, *Reclaiming Populism: How Economic Fairness Can Win Back Disenchanted Voters* (London: Polity, 2022).

[21] Margaret Keck and Kathryn Sikkink, *Activists beyond Borders* (New York, NY: Cornell University Press, 1998), 2. Also see Bob, *The Global Right Wing*; Frank A. Stengel, David B. MacDonald and Dirk Nabers eds., *Populism and World Politics: Exploring Inter-and Transnational Dimensions* (London: Palgrave, 2019); Owen Worth, 'Globalisation and the "Far-Right" Turn in International Affairs', *Irish Studies in International Affairs* 28 (2017), 19–28.

[22] Chenchen Zhang, 'Postcolonial Nationalism and the Global Right', *Geoforum* 144 (2023), 1–5.

they never were, and recent studies have drawn attention to the deep 'imperial globality' of the world, and the manner in which the global is partly constituted inside the national and the local, giving rise to new assemblages that both territorialise and de-territorialise.[23]

Our focus on interconnectedness thus breaks away from established, pre-defined categories of state, nation, and society, recognising their fluid interactions, profound relationality, and the co-constitution of identities. The radical Right, its conditions of possibility, its ideologies, worldviews, and sensibilities, are simultaneously global and local. Thus, the white nationalism of the US and the Hindu nationalism of India are formed in part through transnational dialogues rooted in narratives of race and civilisation that have their origin in colonial knowledge – transnational and transhistorical spaces unseen by conventional methodological nationalism.[24] Or to return to the example of events such as the CPACs, these gatherings are not simply new forms of radical Right networking: they are examples of what Julian Go and George Lawson have called 'contact zones or interstitial spaces' that span the national/international divide and bring together and constitute a range of forces whose power is magnified through their reverberations with each other.[25] As such, they illustrate characteristics of an identifiably global Right that requires a transnational historical sociology to be fully understood.

Second, we argue that today's radical Right is *substantially constituted*, not just structurally enabled, by its relation to the global. It is located not just in opposition to globalisation, but in an ideological relation to the global. Contemporary globalisation involves the construction of transnational structures explicitly designed to operate

---

[23] Tony Ballantyne and Antoinette Burton, *Empires and the Reach of the Global 1870–1945* (Cambridge MA: Belknap Press, 2012); Saskia Sassen, *Territory, Authority, Rights* (Princeton: Princeton University Press, 2006).

[24] Ishan Ashutosh, 'The Transnational Routes of White and Hindu Nationalism', *Ethnic and Racial Studies* 45:2 (2022), 319–339.

[25] Julian Go and George Lawson, 'Introduction: For a Global Historical Sociology', in Julian Go and George Lawson, eds., *Global Historical Sociology* (Cambridge: Cambridge University Press, 2017), 27.

across boundaries and create universal institutions of power and authority beyond national control. The global Right defines itself in diverse but recognisably resonant ways in relation to these structures of power. For example, it opposes (though not without ambivalences) the neoliberal project and its creation of new international structures and elite-dominated institutions insulated from popular pressures and national control.[26] While there are many diverse strands to these analyses, they all demonstrate an engagement with the global as a constitutive condition of a *new* Right. Most importantly, as we will show at length in Chapter 3, the radical Right defines itself in direct opposition to global managerialism and what they perceive as a new global elite. As such these movements and ideas are themselves constituted by the global.[27]

To develop a theoretical framework that can account for both the transnational resonances and the divergences of the global Right, we turn to recent debates surrounding the concept most often associated with the Right: populism. Populism is frequently characterised as a 'thin' ideology that posits a divide between 'the people' and a perfidious 'elite' but that lacks specific content beyond this basic opposition.[28] As a result, populism as a concept can cover a wide range of ideological positions – Left and Right, industrial or agrarian – and is adaptable to many different contexts. Yet despite its popularity, it is not clear that the idea of populism as a thin ideology can bear the weight it has been asked to carry. As Paris Aslanidis has argued, if

---

[26] Quinn Slobodian, *Globalists: The End of Empire and the Birth of Neoliberalism* (Cambridge MA: Harvard University Press, 2018); Ray Kiely, *The Conservative Challenge to Globalization* (New York: Columbia University Press, 2020).

[27] We are not suggesting that the Old Right, including its fascist forms, did not relate to the global. These positions linked their ideas to the impact of international economic, social, and political processes, including global trade, technology transfer, colonialism, migration, and a host of others. Even a cursory glance at the racial theories of Gobineau, the transhistorical assessments of Spengler, or the legal theories of Schmitt easily and quickly reveals the depth of their engagement with global dynamics; and far and fascist Right movements have a long, if uneven, history of attempting to organise internationally. These ideas remain important to parts of the radical Right.

[28] Cas Mudde, 'The Populist Zeitgeist', *Government and Opposition* 39:4 (2004), 542–63.

ideologies are comprised of core and adjacent concepts (liberalism, for instance, has necessary if varying connections to liberty), it is unclear whether in this very attenuated form populism is an ideology at all. How can an ideology, however 'thin', embrace substantially opposed concrete ideologies on both the Left and the Right?[29]

These limitations have led to suggestions that populism is better understood as a specific form of discourse, or a particular discursive framing, that retains the commonplace understanding of populism without getting entangled in the question of whether it is an ideology or not. As Aslanidis puts it, this reformulation yields 'a purely discursive definition: populism modestly becomes a discourse, invoking the supremacy of popular sovereignty to claim that corrupt elites are defrauding "the People" of their rightful political authority. It becomes an anti-elite discourse in the name of the sovereign People.'[30]

This understanding of populism can be traced to the work of Ernesto Laclau, who argued that 'a movement is not populist because in its politics or ideology it presents actual contents identifiable as populistic, but because it shows a particular logic of articulation of those contents – whatever those contents are.'[31] The populist form, or mode of articulation, in turn produces structuring effects that manifest themselves at the level of political representation.[32] In this discursive approach, the division between the elite and the people remains at the heart of populism, but both concepts are 'empty signifiers'. As Aslanidis captures the point:

> The populist form pits a certain "People" against a certain "power bloc", but both subjectivities are "empty signifiers", symbolic vessels filled with particular content depending on the specifics

---

[29] Paris Asladinis, 'Is Populism an Ideology? A Refutation and a New Perspective', *Political Studies* 64:1 (2016), 88–104.

[30] Ibid., 96.

[31] Ernesto Laclau, 'Populism: What's in a Name?', in Francisco Panizza ed., *Populism and the Mirror of Democracy* (London: Verso, 2005), 33. See also Chantal Mouffe, *Toward a Left Populism* (London: Verso, 2019).

[32] Laclau, 'What's in a Name?', 34.

of the political context within which they are invoked and the cultural toolbox at work ... It is those formal components of populist discourse that account for the – almost instinctive – affinity we perceive among the varying phenomena collected under the populist umbrella, while the flexibility of their contents explains the diversity of this ecosystem.[33]

For Laclau, these points are particularly important when one moves from conceptual analysis to political practices and strategies. What if, he asks, 'rather than a clumsy political and ideological operation', populism is a 'performative act endowed with a rationality of its own – that is to say, in some situations, vagueness is a precondition for constructing relevant political meanings?'[34] In this view, the 'people' in populism is never 'a primary datum' and populist discourses do not simply express some kind of original, popular identity. Instead, it constitutes the latter and seeks to bring it into being as a political force.[35] Populism is thus marked by a rhetorical performance, based on metaphor and analogy, containing a structure of basic oppositions. These oppositions do not require a pre-existing sameness or unity. Instead, populism emerges from the 'equivalent articulation of demands making the emergence of the people possible'.[36] Populism is a political practice of 'metaphorical re-aggregation', seeking to allow different groups to 'regroup themselves as equivalent differences around one of the poles of the dichotomy' and to see themselves as part of the same struggle despite the diversity of their social positions and specific demands.[37] In a case of popular opposition to oligarchic domination, for instance, 'the wrongs experienced by various sections of "the people" will be seen as equivalent to each other *vis a vis* the "oligarchy". But this is simply to say that they are all *analogous* with each other in their confrontation with the oligarchic

---

[33] Aslanidis, 'Is Populism an Ideology?', 97.
[34] Ernesto Laclau, *On Populist Reason* (London: Verso, 2005), 17.
[35] Laclau, 'What's in a Name?', 48.
[36] Ibid., 74.
[37] Ibid., 18.

power.'³⁸ Moving away from essentialist visions of classes and class interests in classical Marxist politics, this understanding of populism focuses on its generative practices and strategies. While Laclau and his followers focus primarily on its contributions to leftist politics, it also provides a particularly useful means of thinking about the radical Right and its transnational alliances.

As a form of political discourse, populism can be filled with various kinds of ideological content, whether these are from the Left, the Right, or variations on each. In an important contribution, Marlene Laruelle has argued that discursive views highlighting the ideological 'thinness' of populism address not only conceptual questions but also help explain the pervasiveness of populist movements today – a pervasiveness that reflects the postmodern and globalised conditions of contemporary social and political life itself. In her words, 'thick ideologies' such as socialism or liberalism 'are a product of classical modernity that may not be repeated. Instead, the post-modern world, with its inherent ideological fluidity, may only produce thin ideologies. As such illiberalism does not necessarily present a unified front with a coherent doctrine in its competition with liberalism.'³⁹ From this perspective, 'illiberalism' is, in her felicitous phrase, 'post-postmodern'.⁴⁰

The radical Right embraces these ideological possibilities. It accepts the 'fluid' or 'liquid' sociology of late or post-modernity that renders thick ideological uniformity less politically viable. But it radicalises this acceptance into new forms of willed tradition or modern values: a 'strategic essentialism' that (unlike liberal, Left, or many postcolonial uses of the concept) asserts the truth of these claims even as it rejects modernist views of objectivity. This paradoxical stance is difficult to understand if one remains inside the truth/relativism, modern/postmodern dualisms that dominated controversies

---

[38] *Ibid.*, 19.
[39] Marlene Laruelle, 'Illiberalism: A Conceptual Introduction', *East European Politics* 38:2 (2022), 303–327, 7.
[40] *Ibid.*, 309.

over postmodernism across the social sciences from the 1970s on. As Laruelle notes: 'Post-postmodernism ... offers an appealing context for thinking about illiberalism as a call for a return to modernity against post-modern values or to classic modernity against liquid modernity.'[41]

In the case of the radical Right, Laruelle argues, the content of these discourses (or what she refers to as a discursively reformulated 'thin' ideology) is illiberal – that is, it takes an oppositional stance 'to today's liberalism in all its varied scripts' and represents 'a new ideological universe that, even if doctrinally fluid and context based, is to some degree coherent.' We argue that the global is a crucial element of this framing. Discursive framings of the global provide content for the empty form of populist discourse for today's radical Right ideologies and are key conditions for the globalisation of those ideologies. This two-fold globality is vital and justifies – indeed requires – thinking of today's multiple and diverse radical Rights as simultaneously a global Right.

In our conceptualisation and analysis, this global Right does not require ideological uniformity, institutional hierarchy or even strong network ties. Its strength emerges in part from its ability to *articulate* connections between different agendas and positions. Strict functional or social equivalence – identical economic class relations or specific forms of cultural domination and subordination – between different groups or national settings is *not* required for clustering to emerge around analogically common oppositions to globalisation or the liberal international order. Recall Daryl from the demonstrations in Ottawa; his ready identification of the 'real enemy of this world' as 'the elites, the ones who are controlling what we hear, what we see, what we read, our education system, our monetary system' is part

---

[41] Ibid., 309. On 'liquid modernity', see Zygmunt Bauman, *Liquid Modernity* (Cambridge: Polity Press, 2000), and for an account of how the radical Right embraces a post-postmodern neo-traditionalism, see Jean-François Drolet and Michael C. Williams, 'From Critique to Reaction', *Journal of International Political Theory* 18:1 (2022), 23–45.

of an equivalence chain that situates his position in Canada alongside that of millions of other people around the world. Another striking illustration comes from fieldwork among a right-wing Afrikaner group in rural South Africa, where two supportive visitors from Tennessee explained their presence with the statement 'our situation in the US is the same as that of the Afrikaner minority. We too are a threatened minority.'

These are the terms under which it makes sense to speak of a global Right. They allow us to see articulations between and across national Rights, and between the radical Right and national conservatives. As Mihai Varga and Aron Buzagány have noted, we can distinguish between the radical Right – such as the French New Right, which is often anti-statist and proposes alternatives to the international order beyond the sovereign state system – and national conservatives such as Orbán, whose agendas are based more on national sovereignty and reform of the existing order and its institutions.[42] These are important distinctions; however, they should not distract from the ways that these different positions interact either directly or indirectly within the wider political, social, and cultural field. The multi-valanced nature of right-wing articulations makes the global Right hard to define, but it also gives it its protean nature.

Consider, as an example, how the 'Northeast European' version of the far Right, revealingly analysed by Rogers Brubaker, reverses religious traditionalist convictions and defends LGBTQ+ rights in the name of 'European' values of tolerance that it argues relativistic liberals have abandoned in favour of a multicultural ethos that refuses to defend them, lest it should offend the values of Islamic Traditionalists.[43] Here, the radical Right presents itself as the defender of the true Europe and Western (liberal) values and attacks contemporary liberalism for failing to do so. In

---

[42] Varga and Buzagány, 'The Two Faces of the "Global Right"'.
[43] Rogers Brubaker, 'Between Nationalism and Civilizationism: The European Populist Moment in Comparative Perspective', *Ethnic and Racial Studies* 40:8 (2017), 1191–1226.

Hungary, by contrast, LGBTQ+ rights are rejected in the name of a fusion between Christian traditionalism and nationalism that presents itself as the 'true' basis of European or Western civilisation. Despite their differences, both positions stress the importance of Western or European civilisation as a particular set of values, both are suspicious of Islam and seek radically to limit its influence in their societies, and both oppose the liberals that they present as threatening their societies and values. Analogously, powerful elements of the radical right-wing Hindu diaspora have mobilised anti-racist protests in the US to promote their visions of India as a Hindu community that excludes Muslims.[44] In India itself, the leadership of Rashtriya Swayamsevak Sangh (RSS) has voiced opposition to 'cultural Marxists or Woke' and the 'destructive, all-devouring forces' said to be hobbling India's rise.[45]

The result is not political uniformity, but neither is it nullity: each identifies with and seeks to advance the cause of the radical Right and weaken that of liberal adversaries, sharing some agendas and differing on others. Similarly, they generally eschew revolutionary violence and work within existing political institutions, engaging in counter-hegemonic struggles to radically reform them. Such counter-hegemonic action avoids the 'false dilemma between reform and revolution'[46] that bedevilled the Old Right as well as the Left, while simultaneously enabling a range of agendas that, despite their differences, advance the radical Right.[47]

---

[44] Ashutosh, 'The Transnational Routes of White and Hindu Nationalisms'.
[45] Quotes from RSS leader Mohan Bhagwat's speech at its annual 'Vijayadashami Utsav' event. NDTV, 'Cultural Marxists, Woke Only Want Complete Control', 24 October 2023. The RSS used similar language to dismiss a 2023 BBC documentary critical of the Modi government.
[46] Mouffe, *For a Left Populism*, 45.
[47] This unity in diversity is captured by the US white nationalist Greg Johnson, 'The North American New Right is not a political party or a party-like intellectual sect. We are an informal network that can overlap and penetrate all social institutions, including parties. I maintain contacts with people all over the globe who are involved in various political parties. They know where I stand. Where we disagree, we agree to disagree.' Greg Johnson, 'New Right vs. Old Right', *Counter-Currents* (11 May 2012).

In this book, we trace how the contemporary Right has succeeded in developing an opposition between a global managerial elite and diverse 'people' in multiple geographical locations. This takes many forms, but it is a key discursive structure that anchors the construction and mobilisation of the radical Right across diverse contexts. Uniformity, unanimity, conceptual precision, or centralised organisation are not required in order to craft such performatively loosely shared but still salient and impactful political identities, discourses, and alliances. The unity of the global Right emerges instead from diverse demands articulated in ways that allow its participants to see and feel themselves as engaged in analogically similar struggles against a common enemy. As we will show, within these articulations, African cultural nativists can make common cause with their analogical global allies – as is the case with the radical pan-Africanist Kemi Seba, the *éminence grise* of the French *Nouvelle Droite* Alain de Benoist, and the Russian radical Right ideologue Alexander Dugin. Russians and Iranians, Hungarians and Americans, Swedes and Japanese, Brazilians and Indians, and myriad other social groups and identities can find common rhetorical and affectively mobilising oppositions and affinities despite their divergent economic, cultural, and geographic positions.[48] Similarly, in one of the most striking shifts in recent political discourse, the concept of class – and particularly support for a 'forgotten working class' – has become a key signifier for the radical Right since it is no longer tied to the anti-capitalism of the Left but is defined in opposition to the New Class of liberal globalism. This helps explain why so many right-wing parties now explicitly fight for the votes of the working classes, linking culture, class, and economics within this structuring opposition.

---

[48] There has recently been welcome interest in these global manifestations of the radical Right. See, for example, Priya Chacko and Kanishka Jayasuriya, 'Asia's Conservative Moment: Understanding the Rise of the Right', *Journal of Contemporary Asia* 48:4 (2018), 529–40; Şefika Kumral, 'Globalization, Crisis and Right-Wing Populists in the Global South: The Cases of India and Turkey', *Globalizations* 20:5 (2023), 752–781; Roderigo Duque Estrado Campos, 'The International Turn in Far-Right Studies: A Critical Assessment', *Millennium* 51:3 (2023), 892–919.

There is an important affective, or emotional, aspect to this form of politics, but it is not reducible to emotions alone. Successful populist politics of this kind involves constructing, propagating, and adapting core conceptual oppositions across divergent groups and settings and engaging in educational and organisational initiatives that make this happen. It requires widespread attempts to inspire globe-spanning coalitions of forces able and willing to wage what Gramsci calls a 'war of attrition, trench warfare' against existing common sense. Such war by definition takes decades and requires considerable economic and cultural resources, as well as organisational structures and strategies.

Key right-wing thinkers – especially those associated with the so-called New Right – have, over several decades, theorised and strategically mobilised global economic dislocation and cultural resentment, developing a coherent sociological critique of globalisation. Drawing on the oft-neglected tradition of elite managerialism, New Right ideologues have borrowed freely from Lenin and Schmitt on the power of enmity, as well as from Gramsci and the Frankfurt school on counter-hegemonic strategies. Against the temptation to dismiss right-wing ideas as merely populist and by implication as lacking in ideological and theoretical foundations, we are thus faced with the more challenging task of engaging a position that has already developed its own international political sociology and incorporated it into its political strategies.

THE CHALLENGES OF STUDYING THE RIGHT

Studying the Right is fraught with challenges and studying the global Right even more so. To begin, there is a great deal of disagreement concerning what constitutes a satisfactory and all-encompassing definition of conservatism and the Right, the content of which varies enormously with time and place. Unlike other modern political ideologies, conservatism is not a rigorously developed and cohesive school of thought but a constellation of ideas, attitudes, and thinkers revolving around a series of historically situated rejections of liberal and socialist thought. Even its most committed chroniclers have noted that 'conservatism is inherently resistant to precise definition.'[49] As Karl Mannheim argues, conservatism '*is* a counter movement, and this fact alone already makes it reflective: it is, after all a response, so to speak, to the "self-organisation" and agglomeration of "progressive" elements in experience and thinking.'[50] Against the abstract, speculative tendencies of modern thought, conservatism emphasises the comforting immediacy of shared cultural conventions and self-evident truths. It affirms the importance of historical heritage, collective memory, and the concrete, situated experience of one's particular environment as the main determinant of political thought and action.

This does not mean that conservatism is necessarily committed to maintaining the status quo. Rather, it seeks to prevent the sort of abrupt and disruptive change sought by forces perceived to be of the Left and destructive of what conservatives at a given time want to preserve. Typically, it does this by insisting on the presence of forces (e.g., nature, God, biology, or history) deemed beyond human control, and that impose severe limitations on the perfectibility of the human condition. This preference for stability and continuity over disruptive change is often matched by support for more substantive political concepts such as hierarchy, elitism, religiosity, property rights, free enterprise, and state sovereignty – though naturally not all these are found, or found in the same ways, in conservatism's varying guises.[51]

---

[49] George H. Nash, *The Conservative Intellectual Movement in American since 1945*, Thirtieth-Anniversary ed. (Wilmington: ISI, 2006), xvii; for a massive recent survey, see Edmund Fawcett, *Conservatism: Fight for a Tradition* (Princeton: Princeton University Press, 2020).

[50] Karl Mannheim, *Conservatism: A Contribution to the Sociology of Knowledge* (Abingdon: Routledge, 1936/1997), 84.

[51] Compare Russell Kirk, *The Conservative Mind: From Burke to Elliot* (New York: BN Publishing, 1953/2008), 8–9; Roger Scruton, *A Dictionary of Political Thought* (London: Pan, 1982), 408; Robert Nisbet, *Conservatism* (Milton Keynes: The Open University, 1986), 34; Jennifer Welsh, '"I" is for Ideology: Conservatism in International Affairs', *Global Society* 17:2 (2003), 165–85.

The difficulty in trying to identify a more substantive ideational essence to conservatism arises from the fact that such concepts are open to a wide variety of interpretations and configurations, and they are also not exclusive to the ideological repertoire of the Right.[52] As Michael Freeden argues, 'to ransack conservatism for the substantive core concepts and ideas located in rival progressive ideologies, such as liberty, reason, sociability, or welfare, is to look at the wrong place'. Apart from the morphological consistency provided by its core commitments to organic change and the randomness and uncontrollability of events and human behaviour, 'conservative ideology can only display a substantive coherence that is contingent and time – and space – specific, because that coherence is created solely as a reflection of the substantive internal congruence of the rival ideological structures which the particular conservative discourse aims at rebutting.'[53]

These difficulties are even more fraught when we turn our attention to the adjective 'radical', as in 'the radical Right', a term that has circulated in sociology and political science since the middle years of the twentieth century.[54] Contemporary scholars favour adding – and debating – this and related adjectives (like 'far' and 'extreme') to the nouns Right and conservativism as a way of signalling the challenge of dealing with such a highly context-dependent, contingent, and often rapidly evolving object of study. We think the radical Right draws on a consciously traditionalist and reactionary anti-Enlightenment current that emerged as a response to the breakdown of pre-modern visions of political order underpinned by Providence. It developed as a distinct style of right-wing politics during the late nineteenth and

---

[52] See Roger Eatwell and Noël O'Sullivan eds., *The Nature of the Right* (London: Pinter Publishers, 1989).

[53] Michael Freeden, *Ideologies and Political Theory: A Conceptual Approach* (Oxford: Oxford University Press, 1998), 333.

[54] Seymour M. Lipset, 'The Radical Right: A Problem for American Democracy', *British Journal of Sociology* 6 (1955), 176–209. Telford Taylor, a US lawyer best known for opposing McCarthyism, used the same term even earlier. For further discussions, see Cas Mudde ed., *The Populist Radical Right: A Reader* (London: Routledge, 2017).

twentieth centuries in response to the rise of socialism and the perceived failures of conventional conservatism and bourgeois society to deal with the challenges of mass liberal democracy. As Jerry Muller argues, the 'radical conservative shares many of the concerns of more conventional conservatism, such as the need for institutional authority and continuity with the past, but believes that the processes characteristic of modernity have destroyed the valuable legacy of the past for the present.'[55] This leads to the conclusion that 'a restoration of the virtues of the past' requires abandoning the gradualist attitude of conventional conservatism in favour of a more militant, voluntarist, and programmatic approach that will command the loyalty of individuals and bind them together into an organic whole to a greater extent than existing institutions can be expected to do under present conditions of sociocultural decay.[56]

The threshold delimiting where conventional conservatism ends and radical conservatism begins is often ambiguous, not least because the relationship between tradition and authority determining this continuum of reaction can manifest in many different forms.[57] Contemporary political science suggests that the extreme Right generally refers to right-wing revolutionary movements that reject liberal democratic institutions and tend to embrace violence. The radical Right, by contrast, accepts democracy but is anti-liberal or illiberal in its worldview and transformative ambitions. These ambitions can be reformist or revolutionary in character, but the radical Right tends to acknowledge the importance of institutional means to attain and maintain power. Thus, according to this broad taxonomy, neo-fascist organisations and movements such as the

---

[55] Jerry Z. Muller, 'Carl Schmitt, Hans Freyer and the Radical Conservative Critique of Liberal Democracy in the Weimar Republic', *History of Political Thought* 12:4 (1991), 695–715.

[56] *Ibid.*, 697.

[57] Jeffrey Herf, *Reactionary Modernism* (Cambridge: Cambridge University Press, 1984); Göran Dahl, *Radical Conservatism and the Future of Politics* (London: Sage, 1999); Robert Toplin, *Radical Conservatism: The Right's Political Religion* (Lawrence: University Press of Kansas, 2006); Jane Coaston, 'When Conservatives Turned into Radicals', *New York Times Magazine* (31 October 2017).

Proud Boys, CasaPound, and Golden Dawn would typically be part of the extreme Right, whereas Lega Nord, Fidesz, the Rassemblement National (formerly Front National), the AfD, and Trumpism would be part of the radical Right. Yet as numerous commentators have pointed out, a degree of ambiguity inevitably exists in distinguishing the extreme and radical Rights.[58]

These ambiguities grow once we abandon the national territorial framing and expand the level of analysis to the international. Our study is concerned with the ideological terrain occupied by the radical Right in our present political and sociocultural conditions of globalisation and late liberal modernity. But it does so with the strong caveat that the politics and intellectual commitments of these movements and organisations often exceed and transcend the boundaries of established academic categories and conventions. The Right is an ideological space to be fought over, and we want to make room for this agonistic dimension in our analysis. Yet, at the same time, we argue that today's radical Right *also* contains a systematic and sustained philosophic enterprise that over several decades developed a narrative of globalisation that could equip a renewed radical Right with an analytic, strategic, and affective foundation for its return to political prominence, and even power.

To understand this crucial ideological revision, we must pause over yet another contested term; the New Right. While the label is often attached to the resurgent Right in general, it is more usefully restricted to the assortment of writers, publications, and cultural platforms with strong affinities to the French *Nouvelle Droite*. Established during the late 1960s by Alain de Benoist, Guillaume Faye, Pierre Vial, Dominique Venner, and other militant right-wing intellectuals associated with the *Groupement de recherche*

---

[58] For discussions, see Eatwell and O'Sullivan, *The Nature of the Right*; Cas Mudde, 'The War of Words Defining the Extreme Right Party Family', *West European Politics* 19:2 (1996), 225–248; Nonna Mayer, 'Political Science Approaches to the Far Right', in Stephen D. Ashe, Joel Busher, Graham Macklin, and Aaron Winter eds., *Researching the Far Right: Theory, Method and Practice* (London: Routledge, 2020), 17–31.

et d'études pour la civilization européenne (GRECE), the *Nouvelle Droite* took shape as a response to the rise of the New Left, the student movements, and the realisation that the post-war Right had seriously neglected the importance of cultural and intellectual activism in the maintenance and subversion of political power. Although it remained on the fringe of French political debates until the very end of the Cold War, the *Nouvelle Droite*'s efforts to move the far Right away from historical fascism and the violent anti-intellectualism of skinhead subculture inspired the creation of similar epistemic communities in Italy, Belgium, Germany, Sweden, and elsewhere across Western and Eastern Europe during the 1980s and beyond.[59] The first book written in English about the *Nouvelle Droite* appeared in 1990, indexing trans-oceanic dissemination of GRECE ideas.[60]

In the United States, a similar agenda has been promoted actively in more recent years by cultural enablers such as Greg Johnson, Michael O'Meara, Jared Taylor, Kevin MacDonald, Richard Spencer, and other ideological entrepreneurs gravitating around the publishing and media platforms of the Alt-Right, the North American New Right, American Renaissance, and other agents of white nationalism.[61] The New Right in the US is also closely related to the earlier development of the paleoconservative movement led by intellectuals such as Paul Gottfried, Samuel T. Francis, Thomas Fleming, Clyde N. Wilson, and Donald Livingston. Gottfried and Fleming coined the term paleoconservatism during the early 1980s in an effort

---

[59] Mark Wegierski, 'The New Right in Europe', *Telos* 98/99 (1993–1994), 55–70; Michael O'Meara, *New Culture, New Right: Anti-Liberalism in Postmodern Europe* (London: Arktos, 2004); Jean-Yves Camus and Nicolas Lebourg, *Far-Right Politics in Europe* (Cambridge MA: Harvard University Press, 2017); Roger Griffin, 'Interregnum or Endgame? The Radical Right in the "Post-Fascist" Era', *Journal of Political Ideologies* 5:2 (2000), 163–178; Tamir Bar-On, *Where Have All the Fascists Gone?* (London: Routledge 2016).

[60] Tomislav Sunic, *Against Democracy and Equality: The European New Right* (New York: Peter Lang, 1990). Prefaced by Paul Gottfried, the book was based on a political science dissertation the author, a Croatian émigré, completed in 1988 at the University of California, Santa Barbara.

[61] Johnson, 'New Right vs. Old Right'; see also Thomas J. Main, *The Rise of the Alt-Right* (Washington: Brookings Institution Press, 2018).

to revitalise the agency of the Old Right. The aim was to counter the growing influence of the neoconservative and neoliberal strains of conservatism that were also often designated as the New Right in the US and the UK at the time.[62] Elements of this New Right have for some decades now been among the primary suppliers of high-calibre intellectual ammunition to a wide range of agents and ideological forces challenging the prevailing liberal order nationally and internationally – from the Tea Party and the Alt-Right to Orbánism and Trumpism, and most recently, the National Conservative movement.[63]

Definitional matters are far from the only difficulties confronting the academic study of the Right.[64] In contrast to their predecessors, today's culture wars are globalised and social-mediatised – as well as fuelled by ever-greater sums of political money.[65] They are also shaped by the discursive shifts that have narrowed the space for the most explicit expression of sexism, anti-Semitism, Islamophobia, and anti-Black racism. Thus, rather than inviting their audiences to

---

[62] Thomas Fleming and Paul Gottfried, *The Conservative Movement* (Boston: Twayne Publisher, 1988); Joseph Scotchie, *The Paleoconservatives: New Voices of the Old Right* (New York: Transaction Publishers, 1999); Chris Woltermann, 'What Is Paleoconservatism?', *Telos* 97 (1993), 9–20; Edward Ashbee, 'Politics of Paleoconservatism', *Culture and Society* (March/April 2000), 75–84; Jean-François Drolet and Michael C. Williams, 'America First: Paleoconservatism and the Ideological Struggle for the American Right', *Journal of Political Ideologies* 25:1 (2020), 28–50.

[63] Timothy Shenk, 'The Dark History of Donald Trump's Revolt', *The Guardian* (16 August 2016). Gottfried is credited with co-inventing the term 'alternative right' (alt-right) with Richard Spencer during the first Obama presidency. See Paul Gottfried, 'Some Observations from the Man Who Created the Alt-Right', *Frontpage Magazine* (30 August 2016).

[64] Aurelien Mondon and Aaron Winter, 'From Demonization to Normalisation: Reflecting on Far Right Research', in Stephen D. Ashe, Joel Busher, Graham Macklin, and Aaron Winter eds., *Researching the Far Right: Theory, Method and Practice* (London: Routledge, 2020), 370–382.

[65] The term culture wars invokes not only political struggles over 'cultural' issues but also a Gramscian awareness of the role cultural institutions play in politics. James Davison Hunter, *Culture Wars: The Struggle to Define America* (New York: Basic Books, 1991). On the role of money, see Jane Meyer, *Dark Money: The Hidden History of the Billionaires Behind the Rise of the Radical Right* (New York: Free Press, 2017); Ralph Wilson and Isaac Kamola, *Free Speech and Koch Money: Manufacturing a Campus Culture War* (London: Pluto Press, 2021).

identify themselves with 'white supremacy' or 'the Christian West', contemporary radicals seek to mobilise support by using new terminology and rhetorical inversions. This helps illuminate not only the genealogies and recent popularity of the terms 'white nationalism' and 'the *Judeo*-Christian West' but also a reactionary rearticulation of seemingly centre-liberal discourses of 'not racism' and 'race neutrality'.[66] Along the same lines, we can see why an obligatory renunciation of racism is routinely followed up with a rearticulation of some of its key features under the guise of either evolutionary biology or 'cultural diversity'. For example, radical Right theorists often invoke 'the integrity of cultures' and 'respect for difference' in order to rehabilitate an ethnopolitics discredited by its association with the genocidal violence of the twentieth century, which they argue allows them to make a 'not racist' case against immigration, cultural mixing, and the cosmopolitan hybridity of globalisation.[67] However, even a cursory a look at the radical Right's opus reveals a contemporary segregationism alongside its claims to difference.

The study of the Right is further complicated by mutual suspicion between the contemporary academy and conservative movements. As scholars, it is probably fair to say that we are predisposed not to like right-wing parties and ideas. In fact, our structural position in the academic field gives us a habitus – a deeply sedimented set of expectations, values, and predispositions – that restricts our ability to engage and understand the Right and its supporters.[68] The feeling is reciprocal; for many on the Right, academics belong to the

---

[66] Daniel Geary, Camilla Schofield, and Jennifer Sutton eds., *Global White Nationalism: From Apartheid to Trump* (Manchester: Manchester University Press, 2020); Jelena Subotic, 'Antisemitism in the Global Populist International', *The British Journal of Politics and International Relations* 24:3 (2022), 458–474; Alana Lentin, 'Beyond Denial: "Not Racism" as Racist Violence', *Continuum* 32:4 (2018), 400–414.

[67] Alain De Benoist and Charles Champetier, 'Manifesto of the French New Right in Year 2000', *Telos* 115 (2000), 117–144.

[68] Pierre Bourdieu, *Outline of a Theory of Practice* (Cambridge: Cambridge University Press, 1977); Pierre Bourdieu, 'Participant Objectivation', *The Journal of the Royal Anthropological Institute* 9 (June 2003), 281–294. In the latter, Bourdieu talks about forms of 'academic transcendence' grounded in the post-Kantian metaphysical tradition.

liberal elite. We are part of the problem – part of the enemy. This situation has numerous consequences and creates what Arlie Russell Hochschild calls the 'empathy wall': 'an obstacle to deep understanding of another person, one that can make us feel indifferent and even hostile to those who hold different beliefs or whose childhood is rooted in different circumstances'. Instead of understanding, we settle for 'quick certainties'.[69] Didier Eribon captures this academic inability in his auto-biographical account of his struggles to understand – and empathise – with his own family.[70] Having left his working-class roots in Reims to become a sophisticated, suave Parisian intellectual, he could write eloquently about being gay in France, but not about being working class. The former would earn him academic and symbolic capital, the latter derision and shame. When his family, as so many among the working class in France, turned first to the National Front and then the *Rassemblement National* as the party that best represented their interests, Eribon is confronted with his own structural inability to understand their positions. As a member of the intellectual Left, he is devoid of empathy, structurally prevented from understanding. From this perspective, the problem with accessing the Right entails questions of ethics, politics, and reflexivity – the conditions of knowledge and our own social and political location in its production.

In seeking to take the radical Right, their ideas, and their supporters seriously and subject them to careful academic analysis, we are mindful that some might accuse us of popularising, and possibly naively legitimising them. However, we are convinced that it is essential to take their analytical and political strategies seriously. Not all radical Right schools of thought and movements – let alone all their members – share the views we trace in this book. But many

---

[69] Arlie Russell Hochschild, *Strangers in Their Own Land: Anger and Mourning on the American Right* (New York: The New Press, 2016), 5. For a sceptical view of Hochschild's call for empathy, see Katja Freistein, Frank Gadinger, and Christine Unrau, '*It Just Feels Right*: Visuality and Emotion Norms in Right-Wing Populist Storytelling', *International Political Sociology* 16:4 (2022), 1–23.

[70] Didier Eribon, *Returning to Reims* (New York: Semiotext(e), 2013).

do, and without an understanding of their agendas and global interconnectedness, any attempt to counter these movements will be less robust.

OVERVIEW OF THE BOOK

This book traces key elements of the intellectual strategies and ideological content of the contemporary global Right, their organisational and institutional initiatives, as well as the possible implications for global order. In Chapter 2, we show how the radical Right has turned to the Left's iconic hero Antonio Gramsci for inspiration and guidance on how to launch a counter-hegemonic struggle against liberal cultural and political domination. We argue that Gramsci provides a powerful way to understand the globalisation of the radical Right and show how many of Gramsci's core ideas, particularly those concerning cultural hegemony, historic blocs, and counter-hegemonic movements, have been self-consciously and strategically appropriated by the Right. We do so by tracing the European origins of this project and show the subsequent global spread and adoption of what radical Right intellectuals call metapolitics. This metapolitics provides the radical Right with a global sociological, ideological, and political framing, as well as a political economy with capitalism and class at its centre. It also provides a strategic direction that seeks to mobilise social forces produced and marginalised by liberalism and globalisation by bringing them to self-consciousness, turning them in Marxist parlance from analytically identifiable but political inchoate classes *in* themselves to politically aware and active classes *for* themselves. As we show, recent ideas about the construction of a Gramscian 'postmodern Prince' capture key aspects of what the Right has attempted, and often succeeded, in doing. The global radical Right does not consist of an overarching, universal theory, ideology, or objective that all adherents must subscribe to. Nor does it have centralised controlling institutions. Instead, these counter-hegemonic ideologies enable a range of actors and agendas to find common cause despite their different contexts and concerns. Radical conservative actors and ideas seek to construct transnational chains of equivalences – and at the most basic level, the global Right consists of powerful articulations and equivalences between political subjects that help generate significant political movements.

Chapter 3 provides a detailed analysis of global managerialism, the core ideological content of the radical Right's understanding of the world. In this view, the essence of contemporary world politics is not the age-old story of realist power politics, the liberal tale of progress through institutions, or the corrosive spread of neoliberal capitalism. It is instead the rise to power of a global liberal managerial elite, the so-called New Class of experts and bureaucrats. Detached and unmoored from their national identities and cultures, the interests of this elite lie in yet further globalisation and liberalisation, and work against the interests of traditional national values and local communities. Within this managerialist sociology, the unequal experiences of globalisation and late modern politics are not the unavoidable consequences of anonymous market dynamics or economic modernisation. On the contrary, they are the result of the actions of specific, identifiable agents and institutions that produce, dominate, and benefit from the system. This in turn provides the radical Right with a common enemy – the global liberal elite – which may have different faces in different geographical locations, but which nevertheless facilitates powerful equivalences and transversal alliances than span nations and regions. In this way, liberal managerialism is not only a central part of the radical Right's conception of the world but also the foundation and means of its radicalisation and globalisation.

Chapter 4 shows that the radical Right's initiatives have not been confined to the realm of ideas. Armed with a specific understanding of the deep cultural and social foundations of the liberal hegemonic order, they have diligently embarked on a Gramscian war of position, a patient counter-hegemonic struggle to change the predominant 'common sense' and produce 'organic intellectuals' who can critique the existing order and provide alternatives to it. While the most visible and audible part of this strategy has been their transgressive and often offensive use of digital communication and social media, these activities and their effects have already been extensively analysed.[71] We therefore focus on their equally important but often overlooked efforts to capture the traditional institutions of cultural and political domination via academic publishing, universities, and policy institutes. While diverse and uncoordinated, we argue that these various initiatives serve to create a new legitimacy and acceptability for radical Right ideas, explicitly rewriting intellectual history from a radical conservative perspective and reclaiming it from the academic mainstream. Through new universities and think tanks, their ultimate aim is to replace the liberal, woke, managerial, globalist elite with a Right elite, schooled in the critique of managerialism and critical of the overreach of liberal power and international institutions. This Right elite will then be able to reshape the world in its image.

In Chapter 5, we examine how these counter-hegemonic projects relate to other struggles for power in contemporary world politics and attacks on the so-called LIO. Drawing on recent literature on struggles for recognition within the LIO, we show how the radical Right has built powerful transversal, global alliances based on a logic and discourse of difference and diversity rather than claims to Western superiority. We illustrate this through an analysis of an emerging global alliance in defence of the 'natural family', which seeks to undermine the LIO's progressive family policies and replace them with a new normative global order that is both less liberal and

---

[71] See, for example, Christopher Wylie, *Mindf*ck* (New York, Random House, 2019); Patricia Ann Simpson and Helga Druxes, eds., *Digital Media Strategies of the Far Right in Europe and the United States* (Lanham: Lexington Books, 2015); Anna Leander, with Cristiana Gonzales, Luisa Lobato, and Pedro dos Santos Maia, 'Ripples and Their Returns: Tracing the Regulatory Security State from the EU to Brazil, Back and Beyond', *Journal of European Public Policy* 30:7 (2023), 1379–1405; Chenchen Zhang, 'Right-Wing Populism with Chinese Characteristics? Identity, Otherness and Global Imaginaries in Debating World Politics Online', *European Journal of International Relations* 26:1 (2019), 88–115; Jeffrey J. Hall, *Japan's Nationalist Right in the Internet Age: Online Media and Grassroots Conservative Activism* (Abingdon and New York: Routledge, 2021).

more sovereigntist. The radical Right's civilisationalism and calls for multipolarity also enable complex entanglements with illiberal states such as China and Russia, as well as states and people in the Global South. While the agendas of these actors frequently vary, they are unified in their opposition to Western dominance of the LIO and their desire for recognition within a more multipolar world order. The multipolar, civilisational world order envisioned by these alliances and the radical Right, however, is not anti-hierarchical and inclusive. It legitimises new differences and new forms of exclusion through its claims to cultural diversity. It can both contain and conceal forms of racism, anti-Semitism, and hatred, while supporting new forms of essentialism and exclusionary identities. It is also a more sovereigntist vision of the world in which these more exclusionary illiberal forces would be able to operate with fewer international constraints, be it in the Global North or the Global South.

2 The Gramscian Right, or Turning Gramsci on His Head

Few figures seem less amenable to appropriation by the Right than Antonio Gramsci. An icon of the Left and a key inspiration for 'critical' sociological and political thought and IR theory, Gramsci's ideas about hegemony and political transformation have long been taken as the enemy of conservatism in all its forms. This chapter, by contrast, argues that Gramsci provides a powerful way to understand the globalisation of the Right in part because many of his core ideas, particularly those concerning cultural hegemony, historic blocs, and counter-hegemonic movements, have been self-consciously and strategically appropriated *by* the Right. The near worldwide rise of the Right is in many ways the product of this 'Gramscianism of the Right'. Just as Marx famously quipped that the goal of his historical materialism was to turn Hegelian Idealism 'on its head', so the Right has inverted Gramsci.

This chapter examines the evolution of this project. To be clear, we are not writing from a Gramscian position in the sense of using a self-consciously Gramscian analysis to explain the Right or the crisis of the liberal international order. That would be quite a different undertaking from the one we engage in.[1] Nor are we blaming Gramsci or self-declared Gramscians for the rise of the Right, arguing that the Right is dominated by Gramscian ideas, or claiming that its thinkers and supporters are theoretically rigorous or authentic Gramscians. The Right's use of Gramscian ideas is much more promiscuous and often instrumental, and it is clearly directed

---

[1] For two explorations, see Milan Babic, 'Let's Talk about the Interregnum: Gramsci and the Crisis for the Liberal World Order', *International Affairs* 96:3 (2020), 767–786, and Gillian Hart, 'Why Did It Take So Long? Trump-Bannonism in a Global Conjunctural Frame', *Geografiska Annaler: Series B, Human Geography* 102:3 (2020), 239–266.

towards objectives that Gramsci and his followers would vociferously oppose. Nonetheless, we hold that focusing on its Gramscian dimensions reveals a coherence and an active strategic agency that is often overlooked in discussions of the Right. This in turn has profound implications for domestic and international order.

Below we sketch a series of themes or analytic principles central to Gramsci's exploration of social power and dominant, hegemonic political orders. We then outline how a Gramscian approach provided the radical Right with intellectual and political inspiration for how counter-hegemonic movements might successfully challenge modern liberal orders. Our analysis is not designed to provide a comprehensive or authoritative account of Gramsci's complex ideas. We seek instead to show how these themes illuminate key aspects of the thinking and cultural and political strategies of the Right – in no small part because they draw upon explicitly Gramscian inspirations.

HISTORIC BLOCS AND COUNTER-HEGEMONIC MOVEMENTS

Written largely from his prison cell in fascist Italy in the 1930s, Gramsci's body of work amounts to a comprehensive critique of the capitalist state and the ruling class. A central aspect of his thinking is the close interdependence between ideas, politics, and material production in historically specific structures of social power that he called 'historic blocs'. This analysis proceeds along three dimensions. He begins with the economic, with the mode of production and relations of class power and domination operating in a given historical epoch. These forms and relations of production, he argued, are systematically connected to state structures. Politics, government, and law express and ensure the functioning of economic structures and secure the interests and position of the dominant classes. Much of this followed relatively conventional Marxian tenets, but for Gramsci, social and political orders and their power relations cannot rest on economic and coercive power alone. They depend to a significant extent on the consent or co-optation of the dominated – the operation of what he famously called 'hegemony' – and it is this insight that has proven his most influential contribution, including to the thinking of the radical Right.

In Gramsci's quite nuanced account, it is a degree of consent and ideological consensus that prevents a major clash between the oppressors and the oppressed in any social order. To understand how specific orders and distributions of power and wealth endure, we therefore need to identify the components of a dominant culture that produce this consent: the values, norms, perceptions, beliefs, sentiments, and prejudices that support the existing distribution of material and symbolic goods; the institutions that decide how this distribution occurs; and the permissible range of disagreement about those processes. Culture in the widest sense as a complex of dominant ideas, aesthetics, and even modes of feeling is thus not an ephemeral superstructure mechanistically determined by the material base of economic production, as in the more classic Marxian sense. It is instead an essential, active domain that systematically underpins and supports social orders. To understand a historic bloc is to grasp the connections between the dominant forms of ideological, economic, and state power and the hegemonic culture. As he put it, if these

> are constitutive elements of the world, there must necessarily be, in the theoretical principles, convertibility from the one to the others, a reciprocal translation into the specific language of each constitutive part: each element is implicit in the others and all of them together form a homogenous circle ... For the historian of culture and of ideas, this proposition leads to some important principles of research and criticism.[2]

With this in mind, Gramsci introduced the notion of an organic 'spontaneous philosophy' that permeates society as a whole, and that

---

[2] Quoted in Kyle Murray and Owen Worth, 'Building Consent: Hegemony, "Conceptions of the World" and the Role of Evangelicals in Global Politics', *Political Studies* 61:4 (2013), 731–747, 733; original Antonio Gramsci, in Quintin Hoare and Geoffrey Nowell Smith (trans. and ed.), *Selections from the Prison Notebooks* (London: Lawrence & Wishart, 1929–1935/1971), 403.

is 'spontaneous' in the sense that it is not the result of any systematic educational activity on the part of an already conscious leading group but has been formed through everyday experience illuminated by common sense.[3] Consent and the maintenance of hegemony do not necessarily require active commitment by subordinates to the legitimacy of elite rule. Less powerful people may be thoroughly disaffected. At times they may openly revolt. But normally most people find it difficult, if not impossible, to translate the outlook implicit in their experience into a conception of the world that will directly challenge the hegemonic culture. Consent, for Gramsci, involves a complex psychological mixture of support and apathy, resistance and resignation. The mix varies from individual to individual; some are more socialised than others. In any case, ruling groups never engineer consent with complete success; the outlook of subordinate groups is always divided and ambivalent.

Nevertheless, the deep foundations of a strong hegemonic order mean that direct attacks on it are doomed to failure. Effective opposition must instead be built via a thoroughgoing understanding and critique of that order and the patient construction of ideas and diverse agents capable of confronting it successfully; the creation of a counter-hegemonic movement. Here, the battle of ideas is crucial. Since a hegemonic order is supported not only by common sense but also by organic intellectuals who produce, legitimate, and reproduce its ideological content, a counter-hegemonic movement similarly requires its own intellectuals to undertake a systematic critique of the existing order and provide alternatives to it.

These critical intellectuals and cultural actors must engage in another of Gramsci's most well-known ideas: a 'war of position' in which diverse counter-hegemonic forces operate fluidly to weaken the existing order and build the intellectual, ideological, cultural, and institutional foundations for the new order that will eventually replace the old. In this war of position, the task of the

---

[3] Gramsci, *Prison Notebooks*, 198–199.

intellectual strata is to analyse the structures of liberal power and modern domination, probe their weaknesses, and forge alternatives. But intellectual or cultural agents alone cannot produce a successful counter-hegemonic movement – they must be connected to wider social forces with the interests and, potentially, the will to challenge the existing hegemony. In Gramsci's case, this involved the long and multifaceted strategy of bringing to cultural fruition the Marxian goal of transforming the proletariat from an analytic or sociological class *in* itself into a politically self-conscious and active class *for* itself. In short, what was needed was not only ideas but also a political economy and a symbolic and affective sociology geared towards political mobilisation.

Although Gramsci remained in many ways wedded to the idea of a central guiding role for the Party in these counter-hegemonic struggles, he also developed the innovative notion of spontaneous struggles beyond any central, directing agent. In many cases, such struggles remain purely at the level of reactions against the existing order, and they are therefore unlikely to be effective.[4] However, spontaneous struggles hold the potential for something more powerful if that opposition can be given a more cohesive sense of itself and its situation, as well as an understanding of its adversaries. In such situations, diverse spontaneous actions can become part of movements with real political power. What appear to be spontaneous or purely reactive revolts (as support for right-wing politics is often characterised) may in fact be connected to a wider war of position that transforms purely reactionary opposition into something more coherent and powerful.

[4] According to Gramsci, 'It must be stressed that "pure" spontaneity does not exist in history: it would come to the same thing as "pure" mechanicity. In the "most spontaneous" movement it is simply the case that the elements of "conscious leadership" cannot be checked, have left no reliable document. It may be said that spontaneity is therefore characteristic of the "history of the subaltern classes", and indeed of their most marginal and peripheral elements ... Hence in such movements there exist multiple elements of "conscious leadership" but no one of them is predominant or transcends the level of a given social stratum's "popular science" – its "common sense" or traditional conception of the world.' *Ibid.*, 196–197.

A successful war of position thus contributes to the formation of insurrectionist movements against the dominant order without being the product of central control or direction. While these movements lack centralised leadership, they do not lack a logic. As Gramsci put it in an analysis of the revolutionary movement in Turin in 1920, the success of the rebellion

> testifies to the fact that the leadership given to the movement was both creative and correct. This leadership was not "abstract"; it neither consisted in mechanically repeating scientific or theoretical formulae, nor did it confuse politics, real action, with theoretical disquisition. It applied itself to real men, formed in specific historical relations, with specific feelings, outlooks, fragmentary conceptions of the world, etc. which were the result of "spontaneous" combinations of a given situation of material production with the "fortuitous" agglomeration within it of disparate social elements. The element of "spontaneity" was not neglected and even less despised. It was educated, directed, purged of extraneous contaminations; the aim was to bring it in line with modern theory (marxism) – but in a living and historically effective manner. The leaders themselves spoke of the "spontaneity" of the movement and rightly so. This assertion was a stimulus, a tonic, an element of unification in depth; above all it denied that the movement was arbitrary, a cooked-up venture, and stressed its historical necessity. It gave the masses a "theoretical" consciousness of being creators of historical and institutional values, of being founders of a State. This unity between "spontaneity" and "conscious leadership" or "discipline" is precisely the real political action of the subaltern classes, insofar as this is mass politics and not merely an adventure by groups claiming to represent the masses.[5]

---

[5] We draw these passages from Chris Banbury's exploration of the potential of these ideas for the Left. Chris Banbury, 'Gramsci on Spontaneity, Organization and Leadership', *Counterfire* (30 August 2012).

In Gramsci's analysis, the war of position is a thus long-term struggle, and its success requires the cooperation and coming together of intellectuals, cultural leaders (or influencers in today's parlance), as well as the masses. Merely claiming to represent the ordinary people in the conventional party-political sense is unlikely to overturn existing relations of domination but will instead simply reproduce existing common sense.

A GRAMSCIANISM OF THE RIGHT

Gramsci's strategic analysis of political transformation is generally seen as the intellectual property of the Left. It has, however, been effectively appropriated and in many ways actualised by the Right which has striven, and to a striking extent succeeded, in building a counter-hegemonic project along recognisably similar lines.

Evidence of this appropriation is not difficult to find and dates back nearly half a century.[6] Its historical origins can be traced to the French *Nouvelle Droite*, established during the late 1960s by Alain de Benoist, Guillaume Faye, Dominique Venner, and other militant right-wing intellectuals associated with the *Groupement de recherché et d'etudes pour la civilization européenne* (GRECE). Their aim was nothing less than the development of a 'Gramscianism of the Right', as Venner put it.[7] The *Nouvelle Droite* began as a group of young activists who broke from the older far Right and reinvented themselves as intellectuals and ideological entrepreneurs. Their agenda took shape as a response to the rise of the student movements and New Left counter-cultural forces that expressed passionate commitment to civil rights, free speech, and university reforms, as well as a deep

---

[6] Nor is it limited to the radical Right. For invocations of Gramsci in the discourse of more mainstream conservatives, see George Eaton, 'Why Antonio Gramsci Is the Marxist Thinker for Our Times', *New Statesman* (5 February 2018), and 'The Strange Afterlife of Antonio Gramsci's "Prison Notebooks"', *Economist* (7 November 2017).

[7] See GRECE Collective, 'Pour un gramscisme de droite', *Éléments* 20 (1977), 7–9. A rare early awareness of this move is Rob van Kranenberg, 'Whose Gramsci?: Right-Wing Gramscism', *International Gramsci Society Newsletter* 9 (March 1999), 14–18.

hostility to capitalism, colonialism, and all forms of authoritarianism. This was a 'counter-cultural' revolt insofar as its protagonists sought to completely reshape the cultural *Zeitgeist* in their own image, rather than simply providing an alternative within the existing cultural and political institutions.[8]

In the eyes of the *Nouvelle Droite*, the leftist radicals who undertook their 'long march through the institutions' after the protests of 1968 led the way not towards greater authenticity and emancipation but towards chaotic political anomie and the deracination of all cultural identities. At the same time, however, *Nouvelle Droite* members were deeply struck by the sophistication of the Marxist cultural theories sustaining the revolutionary fervour of students and workers. They realised that the post-war Right had seriously neglected the importance of cultural and intellectual activism in the maintenance and subversion of political power. The *Nouvelle Droite* found its mission in addressing this important failure. Instead of planning a political revolution or an electoral victory, its leading figures proceeded to establish new research networks and journals of ideas to renew the conservative critique of liberal modernity and forge sympathies in the realms of education, media, and the arts.

This self-conscious appropriation of Gramsci's revolutionary legacy marked a major change of tactics within the French radical Right, which until then had been guided by the 'integral nationalism' of *Action Française* philosopher Charles Maurras. Whereas Maurras insisted on the importance of decisive and confrontational political

---

[8] See Andrea Mammone, *Transnational Fascism in France and Italy* (Cambridge: Cambridge University Press, 2015), Chapter 5 especially; Michael Seidman, *The Imaginary Revolution: Parisian Students and Workers in 1968* (New York: Berghahn, 2004). For a conservative reading of how the Left has used Gramscian strategies in the American culture wars, see Angelo Codevilla, 'The Rise of Political Correctness: From Marx to Gramsci to Trump', *Claremont Review* 16:4 (2016). In a similar vein, Jack Snyder has suggested that the rise of the Right 'might better be called a rising, illiberal Gramscian hegemony' and that focusing on its 'ideology' is a 'more productive' way of analysing its dynamics; Snyder, 'Is There a Coherent Ideology of Illiberal Modernity, and Is It a Source of Soft Power?', in Burcu Baykurt and Victoria de Grazia, eds., *Soft-Power Internationalism* (New York: Columbia University Press, 2021), 274–300.

engagement, members of the *Nouvelle Droite* were convinced that a wide range of intellectual and cultural activities were preconditions for successful political action. Organised around the GRECE networks, they abandoned the extra-parliamentary militancy of the extreme Right to pursue a long-term strategy premised on the notion that all great political revolutions in modern European history were the actualisations of developments that had already taken place in the realms of thought and culture.

The appropriation of Gramscian themes provided the *Nouvelle Droite* with novel strategic insights and facilitated its attempts to blur the traditional distinctions between Left and Right in ways that could neutralise the polemical force of left-wing usages of Gramscian tropes. At the same time, it adorned radical right-wing positions with a certain revolutionary appeal and a new post-fascist intellectual credibility.[9] As Guillaume Faye recalls in his *Manifesto of the European Resistance*, this post-1968 *Nouvelle Droite* set out to selectively appropriate Gramscian ideas, focusing on the dissemination of cultural values, ideas, and mentalities with the aim of instigating long-term political change by first shifting the boundaries of acceptable discourse within society.[10] Gramsci was by no means the only left-wing thinker who attracted the attention of *Nouvelle Droite* intellectuals. Adorno, Horkheimer, Marcuse, Althusser, and Marx himself also became part of a 'counter-encyclopaedic' pedagogy of the Right designed 'to draw historical lessons by analysing the

---

[9] See the statements by Alain de Benoist, 'Ce que nous disons', *Le Monde* (29 September 1979), 2; Pierre Vial, 'Le GRECE et la Revolution du XXI Siècle', *Le Monde* (24 August 1979), 5. For analytical overviews, see Pierre-André Taguieff, 'La stratégie culturelle de la "Nouvelle Droite" en France (1968–1983)', in Robert Badinter ed., *Vous Avez Dit Fascismes?* (Paris: Montalba, 1984), 13–152; Vito Carofiglio and Carmela Ferrandes, 'Les aventures de la droite française et les avatars de Gramsci', *Mots* 12 (1996), 191–203; Anne-Marie Duranton-Grabol, 'La "Nouvelle Droite" Entre Printemps et Automne, 1968–1986', *Vingtième Siècle. Revue D'Histoire* 17 (1988), 39–50; Roger Griffin, 'Between Metapolitics and Apoliteia: The Nouvelle Droite Strategy for Conserving the Fascist Vision in the Interregnum', *Modern and Contemporary France* 8 (2000), 35–53.

[10] Guillaume Faye, *Why We Fight: Manifesto of the European Resistance* (London: Arktos Media, 2011), 190.

mechanisms that allowed egalitarian ideas to implant themselves so successfully in Europe during the twentieth century'.[11] But what distinguished Gramsci from other left-wing thinkers was the non-egalitarian potential of his theory of cultural power, along with the organisational lessons that conservative forces could derive from it in their struggle against liberal modernity.

Nearly three decades later, this strategic orientation continues to inspire the Right in France. During the 2022 French Presidential elections, for example, *The New York Times* observed somewhat incredulously that the two right-wing candidates Eric Zemmour and Marion Maréchal frequently denounced the liberalism of cultural institutions, particularly the media and academia. 'Paradoxically', the newspaper noted, 'they cite Antonio Gramsci, the Italian Marxist philosopher, and his theory of "cultural hegemony" to explain how beliefs expressed by the ruling class trickle down to become cultural norms. They have taken up the battle of ideas within mainstream institutions with zeal'.[12] In other European countries too, the radical Right regularly recognises Gramsci as an inspiration. The leader of the Dutch right-wing FVD party, Thierry Baudet, concluded his speech at a conference organised by the American Freedom Alliance with his own declaration of admiration for Gramsci.[13] 'Antonio Gramsci', he exhorted

> was a far greater revolutionary than Lenin ... he said that ... we shouldn't be merely taking over power as the Leninists had done in Russia because power can be toppled, revolutions can be

---

[11] GRECE Collective, *Dix Ans de Combat Culturel pour une Renaissance* (Paris: GRECE, 1977), 7; see also Alain de Benoist, *Beyond Human Rights: Defending Freedoms* (London: Arktos, 2001).

[12] Elisabeth Zerofsky, 'France's Far Right Turn', *New York Times* (5 April 2022).

[13] Baudet is no theoretical novice. His PhD supervisor was the English conservative philosopher Roger Scruton, one of the greatest influences on today's intellectual Right, particularly in North and Central Europe. Scruton's views on Gramsci can be found in his *Fools, Frauds, and Firebrands* (London: Bloomsbury, 2015). The influence of his conservatism has recently been given physical expression with the opening of a Scruton-themed *Café Scruton*, in Budapest. See John O'Sullivan, 'A Moveable Feast?', *National Review* (27 November 2020).

orchestrated, governments can change, but we need to get into the institutions of society ... he said that the electorate and power comes and goes like the tides of the sea. You have high tide and low tide and these are somewhat like the polls we experience with our several political movements ... But we need to get to the undertide ... the stream under the tides of the sea, the deep stream, where actually power can be institutionalized in a much more stable manner. And that's why I think it is so important what we're doing here. Because we're creating not just a political narrative and political alliances, but cultural and societal alliances.[14]

In Greece in 2013, the controversial right-wing politician and sometime government minister Makis Voridis justified the decision to shut down the public broadcaster with reference to Gramsci. 'While he was imprisoned by Mussolini', Voridis argued, 'Antonio Gramsci had plenty of time to think about the weaknesses of Communism. He soon realised that no political party can gain power without ensuring its ideological hegemony through ideological mechanisms ... We forgot how hegemony worked during the '80s and allowed the left's organic intellectuals and supporters to dominate ... and propagate a reversed reality.'[15]

The appropriation of Gramsci is also evident outside Europe. In India, the RSS ideologue Ram Madhav has made explicit connections between cultural Marxism and Gramsci, and joined the RSS leader in blaming 'cultural Marxists or wokes' for capturing the media and academe, and plunging India's educational, cultural, political, and social environment into chaos.[16] In Brazil, the maverick intellectual and

---

[14] Quoted in Tinus Sloen, 'Right-Wing Gramscianism: The Hegemonic Project of Thierry Baudet', *Digit Magazine* (29 March 2021).

[15] In a later speech, Voridis asked: 'Leftist propaganda: Why is it so successful? The answer was given by Antonio Gramsci. What is hegemony? It is not political dominance; it is possession of the state's ideological mechanisms.' Quoted in Salomi Boukala, '"We Need to Talk about the Hegemony of the Left": The Normalization of Extreme Right Discourse in Greece', *Journal of Language and Politics* 20:3 (2021), 361–382, and 369–371.

[16] Ram Madhav, 'Mohan Bhagwat Has a Solution for "Wokeism"', *Indian Express* (28 October 2023).

confidant of former President Jair Bolsonaro, Olavo de Carvalho, has been described as 'the Gramsci of the Brazilian Right'.[17] Carvalho, who died in 2022, provided his own idiosyncratic reading of the Italian thinker to explain both the previous dominance of the Left and the need to create a movement of right-wing intellectuals that would gradually transform the population's thinking. In *The New Era and the Cultural Revolution*, originally published in 1994, he identifies the Left's intellectual conversion to Gramsci's strategy as 'the most relevant fact in the national history of the last thirty years'. For the Brazilian Right, this means a patient struggle is needed: 'The steps are as follows: in the first step, it is necessary to create a movement of intellectuals who will intensely discuss the situation and create a kind of consensual diagnosis. In the second stage, money has to be collected to form a militancy. The third stage is the formation of the militancy itself. The fourth stage is penetration into society. How long would it take to do all this? Twenty years.'[18] On Carvalho's advice, a group of 'olavistas' obtained influential positions in Bolsonaro's government, and not surprisingly, one of their main targets was the university sector and its left-wing intellectuals.

In Argentina, the Right has long admired Gramsci and adopted a war of position in their efforts to counter the Left. According to Mark Osiel, Argentina's 'far Right' started reading Gramsci in the 1980s. He recalls the 'bizarre' experience of interviewing Argentine military officers in the late 1980s and hearing 'them quote chapter and verse from the same Gramsci passages one had pondered in graduate school'.[19] The newly elected libertarian anarcho-capitalist Javier Milei is also a

---

[17] Mitchell Abidor, 'The Gramsci of the Brazilian Right', *Dissent* (Summer 2020); Carvalho's connection to the American radical Right, including Steve Bannon, is explored in Benjamin Teitelbaum, *War for Eternity: The Return of Traditionalism and the Rise of the Populist Right* (New York: Harper Collins, 2020).

[18] Quoted in Marcus Vinícius Furtado da Silva Oliveira, 'Gramsci in the Garden of Afflictions', unpublished paper, 2022, 9; See also Camilo Negria, Rebecca Lemos Igreja and Simone Roderigues Pinto, 'It Happened in Brazil Too: The Radical Right's Capture of Networks of Hope', *Cahiers des Amériques Latines* 92 (2019), 17–38.

[19] Mark Osiel, *Mass Atrocity, Ordinary Evil, and Hannah Arendt: Criminal Consciousness in Argentina's Dirty War* (New Haven: Yale University Press, 2001). See also Donald C. Hodges, *Argentina's 'Dirty War': An Intellectual Biography* (Austin: University of Texas Press, 1991).

Gramscian of the Right. As he explained in an interview with Tucker Carlson shortly before his election, the Right has to 'wage a culture-war every single day – and we have to be careful because they [the Left] have no problem with getting inside the state and employing Gramsci's techniques: seducing the artists, seducing the culture, seducing the media or meddling in educational content'.[20] While Milei's aggressively neoliberal approach to the economy differs from many other radical Right positions, he is a committed culture warrior dedicated to the fight against liberal values and policies on abortion, gender rights, and racial justice. To this end, he has established ties with Spain's Vox party, right-wing leaders in Latin America, as well as the Madrid Forum that seeks to bring together right-wing parties within the Iberosphere.

In the United States, the evolution and influence of right-wing Gramscianism was articulated in the early 1990s by the prominent paleoconservative Sam Francis. Like the European New Right, Francis stressed the importance of adopting a cultural struggle against the prevailing liberal order. As he saw it, the problem was that although the conservative tradition had much to say about what it wanted to conserve and why, it provided little strategic guidance on how to achieve those ends. As a consequence, to 'understand how a politically subordinated and culturally dispossessed majority of Americans can recover its rightful position as the dominant and creative core of American society', conservatives needed to look to the Left:

> By far the most relevant figure on the left in the 20th century for this purpose is the Italian communist Antonio Gramsci, whose idea of "cultural hegemony" has facilitated the cultural revolution that the enemies of American civilization have pulled

---

[20] Quoted in Aleks Phillips, 'Javier Milei's Ominous Warning to Americans', *Newsweek* (20 November 2023); see also Uki Goñi, 'Argentina's New Leader Is a Snake-Oil Salesman with Extreme Views on Abortion, Gay Rights and More. I Fear for My Country', *The Guardian* (21 November 2023). According to reports, the Milei–Carlson interview was watched 420 million times after being mentioned by Elon Musk on X. William Callison, 'Milei's Chainsaw', *Sidecar* (5 October 2023).

off in the last half century. I do not claim that Gramsci's ideas were consciously followed by those who seized cultural power in the United States – indeed, the beginnings of the cultural revolution of the left long predated Gramsci's influence – but it is true that the process by which that revolution occurred resembled the strategic and tactical ideas that Gramsci later articulated. Besides, most successful revolutionaries possess an instinctive understanding of these ideas and know how to apply them. If the cultural right in the United States is to take back its culture from those who have usurped it, it will find a study of Gramsci's ideas rewarding.[21]

The most important of these ideas involved cultural hegemony. Conservatives, Francis argued, have ceded control of cultural institutions, products, and power to liberal elites. As a result, even when they achieve electoral success, conservatives fail to exercise real political power. 'What is important to understand about Gramsci's strategy of cultural hegemony', Francis explained, is 'first, that it recognizes that political power is ultimately dependent on cultural power – that human beings obey because they share, perhaps unconsciously, many of the assumptions, values, and goals of those who are giving them orders – and, second, that in order to challenge the dominance of any established authority, it is necessary to construct a countervailing cultural establishment, a "counter-hegemony" (or, as the New Left called it, a "counterculture") that is independent of the dominant cultural apparatus and is able to generate its own system of beliefs'.[22]

Francis was not alone. Andrew Breitbart, whose eponymous website Breitbart News played so important a role in the early rise of the Alt-Right and Donald Trump, similarly accorded an important place to Gramsci in his belief that 'politics is downstream from culture' and his attacks on the hegemony of the Left's

---

[21] Samuel T. Francis, 'Principalities and Power', *Chronicles* (December 1991), 9–11.
[22] Samuel T. Francis, 'Winning the Culture Wars', *Chronicles* (December 1993), 2.

'cultural Marxism'.[23] Breitbart's even more famous and influential protégé and collaborator, Steve Bannon, adopts a similar position when discussing his desire to 'deconstruct the administrative state' – an idea whose genealogy and centrality we trace in the next chapter.[24]

METAPOLITICS

These diverse calls to cultural arms provide a useful framing for understanding wider intellectual moves on the Right, which can be read in terms of Gramsci's tripartite focus on philosophy, politics, and economics. Their stress on philosophy is most strikingly illustrated in the intense engagement with what Alain de Benoist, the key intellectual figure in the French *Nouvelle Droite*, labelled 'metapolitics': the need for a deep critique of modernity in general, and of liberalism in particular, as part of a wider project of intellectual and cultural counter-hegemony.[25] Although culture and its relationship to political power played a major role in the philosophy of the counter-Enlightenment, de Benoist and his GRECE colleagues believed that the post-war Right had seriously neglected this relationship. In its obsession with fighting communism, it had come to embrace the free-market catechism of the United States, along with its consumerist culture of cheap entertainment and technological fetishism. By contrast, the *Nouvelle Droite* undertook a wide-ranging re-evaluation and critique of modernity, including a modulated scepticism towards capitalism. At the heart of this critique lie several interrelated themes – most notably, the commercialisation of culture

---

[23] See Andrew Breitbart, *Righteous Indignation: Excuse Me While I Save the World* (New York: Grand Central Publishing, 2011) and Leif Weatherby, 'Politics Is Downstream from Culture, Part 2: Hegel to Obama', *The Hedgehog Review* (18 April 2017).
[24] An intriguing reading of Bannon's and the Right's use of Marxian political strategies is Cihan Tuğal, 'The Counter-Revolution's Long March: The American Right's Shift from Primitive to Advanced Leninism', *Critical Sociology* 46:3 (2020), 343–358.
[25] Alain de Benoist, 'The European New Right Forty Years Later: Tomislav Sunic's against Democracy and Equality', *The Occidental Quarterly* 9:1 (2009), 61–74.

by the consumerist society and the danger of uniformity.[26] Speaking in no uncertain terms about the dangers of importing free-market cultural institutions such as Disneyland, de Benoist called for Europe to move away from the United States. In his words, 'cultural war has been declared'.[27]

The *Nouvelle Droite* theorists channelled this strategy in different ways. Collectively, however, they shared the conviction that the cultural revolutions of the 1960s had succeeded in politicising all areas of human activity; that parliamentary debates and government policies would from now on merely confirm the results of the culture wars; and that the egalitarian principles of the Left had become hegemonic in practically all civil society, state, and international institutions.[28] Under these conditions, members of the *Nouvelle Droite* concluded that the only viable strategy to challenge the 'cultural power' of its adversaries was to provide a critique of ideology that turned the Left's own methods against it. The aim was to 'de-naturalise' the egalitarian categories and universalist claims of the Left, and reshape public debates on a theoretical meta-level by re-articulating the ideas, concepts, and meanings which people use to make sense of and define the world around them.[29]

---

[26] Alain de Benoist, 'Une remise en cause salutaire des valeurs marchandes', *Éléments* 66 (September/October 1989); Paul Masquelier, 'Le capitalisme aime habiller les jeunes', *Éléments* 115 (Winter 2004–2005), 40–44.

[27] Alain de Benoist, 'Vers l'indépendence. Pour une Europe souveraine et liberée de blocs', in *Le Défi de Disneyland. Actes du 20e Colloque National de la Revue Éléments* (Paris: Le Labyrinthe, 1987), 94–95.

[28] GRECE Collective, *Dix Ans de Combat Culturel pour une Renaissance*.

[29] As de Benoist declared on behalf of the GRECE collective in 1977: 'We are convinced that the only way of fighting the subversion that is presently taking place in all spheres of the social structure is to provide a worldview which deprives this subversion of all its appeals ... Our metapolitical action on society responds to the "cultural power" of the Left by developing a counter-cultural power based on the same characteristics, the same strategy and ambitions.' De Benoist was writing under the pseudonym Robert de Herte, 'La "Revolution Conservatrice"', *Éléments* 20 (1977), 3. Our translation. See also GRECE Collective, 'Pour un gramscisme de droite', *Éléments* (1982); Alain de Benoist, 'Le pouvoir culturel', in *Les Idées à l'Endroit* (Paris: Editions Libres-Hallier, 1979), 250–259; Pierre Vial, *Pour une Renaissance Culturelle: Le GRECE Prend la Parole* (Paris: Copernic, 1979); Marco Tarchi, 'Italie: Une nouvelle droite pour aller plus loin', *Totalité* 11 (1980), 39–46.

These metapolitical endeavours take many forms, ranging from philology and the esoteric to the more conventionally philosophic. They are far from unified, and many are in respects conceptually at odds with one another.[30] Their diversity, and at times incoherence, should not however deflect from their more basic strategic orientation and political objectives, for these are rarely abstract scholarly endeavours alone. Instead, they aim to provide the bases for a thoroughgoing critique of liberal modernity so as to reveal the deep and powerful interconnections between thought, culture, and power that underpin liberal domination – and in so doing, provide the means of resisting and gradually overturning it.

In the major ideological realignments of the 1970s, metapolitics became a key resource in reorienting the radical Right away from its association with historical fascism and the violent anti-intellectualism of skinhead subculture. The *Nouvelle Droite* instead pointed to the more ambiguous constellation of interwar philosophical explorations and anti-liberal political experimentations that has come to be known as the German Conservative Revolution as its main ideological forebearers.[31] By the 1980s, the strategy had inspired the creation of similar movements in Italy, Belgium, Germany, and other countries across Western Europe.[32] The further expansion of those networks across

---

[30] See, for instance, Matthew Rose, *A World after Liberalism: Philosophers of the New Right* (New Haven: Yale University Press, 2021) and Mark Sedgwick ed., *Key Thinkers of the Radical Right* (Oxford: Oxford University Press, 2019).

[31] Some of the most well-known representatives of the Conservative Revolution include Oswald Spengler, Carl Schmitt, Arthur Moeller van den Bruck, Ernst Jünger, Hans Freyer, and Ernst Niekisch. Despite important differences, what those thinkers had in common was the belief that conventional efforts to regenerate the legacy of the ancient regime had failed and that efforts to build a conservative non-liberal alternative had to radicalise and transform – rather than reject – the aesthetic voluntarism of modernity. On the New Right and the German conservative revolution, see Sunic, *Against Democracy and Equality*, 75–82; Michael O'Meara, *New Culture, New Right: Anti-Liberalism in Postmodern Europe* (London: Arktos, 2013), 46–50; Troy Southgate, *Tradition and Revolution: Collected Writings of Troy Southgate* (London: Arktos, 2011); Armin Mohler, *The Conservative Revolution in Germany* (Whitefish, MT: Washington Summit Publishers, 1950/2018).

[32] On the Europeanisation of the New Right, see Mark Wegierski, 'The New Right in Europe', *Telos* 98–99 (1993), 55–69; O'Meara, *New Culture, New Right*; Eva

Scandinavia, Eastern Europe, and Russia after the end of the Cold War in turn led to the development of a significant transnational network of publications, publishing companies, study groups, conferences, front organisations, and online platforms that make up what participants and observers today simply call the European New Right. We trace a number of these initiatives further in Chapter 4.

In the United States, the emergence and consolidation of a similar metapolitical agenda is again closely linked to the historical development of the paleoconservative movement led by intellectuals like Paul Gottfried, Thomas Fleming, and Sam Francis. The term paleoconservatism emerged and gained traction during the mid-1980s, designating a diverse group of traditional conservatives dissatisfied with the growing influence within the Republican establishment of neoconservative and neoliberal strains of conservatism that were often at the time designated as the New Right.[33] For paleoconservatives, these developments were symptomatic of the moral and political degeneration of the American conservative movement itself, which they believed had wholeheartedly embraced the hedonistic commercial culture of late-modern capitalism while accommodating the political correctness of the Left and dismissing traditional conservative positions as political liabilities.[34]

Gianoncelli, 'The Unification of the "New Right"? On Europe, Identity Politics and Reactionary Ideologies', *New Perspectives* 29:4 (2021), 364–375. See also Franco Sacchi, 'The Italian New Right, *Telos* 98–99 (1993), 71–80; Marina Peunova, 'An Eastern Incarnation of the European New Right: Aleksandr Panarin and New Eurasianist Discourse in Contemporary Russia', *Journal of Contemporary European Studies* 16:3 (2008), 407–419; Volker Weiss, *Die Autoritäre Revolte: Die Neue Rechte und der Untergang des Abendlandes* (Stuttgart: Klett-Cotta Verlag, 2017); Sumi Somaskanda, 'A New, New Right Rises in Germany', *The Atlantic* (22 June 2017).

[33] Thomas Fleming and Paul Gottfried, *The Conservative Movement* (Boston: Twayne Publisher, 1988); Joseph Scotchie, *The Paleoconservatives: New Voices of the Old Right* (New York: Transaction Publishers, 1999); Jean-François Drolet and Michael C. Williams, 'America First: Paleoconservatism and the Ideological Struggle for the American Right', *Journal of Political Ideologies* 25:1 (2019), 28–50.

[34] See Paul Gottfried and Richard Spencer, *The Great Purge: The Deformation of the Conservative Movement* (Washington, DC: Washington Summit Publishers, 2015); Samuel T. Francis, 'The Paleo Persuasion', *The American Conservative* (12 December 2002).

Long before Trump, paleoconservatives predicted and sought to foment a populist revolt that would radicalise conservative positions in the domestic and global culture wars. They saw the first glimmers of this revolt in Pat Buchanan's 'America First' challenge to the incumbent President George H.W. Bush in the presidential primaries of 1992.[35] The aim was not so much a return to classical conservatism as the creation of a New Fusionism that would combine traditionalism with the modernist rebellious spirit that yielded the American Revolution.[36] Paleoconservatives, however, were under no illusions that winning elections would be sufficient to overthrow the incumbent regime. If the dissident Right was to lead a revolt, Francis wrote at the time, it was 'necessary to construct a countervailing cultural establishment, a "counter-hegemony" ... that is independent of the dominant cultural apparatus and is able to generate its own system of beliefs'.[37] Drawing on Gramsci, Francis saw Middle American Radicalism (MARS) as an untapped and potentially game-changing source of 'post-bourgeois resistance' against the dominant 'liberal' culture, as well as economic globalisation and the follies of internationalist foreign policies.[38]

The Buchanan Revolution never really materialised, but in the following decades, paleoconservatives continued to provide intellectual ammunition to a wide range of agents and ideological forces challenging the prevailing liberal order nationally and internationally.[39] This constellation of conservative voices sees itself as part of an ideological vanguard charged with fighting a long war of position

---

[35] Pat Buchanan, 'America First – and Second and Third', *The National Interest* 19 (Spring 1990), 77–82; Samuel T. Francis, 'The Buchanan Revolution, Part I', *Chronicles* (July 1992), 11; Thomas Fleming, 'America First 1941/1991', *Chronicles* (December 1991), 12–14.

[36] Thomas Fleming, 'The New Fusionism', *Chronicles* (May 1991), 9.

[37] Francis, 'Principalities and Power', 2.

[38] Jean-François Drolet and Michael C. Williams, 'The View from MARS: US Paleoconservatism and Ideological Challenges to the Liberal World Order', *International Journal* 74:1 (2019), 15–31.

[39] Samuel T. Francis, 'Beyond Conservatism', *Chronicles* (January 2000), 21.

on behalf of the large culturally conservative populations it claims to represent. As Francis saw it:

> The main focus should be the reclamation of cultural power, the patient elaboration of an alternative culture within but against the regime – within the belly of the beast but indigestible by it. Instead of the uselessness of a Diogenes' search for an honest presidential candidate or a Fabian quest for a career in the bureaucracy, a Middle American Right should begin working in and with schools, churches, clubs, women's groups, youth organizations, civic and professional associations, the military and police forces, and even in the much dreaded labor unions to create a radicalized Middle American consciousness that can perceive the ways in which exploitation of the middle classes is institutionalized and understand how it can be resisted.[40]

These perspectives have also provided a means of bringing issues of race back into explicit discussion. Francis often invoked race, although until later in life he generally did so with some caution, frequently formulating questions of race relations within a wider defence of the culture of the anti-bellum American South. More recently, Greg Johnson, a leading figure in the North American New Right, articulates a more explicitly 'race-focused' metapolitical strategy:

> Because of the blending of European stocks and breakdown of more compact European national identities in North America, we are forced to stress the deeper roots of common European identity, including racial identity ... The primary metapolitical project of the North American New Right is to challenge and replace the hegemony of anti-white ideas throughout our culture and political system. The entire cultural and political mainstream – including every shade of the "respectable" political spectrum – treats white racial consciousness and white self-assertion as evil. Our goal is to critique and destroy this

---

[40] Samuel T. Francis, 'Beautiful Losers', *Chronicles* (May 1991), 17.

consensus and make white racial consciousness and self-assertion hegemonic instead, so that no matter what political party wins office, white interests will be secured. Our goal is a pluralistic white society in which there is disagreement and debate about a whole range of issues. But white survival will not be among them.[41]

Race is thus an important element in much radical Right thinking, but their metapolitics is not reducible to race alone. Not all those sympathetic to the American New Right subscribe to its racist, white nationalist, or supremacist variants, something that is even more true of those who are not explicitly part of the 'movement' but sympathise with some of its cultural or economic positions. As we discuss in the next chapter, capturing this diversity and the strategic potential it holds for the radical Right requires a rather different understanding of its unifying ideas.

THE END OF ENLIGHTENMENT (AND LIBERALISM)

Conservatism has long been identified with hostility towards Enlightenment Reason.[42] Against the abstract, speculative tendencies of modern thought, conservatism emphasises the comforting immediacy of shared cultural conventions and self-evident truths. It affirms the importance of historical heritage, collective memory, and the concrete, situated experience of one's particular environment as the main determinant of political thought and action. Yet this has also long left conservatives in a dilemma, inhabiting a world that they can only respond to with what seems like an increasingly nostalgic (or worse, authoritarian) yearning for long-lost verities.

---

[41] Greg Johnson, 'New Right vs. Old Right', *Counter-Currents* (11 May 2012). Francis' racist views eventually led to the termination of his position as a columnist for the *Washington Times*. On his rehabilitation on the Right, see Alec Dent, 'The Right's Quiet Uncancelling of a Dead White Supremacist', *Vanity Fair* (14 October 2022).

[42] See Darren McMahon, *Enemies of the Enlightenment* (Oxford: Oxford University Press, 2001).

What marks the radical Right is both a foundational critique of liberal modernity and an attempt to build a non-liberal alternative by radicalising rather than rejecting some of modernity's most powerful dynamics.[43]

This is most strikingly seen in the attitude of wide parts of the radical Right towards postmodernism. In many of the culture wars that wracked Western societies in the late twentieth and early twenty-first centuries, postmodernism played the role of a cultural bogeyman in conservative circles – a decadent destroyer of values that threatened to undermine traditional values, social structures, and reason. Indeed, hostility towards postmodernism was a rare issue on which many mainstream liberals and conservatives found common ground. However, this is not the case for important parts of the radical Right, which instead find much to use and value in postmodern views.[44] As one of their leading theorists explains, influential postmodern positions like that of Jean-François Lyotard are characterised by an ironic, fatalistic, and pluralist incredulity regarding metanarratives and a scepticism towards liberal morality and Enlightenment Reason shared by many radical conservatives.[45] In this account, what makes our era 'post' modern is precisely the fact that the Enlightenment narrative remains central to the reproduction

---

[43] It is this synthetic, forward-looking dimension that attracts many radical conservative intellectuals to the political theory of the conservative revolution. See, for instance, Alain de Benoist, *Quatres Figures de la Révolution Conservatrice Allemande: Werner Sombart, Arthur Moeller van den Bruck, Ernst Niekisch, Oswald Spengler* (Paris: Les Amis d'Alain de Benoist, 2014); Sunic, *Against Democracy and Equality*, 75–82; O'Meara, *New Culture, New Right*, 46–50; Michael Minkenberg, 'The New Right in France and Germany: Nouvelle Droite, Neue Rechte, and the New Right Radical Right Parties', in Peter H. Merkl and Leonard Weinberg eds., *The Revival of Right-Wing Extremism in the Nineties* (London: Frank Cass, 1997); Kurt Lenk, Günter Meuter, and Henrique Ricardo Otten, *Vordenker der Neuen Rechten* (Frankfurt: Campus, 1997).

[44] On the surprising yet revealing familiarity with Critical Theory displayed by a number of individuals with links to the Trump administration, see Geoff Schullenberger, 'Theorycels in Trumpworld', *Outsider Theory* (5 January 2021).

[45] Robert Steuckers, 'Post-Modern Challenges: Between Faust and Narcissus', in Greg Johnson, ed., *North American New Right, vol. 1* (San Francisco: Counter-Currents Publishing, 2012), 250.

of contemporary liberal orders, despite having lost all metaphysical credibility: 'It persists', according to Robert Steuckers, 'by dint of force and propaganda. But in the sphere of thought, poetry, music, art or letters, this metanarrative says and inspires nothing. It has not moved a great mind for 100 or 150 years'.[46]

For the radical Right, this incredulity towards the Enlightenment does not open up a vast new vista of political tolerance and the proliferation and play of difference. Instead, 'provincializing'[47] Europe's false Enlightenment universalism provides an opportunity to unapologetically revive the West's essential and unique historical identity, which lies not in liberal Reason but in 'a return of the Dionysian, the irrational, the carnal, the turbid, and disconcerting areas of the human soul revealed by Bataille or Caillois, opening up the possibility for a revival of myth and the tragic, agonistic worldview laying at the origins of Western civilisation and its best cultural achievements – what Spengler called the "Faustian spirit"'.[48] As de Benoist and Champetier emphasise, this affirmation of mysticism and the transgressive, emotional aspects of Western culture is not a question of overcoming the crisis of modernity by returning to the past, but of recovering 'certain premodern values in a decisively postmodern dimension'.[49] In their view, 'it is only at the price of such a radical restructuring that anomie and contemporary nihilism will be exorcised'. In this context, the end of the Enlightenment project heralded by postmodernism is transformed by radical Right intellectuals into

---

[46] Steuckers, 'Post-Modern Challenges', 250; see also Domitius Corbulo, 'The Enlightenment from a New Right Perspective', in Greg Johnson, ed., *North American New Right, vol. 2* (San Francisco: Counter-Currents Publishing, 2017), 7–32.

[47] Dipesh Chakrabarti, *Provincializing Europe: Postcolonial Thought and Historical Difference* (Princeton: Princeton University Press, 2000).

[48] Steuckers, 'Post-Modern Challenges', 248–249.

[49] Alain de Benoist and Charles Champetier, *Manifesto for a European Renaissance* (London: Arktos, 2012), 2. From another perspective, often associated with Traditionalism, the distinction between pre-modern and modern (and with it, the post-modern) is itself a misconception. The Traditionalist position is broad and we do not engage it directly, but see Mark Sedgwick, *Against the Modern World* (Oxford: Oxford University Press, 2009).

an opportunity for the reconstitution of an organic populism. This reconstitution seeks to rehabilitate an ethno-politics disgraced by its association with eugenics and historical fascism by re-articulating this position in the somewhat less offensive language of cultural relativism, fashioned conceptually through an 'identitarian' theory of individual and collective self-determination that frames identity as a process of constant becoming within the limitations of historical experiences and material conditions. In this framework, identity 'is not what never changes, but on the contrary, it is what allows one to constantly change without giving up who one is' – that is, without losing the sense of ontological security afforded by our existence as member of a distinct community of fate.[50]

Identitarianism thus affirms the value and importance of recognising differences between cultures, ethnic groups, races, and civilisations, along with the political processes and ideological mechanisms that maintain a healthy degree of segregation and estrangement between them: 'The group and the individual', de Benoist argues, 'both need to be confronted by "significant others"'.[51] This is what radical Rightists call 'differentialism', or the 'right to difference'. While asserting the absence of objective criteria for determining a hierarchy of cultures, races, or ethnic groups, differentialism casts itself as an ethico-political response to the perceived threat posed by liberal multiculturalism and ethnic and racial miscegenation. As Lucian Tudor emphasises in a sympathetic survey: 'When total openness and mixing occur, peoples do not merely change in the normal sense, but lose who they are or merge with another people entirely, thus resulting in the elimination of their identity.'[52] These views are

---

[50] Alain de Benoist, 'On Identity', *Telos* 128 (2004), 41.
[51] Ibid., 39.
[52] Lucian Tudor, 'The Philosophy of Identity: Ethnicity, Culture, and Race in Identitarian Thought', *The Occidental Quarterly* 14:3 (2014), 88–89; see also Sunic, *Against Democracy and Equality*; Markus Willinger, *Generation Identity* (London: Arktos, 2013), more broadly, see José Pedro Zúquete, *The Identitarians: The Movement against Globalism and Islam in Europe* (South Bend: Notre Dame University Press, 2018).

reflected in frequent racism and hostility towards mass migration, as well as the popularity of the idea of the 'great replacement' whereby 'native' populations are being divested of their 'indigenous' cultural traits. Importantly, as we argue in the next chapter, these views are not simply a critique of population movements: the great replacement is seen as the outcome of the policies and interests of specific agents and is linked to a wider assault on liberal power.

It is safe to say that this fusion of poststructuralist tropes on the disenfranchisement of alternative subjectivities will not satisfy many sociologists within professional academic circles. But as we will see in Chapter 4, identitarians have their own para-academic outlets and alternative epistemic communities through which they can challenge liberal 'regimes of truth' and disseminate their own. As Michael O'Meara cheerfully acknowledges, the revolutionary conservatism of today's radical Right, in this sense, does indeed unfold within the cultural horizon of postmodernism:

> Accepting the world's intrinsic lack of coherence and the relativity of its different orders of value need not trivialize or discredit the European heritage. From the identitarian's perspective, postmodernism's broadsides constitute an emphatic justification of tradition's particularity and the fact that we are who we are only because we make certain decisions to identify with and defend *our* particular system of truth. The constructed (that is, the human or cultural) character of the historical narrative, the multiplicity of these narratives, and their absence of closure are cause for commitment, not despair, for the culturally relative "truths" born of one's own identity are necessarily more meaningful than those that are not. The art of historical survival consequently dictates that a people jealously, intolerantly if need be, defend its myths, beliefs, lifestyles, language, institutions, and, above all, its genetic heritage, for these alone enable it to be what it is and what it might be.[53]

[53] O'Meara, *New Culture, New Right*, 261–262.

According to radical Right thinkers, the disorientating temporalities and disastrous demographic and environmental consequences of globalisation have made the renewal of traditions and revitalisation of local communities imperative. The vision of universal progress and development that is at the heart of liberal globalisation is fundamentally flawed since it detaches 'man [sic] from the soil, reduces his beliefs to superstitions, denounces political sovereignty as despotism, atomises society, reducing it to individual and interchangeable economic actors'.[54]

By contrast, as de Benoist and Champetier argue: 'Fostering social interaction and a sense of celebration, traditions inculcate a sense of life's cycles and provide temporal landmarks. Emphasising rhythmic passing of the ages and of the seasons, great moments in life, and the stages of the passing year, they nourish symbolic imagination and create social bonds. These traditions must never be frozen in time but must always be in a state of renewal.'[55] Appropriating the language of Indigenous Sovereignty and environmentalism, some radical Rightists insist on the close link between historical heritage, collective memory, and spiritual rootedness in ancestral lands against the utopian vision of a cosmopolitan elite that has no concrete ties to the earth. In their eyes, the protection of the ecosystem is inseparable from territorial sovereignty and the defence of 'indigenous' white populations.

Progress is the guiding ideology of modernity. The idea of a future open to social and technological innovation and reformation is among its most powerful philosophical underpinnings. The power of progress as a metaphysic and a political ideology has always presented conservatives with a dilemma. Many found their only response in forms of reaction that rejected modernity in favour of a nostalgic return to the past. Today's radical Right has no such illusions. It

---

[54] Alain de Benoist, *Europe, Tiers Monde, Même Combat* (Paris: Robert Laffont, 1986), 125–126.

[55] De Benoist and Champetier, *Manifesto*, section 10; see also Alain de Benoist, 'Tradition?', *Telos* 94 (1992), 82–88.

recognises that the ideology of progress and the power of technology cannot be denied; the challenge is to rework their directions, transforming them into bases for neo-reactionary alternatives. Whereas the counter-revolutionary conservative rejects the demagoguery of modern democratic politics unconditionally, the revolutionary conservative accepts democracy as a *fait accompli* and seeks to redirect mechanisms of popular mobilisation against liberal-democratic institutions. For the theorists of the French *Nouvelle Droite*, as for Alexander Dugin in Russia and Greg Johnson and his acolytes in *American Renaissance*, the challenges of the twenty-first century demand a new synthesis of tradition and technology that will break decisively with modern egalitarianism and restructure the relationship between the local and the global.[56] As Ruuben Kaalep and August Meister argue in their 'ethnofuturist' manifesto for the Baltic New Right: 'Maybe the defeat of fascism and the transformation of Marxism into its post-modernist absurdities was necessary for the next leap in our history. The new ideology to make this leap possible would include elements of other organic ideologies merged with a futuristic vision of the world and political methods of the postmodernists ("fight fire with fire"), but with a metaphysical and traditionalist core.'[57] Faye calls his own influential version of this synthesis *Archeofuturism*:

> To envisage a future society that combines techno-scientific progress with a return to the traditional answers that stretch back into the mists of time. This is perhaps the true face of postmodernity ... Could we not imagine and foresee a scenario where most of humanity reverts to living in traditional societies

---

[56] Alexander Dugin, *The Fourth Political Theory* (London: Arktos, 2012); Greg Johnson, *Towards a New Nationalism* (San Francisco: Counter-Current Publishing, 2018); Philip Santoro, 'White Environmentalism', *American Renaissance* (29 April 2017)/; Jared Taylor, *The Real American Dilemma: Race, Immigration and the Future of America* (Oakton, VA: New Century Books, 1998).

[57] Ruuben Kaalep and August Meister, *Rebirth of Europe: The Ethnofuturist Manifesto* (London: Arktos, 2020), 37.

that consume little energy, and are socially more stable and happy, while – in the context of globalisation – a minority continues to live according to the techno-industrial model? Might there be two parallel worlds in the future, the worlds of a new Middle Ages and of Hyperscience? Who would be living in each of these worlds, and in what numbers? All daring and creative thought must think the unthinkable. I believe that *Archeofuturism*, an explosive meeting of opposites, is the key to the future, simply because the paradigm of modernity is no longer viable on a global scale.[58]

CONCLUSION

Over the past half-century, the radical Right has generated a range of critiques of liberal power and its weaknesses as part of constructing a cultural strategy – a vision of political identity and ideology – capable of overcoming it. Yet they are well aware that a purely cultural strategy is not enough. For Francis, a close student of Marx as well as Gramsci, and a follower of the ex-Trotskyist turned arch-conservative James Burnham, a project of cultural hegemony would only succeed if linked to concrete social forces. Here, he argued, conservatism actually had a decisive advantage over both liberalism and the Left. The proletarian agency expected by Marxian theory has failed to materialise. Yet, as we detail in the next chapter, the radical Right sees the dynamics of global capitalism with its attendant economic, normative, and cultural dislocation of key social classes, combined with resentment towards the power of the dominant New Class of liberal elites, as creating the economic, social, and cultural-ideological conditions for a genuine conservative revolution.

This provides the radical Right with a global sociological, ideological, and political framing, a political economy with capitalism and class at its centre, and a strategic direction. It seeks to mobilise social

---

[58] Guillaume Faye, *Archeofuturism: European Visions of the Post-Catastrophic Age* (London: Arktos, 2010), 45–46.

forces produced and marginalised by liberalism and globalisation by bringing them to self-consciousness, turning them from analytically identifiable but political inchoate classes *in* themselves to politically aware and active classes *for* themselves. Ideas and the activities of 'organic intellectuals' are central to this process, as is the mobilisation of wider forces of cultural resistance into diverse counter-hegemonic movements. As de Benoist argues, the aim of this strategy is not simply to displace the democratic consensus from Left to Right, but to use that displacement to position the radical Right as a plausible partner to the working class and other social positions and allow it eventually to replace the liberal elite with its own leadership cadres.[59]

In intriguing ways, this process resembles (albeit in politically very different ways) what a number of Gramscian-inspired thinkers have theorised as the project of a 'postmodern Prince ... a political subject that could form a collective will out of diversity and difference, in a social, cultural, and political context defined by postmodern subjectivities and a post-Fordist mode of production'.[60] Instead of relying on a single source (the proletariat or the Party) as the agent of historical transformation, these views call for diffuse, yet not disconnected, forms of political struggle, complex processes of political resistance and transformation that unite diverse social actors against shared structures of oppression. These ideas are most prominent in attempts to develop a 'Left populism',[61] but the idea of a postmodern Prince also sheds revealing light on the activities of the Right.

---

[59] Alain de Benoist, writing as Robert de Herte, 'La revolution conservatrice', *Éléments* 20 (1977), 3.

[60] Marco Brizzarelli, 'Podemos' Twofold Assault on Hegemony: The Possibilities of the Post-Modern Prince and the Perils of Passive Revolution', in Oscar Garcia and Marco Brizzarelli eds., *Podemos and the New Political Cycle: Left-Wing Populism and Anti-Establishment Politics* (New York: Palgrave, 2017), 116. See also John Sanbonmatsu, *The Postmodern Prince: Critical Theory, Left Strategy, and the Making of a New Political Subject* (New York: Monthly Review Press, 2004). An interesting perspective is Perry Anderson, 'The Heirs of Gramsci', *New Left Review* 100 (2016), 71–97.

[61] For instance, Chantal Mouffe, *For a Left Populism* (London: Verso, 2018) and Ernesto Laclau, *On Populist Reason* (London: Verso, 2004). In IR, the idea has been suggested in Stephen Gill, 'Toward a Postmodern Prince? The Battle in Seattle as a Moment in the New Politics of Globalisation', *Millennium* 29:1 (2000), 131–140.

This is the sense, for example, in which the radical Right represents an 'internationalist nationalism'. It mobilises what Kyle Murray and Owen Worth have called Gramsci's notion of the 'conception of the world' through which 'certain social groups and individuals within them understand the world and their place in it', and seeks to construct discursive and organisational structures through which 'different narratives can be harmonised across different levels of international society'.[62] In the era of a global Right, these conceptions of the world can be actively and strategically produced and promoted to generate transnational equivalences and effects. Just as the conditions and structures of liberal power and domination are in important ways global, so too must be the resistance. The global Right thus seeks to create what Robert Cox called 'transnational social forces' by mobilising national social forces within a transnational framing set against a global (and globalising) enemy. This is not a unified movement in the sense of traditional Marxian conceptions of the international working class. It draws instead on the idea that similar or similarly positioned groups within states are being marginalised by the powers of liberalism and by national and international processes of globalisation, and that they can be brought to awareness of the common causes of their plight and their common cause in resisting it.

As we discussed in Chapter 1, some of the most powerful insights into such strategies come from attempts to use Gramscian ideas to build counter-hegemonic movements on the Left. In her call *For a Left Populism*, for example, Chantal Mouffe argues that a successful populist movement must construct a 'people' through a series of discursive oppositions, a strategy that 'consists in disarticulating the sedimented structure of an existing formation and, through the transformation of these practices and the instauration of new ones, establishing the nodal points of a new hegemonic formation'.[63] Crucial to a counter-hegemonic

---

[62] Murray and Worth, 'Building Consent', 733.
[63] Chantal Mouffe, *For a Left Populism* (London: Verso, 2018), 44; drawing also on Laclau, *On Populist Reason*.

movement is its ability to generate discursive 'chains of equivalence' between different groups and struggles in relation to a unifying negativity or opposition. As Mark Purcell summarises the idea:

> The groups in the chain each have their own distinct relation to the existing hegemony, and each group's experience and interests are irreducible to the others. Each retains their difference. However, they are able to act in concert around an agenda of equivalence. That is, they see themselves as equivalently disadvantaged by existing power relations. "Equivalent" in this case does not mean identical. They are not disadvantaged in precisely the same way, and it is necessary to explicitly reject the old-style social movements that reduced participants to a single social position (usually class). Each link in the chain remains distinct, but they operate together, in concert.[64]

Perhaps ironically, these ideas are more effective in helping understand the successes of the radical global Right than they have been in building a Left internationalism. As we will show, they help capture what the Right has attempted, and often succeeded, in doing. The global, cast as managerial liberalism, is a key element in this oppositional conservative discourse that can operate globally, capable of being mobilised in different forms and contexts. In contrast to some historical forms of fascism (or for the matter, the Marxian tradition in which Gramsci is rather awkwardly located), the global Right does not consist of an overarching, universal theory, ideology, or zobjective that all adherents must subscribe to. Instead, it involves the construction of myriad chains of equivalence between the positions, concerns, and objectives of diverse agents. Its objective, as

---

[64] Mark Purcell, 'Resisting Neoliberalization: Communicative Planning or Counter-Hegemonic Movements?', *Planning Theory* 8:2 (2009), 140–165. The idea originates in Ernesto Laclau and Chantal Mouffe, *Hegemony and Socialist Strategy* (London: Verso, 1985). For an application to the radical Right, see Christian Lamour, 'The League of Leagues: Meta-Populism and the "Chain of Equivalence" in a Cross-Border Alpine Area', *Political Geography* 81 (2020), 1–11.

Mouffe outlines from her Left populist position, is 'the creation of a popular majority to come to power' However

> 'there is no blueprint for how this will take place or a final destination'. The chain of equivalence through which "the people" is going to be constituted will depend on the historical circumstances. Its dynamics cannot be determined in isolation from all contextual references. The same is true for the shape of the new hegemony that this strategy seeks to bring about. What is in question is not the establishment of a "populist regime" with a pre-defined programme but the creation of a hegemonic formation.[65]

Such a strategy may seem suspiciously vague, and within projects that ultimately seek a unified, universal goal it may well be. However, it is particularly well suited for a radical Right that does not seek universality but works instead to generate a range of mutually supportive yet distinct conservative visions of global plurality – as expressed, for example, in the combination of various essentialisms (Tradition, People, Nation, Civilisation) adopted by diverse radical Right movements across the world. That these diverse ideological positions lack ideological conformity and centralised, tightly structured hierarchical organisations should not blind us to the continual efforts and capacity to establish between them mutually reinforcing affinities or 'articulations'. To quote Mouffe once more, 'To deny the existence of a priori, necessary link between subject positions does not mean that there is no constant effort to establish between them historical, contingent, and variable links ... Even though there is no necessary link between different subject positions, in the field of politics there are always discourses that try to provide an articulation from different standpoints.'[66]

Seen in this way, counter-hegemonic ideologies enable a range of actors and agendas to find common cause despite their different

---

[65] Mouffe, *For a Left Populism*, 30–31.
[66] Ibid., 89–90.

contexts and concerns. Radical conservative actors and ideas seek to construct transnational chains of equivalence between different movements – and at the most basic level, the global Right consists of precisely such articulations. In the North, this is strikingly evident in articulations linking working-class material interests and discontent, the predations of economic globalisation, cultural and symbolic opposition to liberal elites and 'wokeism', and the privileged positions of experts and expert institutions. In the South, as Marlene Laruelle points out and as we show in the final chapter, they are often connected to critiques of liberal imperialism and domination.[67] These diverse articulations are deeply relational and globally connected, and even if the equivalences and political alliances are disparate and their ends on closer inspection perhaps incompatible, they can become socially and politically powerful in their shared opposition to liberal globalisation as a socio-economic and political agenda.

[67] Marlene Laruelle, 'Illiberalism: A Conceptual Introduction', *East European Politics* 38:2 (2022), 303–327, 313.

3 Deconstructing the Global Administrative State

The national and international politics articulated by the contemporary radical Right did not emerge overnight with the recent election of right-wing leaders into positions of power. Instead, the Right's rise to prominence is in important ways the product of decades-long attempts to craft philosophical positions capable of mounting an intellectual challenge to liberal orders, fostering political movements dedicated to their destruction and supporting alternative political projects at the national, regional, and global levels. This chapter outlines and analyses the arguments of the intellectual vanguard at the helm of this metapolitical strategy in Europe, North America, and beyond since the end of the Cold War. Despite their considerable diversity, these various thinkers and movements share a recognisably similar vision of the global and of globalisation, based in a managerial sociology that provides a wide-ranging critique of the administrative state and liberal power. In this view, the essence of globalisation is the planetary spread of the liberal managerial society, the administrative state, and the New Class that dominates and benefits from both. This argument, in turn, is itself central to the globalisation of the radical Right.

In both a practical and an ideological sense, managerialism has become an essential part of the radical Right's conception of the world, imparting coherence to its radicalisation and transnationalisation. It provides an account of how the world works, supplying a framing of people's economic situations, cultural settings, and even their individual feelings or affects. It provides an account of power – of who has it and how they exercise it, of who benefits and who loses; a vision of us and them. And it provides a sense of possibility and, crucially, of hope: ideas of collective causes, of strategic political mobilisation, and plans of action. It also provides a unifying conception of the political possibility and necessity of bringing together – nationally and internationally – groups and individuals otherwise divided by class, culture, distance, and even on occasion race. Religious traditionalists, conservative nationalists, disaffected parts of the working class, disillusioned liberals and progressives, as well as those closer to more extremist concerns with ethnicity and race, find ideologically powerful elements in the managerial conception of the world.

The ideological unity of the radical Right is uneven, and their adherence to managerialism is frequently not explicit or systematic. In some guises, this ideological framework is articulated in formal philosophical, theoretical, and analytic principles, but it need not be. Nor does it underpin a rigidly shared agenda; different groups have different aspirations and operate in different national contexts. In this way, managerialism functions as a 'core concept' that provides a unifying conception within which explicitly diverse national agendas can be pursued and through which they can be furthered.[1] Similarly, at the international level, the same core concept serves to identify the global spread and devastating impact of managerialist power. As such it is crucial to the globalisation of radical Right ideas and movements, stimulating new, nationally or locally rooted critiques of managerialism. While the origin and centre of gravity of this ideology is in the Global North, it has increasingly radiated outwards through recursive interactions, alliances, and international networks.

In what follows, we trace the development and spread of the view that globalisation should be understood as the expansion of liberal managerial society, the administrative state, and the New Class. We make two tightly connected moves. First, we outline the specific, managerialist sociology that provides the radical Right with an analytic frame of how the world works, a map allowing people to understand

---

[1] Michael Freeden, *Ideologies and Political Theory: A Conceptual Approach* (Oxford: Oxford University Press, 1998).

what has happened and is happening to them – or, more specifically, the divergent fortunes, experiences, and prospects of different social groups and (in a language that the radical Right is much more comfortable with than its mainstream conservative competitors) classes. Second, we show how this sociology provides the foundations for a recognisably similar set of political strategies in different geographical locations. In this vision, the unequal experiences of globalisation and late modern politics are not the unavoidable consequences of anonymous market dynamics or economic modernisation. On the contrary, there are specific, identifiable agents and institutions that produce, dominate, and benefit from the system. Thus, when thinkers and political actors on the radical Right refer to 'global elites' or 'globalists', it is not simply a loose application of the standard populist opposition between the 'elite' and 'the people' with the prefix 'global' added. It marks a specific political sociology that identifies actors to be blamed, institutions to be opposed and targeted, thus focusing discontent and resentment. It also helps identify groups or constituencies to be mobilised, alliances to be constructed, rhetorical and discursive tropes to be employed, and strategies to be pursued. In Gramscian terms, the New Class is the present-day historic bloc, whose hegemonic order must be carefully deconstructed and critiqued in preparation for a successful counter-hegemonic movement to emerge.

THE NEW LIBERALISM

The radical Right's critique of globalisation rests on an interpretation of the relationship between liberalism and wider transformations in social power, institutional structures, and mass communications since the late nineteenth century. In many ways, this analysis draws upon and expands the diagnoses of earlier critics of liberal democracy and the perceived decay of Western civilisation.[2] Despite significant

---

[2] These include Vilfredo Pareto, Gaetano Mosca, Robert Michels, Oswald Spengler, Carl Schmitt, Ernst Jünger, and many others. For surveys from different radical Right perspectives, see Alain de Benoist, *View from the Right: A Critical Anthology of*

differences between these critiques, a claim common to them all – and central to many radical conservatives today – is that popular understandings of liberal democracy in the public domain are little more than the ideological reflection (or obfuscation) of a bourgeois world that long ago disappeared. In this idealised (indeed ideologised) representation, the bourgeois world of classical liberalism envisaged politics as a relatively clearly delimited public domain reserved for educated and civic-minded (male) individuals who represented the nation through rational deliberation on the nature of the common good in light of natural law. These bourgeois political, economic, and cultural structures valued and promoted individual restraint and responsibility; social solidarity based on the family, local community, and nation; and 'virtuous' forms of capitalism that blended individual achievement and local benefaction.[3] Some classical liberals and other reformers sought to improve this system by making the representatives more responsive to the people's will by increasing popular participation and cultivating progressive commitments to the idea of civilisation as the collective achievement of nations, but they remained within its recognisable confines.

According to the radical Right, this order was rendered obsolete by the development of modern industrial society. The emergence of large-scale corporations and other administrative organisations swallowed individuals into the rule-bound and hierarchical structures of bureaucratic agencies, replacing the entrepreneur with the administrator and reducing workers from skilled craftsmen to

Contemporary Ideas, 3 vols. (London: Arktos, 1977/2017–19); Alain de Benoist, *The Problem of Democracy* (London: Arktos 2011); Tomislav Sunic, *Against Democracy and Equality: The European New Right* (London: Arktos, 2011); Paul Gottfried, *After Liberalism: Mass Democracy in the Managerial State* (Princeton, NJ: Princeton University Press, 2001); Samuel T. Francis, *Leviathan and Its Enemies* (Arlington, VA: Radix/Washington Summit Publishers, 2016); Joakim Andersen, *Rising from the Ruins: The Right in the Twenty First Century* (London: Arktos, 2018).

[3] The contrast between this somewhat bucolic image and the contemporary global system in Steve Bannon's distinction between 'productive' and destructive forms of capitalism is traced in Jens Steffek and Yannick Lasshof, 'Steve Bannon on "Productive Capitalism": Investigating the Economic Ideology of the American Populist Right', *Journal of Political Ideologies* (Online first 2022).

replaceable cogs in vast, technologically dominated industrial and commercial organisations. At the same time, the increased functional differentiation and complexity of industrial societies and the ensuing sociocultural diversity combined to erode the unifying normative framework of bourgeois society. The social homogeneity presupposed by the bourgeois model of liberal democracy faded as individuals became caught up within the constraints of their social roles and functions and therefore lacked the expertise, time, and organisational capacity required to contribute meaningfully to public political debates. Although liberalism extended the franchise, this did not empower the average citizen because it was accompanied by social innovations that instead strengthened the power of professional politicians, managers in charge of party machines, and civil servants tasked with running the expanding state bureaucracy in an age of mass politics.

In this interpretation, liberalism as a bourgeois ideology had failed to provide the political and procedural predictability indispensable for capitalist development under conditions of modernity. Many traditional conservatives were convinced that this would lead to liberalism's collapse. By contrast, today's radical Right contends that it marked the emergence of a 'New Class managerialism' – a novel, more intrusive, and totalising form of technocratic liberal ordering that would erode temporal and geographical particularity and integrate the planet on a scale never seen before.

The concept of the New Class has its origins in late nineteenth-century anarchist critiques of communism.[4] It was developed into a more substantive political sociology in the later work of Adolph Berle and Gardiner Means, Bruno Rizzi, and especially the political theorist James Burnham.[5] Turning his back on

---

[4] Exemplified by the writings of Polish revolutionary Jan Waclaw Machajski. See Marshall S. Shatz, *Jan Waclaw Machajski: A Radical Critic of the Russian Intelligentsia and Socialism* (Pittsburgh, PA: University of Pittsburgh Press, 1999).

[5] Bruno Rizzi, *The Bureaucratisation of the World* (New York: Free Press, 1939/1985); Adolph Berle and Gardiner Means, *The Modern Corporation and Private Property* (New York: Harcourt, Brace, and World, 1932/1967); James Burnham, *The Managerial*

Trotskyism in 1940, Burnham, in alliance with other conservatives such as William F. Buckley, became one of the leading public intellectuals behind the rise of the American Right during the Cold War and the civil rights era.[6] He supported hard-core anti-communism, generally opposed Great Society social programmes, was at best ambivalent towards racial reforms, and in his later years warned in quasi-Spenglerian terms that liberal cultural decay was leading to the 'suicide of the West'.[7] Perhaps for these reasons, Burnham receded into relative obscurity towards the end of the century. Recent years, however, have seen a remarkable resurgence of interest in his writings, a revival that testifies to the significance of managerialist themes on the Right.[8] In *The Managerial Revolution*, published in 1941, Burnham analysed the new mass societies and ever-increasing concentration of industrial and financial power that he saw emerging around the world. Identifying similarities between the political-economic formations of Stalinist Russia, Nazi Germany, and the United States under Roosevelt's New Deal liberalism, he argued that since 1914, a trend of economic organisation had been developing in industrialised countries in which a New Class of technically skilled managers, administrators, engineers,

Revolution: What Is Happening in the World (New York: John Day Co., 1941). See also Milovan Djilas, *The New Class: An Analysis of the Communist System* (New York: Harcourt, Brace, Jovanovich, 1957); Barry Bruce-Briggs ed., *The New Class?* (New Brunswick, NJ: Transaction Books, 1978); Alvin W. Gouldner, *The Future of Intellectuals and the Rise of the New Class* (London: MacMillan Press, 1979).

[6] Along with Buckley and Frank Meyer, Burnham was a key figure in developing the 'fusionist' conservatism that fostered unstable but powerful common cause between religious traditionalists, libertarians, free marketeers, and anti-communists from the 1950s to the 1980s. Fusionism was crucial to the Republican's electoral success through the early twenty-first century, and its breakdown is a key aspect of today's tumult on the American Right. For an illustration, see the collective statement 'Against the Dead Consensus', *First Things* (21 March 2019), and for a conservative overview, see Matthew Continetti, *The Right: The One Hundred Year War for American Conservatism* (New York: Basic Books, 2022).

[7] James Burnham, *The Suicide of the West* (New York: John Day, 1964).

[8] As illustrations, see Michael Lind, 'The Importance of James Burnham', *Tablet Magazine* (1 September 2021); and Julius Krein, 'James Burnham's Managerial Elite', *American Affairs* 1 (Spring 2017). See also Michael Lind, *The New Class War* (New York: Penguin, 2020).

and bureaucrats of all sorts were engaged in a 'drive for social dominance, for power and privilege, for the position of ruling class'.⁹

This New Class was usurping the power of the traditional bourgeois elites that lacked the technical expertise required to direct the large organisations and enterprises of twentieth-century societies. In this emerging order, the distinction between the ruling managerial elite and the masses no longer hinged on the actual *ownership* of the means of production, but rather on the control – the management – of the means of production and communication, and the ability of the elites to influence and direct state-authorised mechanisms of mass organisation and economic distribution. Generally, the interests of these new managerial elites consisted in maintaining and extending the institutions they controlled, and in ensuring that the demand – and the rewards – for their technical skills were steadily increased.

Burnham held that in contrast to the authoritarian strands of managerialism prevailing in communist and fascist regimes, elites in liberal democratic societies tended to rely on the manipulation of cultural symbols, desires, and material incentives rather than on direct coercion. These experimental technologies of government were closely associated with the rise of the welfare state and the reformist, social democratic strands of liberalism that gained ascendency in Anglo-American countries during the late nineteenth and early twentieth centuries. Championed by the likes of T. H. Green, John Hobson, and John Dewey, this new liberalism presents itself as an ethical sociocultural response to the evils spawned by the mass industrialised society that the bourgeoisie had created. In the words of Sam Francis, one of Burnham's most assiduous and influential followers, a key feature of the old bourgeois regime was the moral framework

> by which the virtues of work, thrift, duty, and deferral of gratification were inculcated and upheld. This ethic, institutionalised in bourgeois economic and social codes of

---
⁹ Burnham, *Managerial Revolution*, 71.

socially rooted or ascetic individualism, was perceived by many Progressivist liberals as responsible for a callous and brutalizing society that ignored or exploited human needs and was indifferent or hostile to the possibilities of social reform and the merits of the intellectually and morally deserving.[10]

The new liberalism therefore abandoned the bourgeois view of the state as an impediment to individual self-realisation and instead emphasised the collective nature of human improvement and responsibilities under conditions of large-scale industrialisation and growing interdependence. These ideological shifts were further buttressed by new conceptions of knowledge, such as pragmatism, that stressed the contingent character of truth and presented individuals and groups as capable of continual adaptation and re-fashioning in a social world characterised by constant change and transformation.[11]

Contemporary radical Right dismissals of the 'managerial elites' or the 'managerial regime' are thus not simply a standard populist dislike of politicians and experts but also a sociological critique of the annexation of reformist liberalism by a New Class that successfully overcame bourgeois opposition and solidified its power in the Euro-Atlantic world and beyond over the course of the twentieth century.[12] Just as classical liberalism had rationalised bourgeois interests during the nineteenth century, the new liberalism provided the emerging New Class with the ideological combination of utopianism, meliorism, scientism, secularism, hedonism, and cosmopolitanism that reflected and justified the functional imperatives of the managerial revolution: the merger of state and economy, the

---

[10] Francis, *Leviathan*, 200.
[11] The links between Progressivism and the rise of the administrative state are explored extensively in Ronald J. Pestritto, *America Transformed: The Rise and Legacy of American Progressivism* (New York: Encounter Books, 2021).
[12] For substantive analytical statements, see Gottfried, *After Liberalism*; Francis, *Leviathan*; Kaalep and Meister, *Rebirth of Europe*. See also Michael O'Meara, *New Culture, New Right: Anti-Liberalism in Postmodern Europe* (London: Arktos, 2013); Alain de Benoist and Charles Champetier, *Manifesto for a European Renaissance* (London: Arktos, 2012).

centralisation of government at the expense of local authority and mediating institutions, the diffusion of mass education, consumerism, the mass media, and so on. Whereas classical liberalism emphasised the merits of distributed powers, the virtues of self-government, natural rights, and the importance of protecting civil society from state interference, managerial liberalism promotes the application of expert knowledge to solve social problems and cultivates commitments to humanity designed to undermine bourgeois attachments to particular national, regional, social, and biological identities and hierarchies.

In this view, managerialism has become the dominant institutional form across the West and beyond, spanning commerce and culture, as well as the domestic/international divide. The New Class in this post-68 context includes corporate elites, civil servants, journalists, lawyers, information technologists, engineers, therapists, academics, consultants, and bureaucrats of all sorts who occupy positions of economic and political power in the post-industrial 'information' society. Although they often hold conflicting political opinions on the matters of the day, these professionals constitute a New Class insofar as their livelihoods do not rest on the ownership of property, but on knowledge, expertise, and the reproduction of a globalised capitalist economy in which the progressive values of education, cultural capital, mobility, technical sophistication, and connections to cosmopolitan networks have become the primary determinants of salary, status, and social advancement. These skills and positions, as well as the New Class that wields and benefits from them, are increasingly global and disconnected from locality, tradition, or nation.

The radical Right associates this constellation of power with liberalism insofar as its continuous expansion hinges on a series of declared commitments to the interests and well-being of others, to universal justice, equality, and human rights, but without significant economic or social reforms that would threaten the interests of the incumbent managerial elites. These elites see themselves as the antidote to the bigoted, parochial, and repressive worldviews and attitudes that they associate with the 'heartland' and the mindless flag-waving patriotism of working and lower middle-class suburbs and rural locations. Through intrusive taxation, anti-racist 'empowerment campaigns', 'sensitivity training', 'decolonised curricula', and a whole range of other correctional interventions, its re-educative mindset encroaches into practically all aspects of individual, social, and family life. In the name of pluralism, the New Class reduces all values to subjective 'lifestyles' and then subjects those lifestyles to their manipulation by the market and regulation by bureaucratic, therapeutic, and cultural experts who prescribe acceptable forms of subjectivity and diversity and proscribe those they find offensive or politically incorrect. As Francis argues in the American context:

> The managerial ruling class, lodged primarily in the state and the other massive bureaucratic structures that dominate the economy and mass culture, must undermine such institutions of traditional social life if its power and interests are to prevail. Disparities between races – rebaptized as "prejudice", "discrimination", "white supremacy", and "hate" to which state and local governments and private institutions are indifferent or in which they are allegedly complicit – provide constant targets of convenience for managerial attack on local, private, and social relationships. Seen in this perspective, as a means of subverting traditional society and enhancing the dominance of a new elite and its own social forms, the crusade for racial "liberation" is not distinctly different from other phases of the same conflict that involve attacks on the family, community, class, and religion.[13]

The challenges that managerialism presents in the eyes of the radical Right thus go far beyond conservatism's usual lament about the loss of traditional values, solidarity, and authority. As Hungarian

---

[13] Samuel T. Francis, 'Paleoconservatism and Race', *Chronicles* (December 2000), 9. For a recent statement of similar themes, see Michael Anton, 'Draining the Swamp', *Claremont Review of Books* (Winter 2019).

Prime Minister Viktor Orbán put it in a highly publicised speech to the American Conservative Political Action Committee's meeting in Budapest in May 2022, the problem is 'the domination of public life by progressive liberals. The problem is the fact that they hold the most important positions in the most important institutions, that they occupy the dominant positions in the media, and that they produce all the politically indoctrinating works of high and mass culture. They – the progressive left – tell us what is the truth and what is not, what is right and what is wrong. And as conservatives, our lot is to feel about our nations' public life as Sting felt in New York: like a "legal alien".'[14]

Rather than leading almost inevitably to state entropy or weakness, as earlier conservative thinkers such as Schmitt, Spengler, and Strauss believed, the radical Right holds that the new liberalism generates novel and ever more pervasive forms of state and elite power. Having emptied social life of all concrete, positive content previously embedded in local traditions, inherited institutions, and shared values, the rights and values of modern liberal democracies are abstract, empty vessels. The meaning of equality and the content of rights, and more recently diversity, is therefore determined by those groups dominating the intellectual, social, and institutional structures that decide on the content of these rights. Formal pluralism disguises the fact that these structures are dominated by a liberal elite that controls both the parameters of acceptable discourse and the key decision-making organisations, exercising subtle yet pervasive forms of power and domination. In this view, for example, the supposed legislative gridlock generated by the US electoral system obscures the exercise of power by the 'fourth branch' of government – rule by unelected experts, bureaucrats, and regulators. As Paul Gottfried puts it, the liberal state 'is becoming the instrument of a political class marked by a common access to power and a shared vision of change. Seizing

---

[14] Viktor Orbán, 'Speech at the CPAC on 19 May 2022', *Visegrad Post* (24 May 2022). As discussed in Chapter 1, this was the first time CPAC met outside the United States.

opportunities to transform society, this class has used entitlements to gain leverage over citizens. But it also conceals its power and designs by presenting itself as perpetually caught between interest groups.'[15]

In recent years, these themes have been most systematically pursued in the United States under the overarching concept of the 'administrative state'. Given public prominence by Trump advisor Steve Bannon's 2017 declaration that one of the President's goals was to 'deconstruct the administrative state', the term represents a more detailed offshoot of managerialist theory, developed primarily by thinkers associated with the Claremont Institute.[16] Writing in the Institute's magazine *The American Mind*, John Fonte, Senior Fellow at the Heritage Foundation, brings these themes together revealingly:

> The authority of the administrative state does not rest on raw power alone; like any political regime, it needs moral and intellectual legitimacy. This moral-intellectual legitimacy is rooted in a system of principles, values, mores, norms, and cultural habits that together constitute what Antonio Gramsci called ideological hegemony. What could be described as the "cultural leviathan" provides moral-intellectual legitimacy to the administrative state. The cultural leviathan consists of the vast network of universities, mainstream media, corporate human resources departments, public schools, and the entertainment industry that promotes, creates, and polices, norms and opinions. The cultural leviathan bolsters the moral-intellectual legitimacy of the administrative state by exercising ideological hegemony through the advancement of what is euphemistically called "diversity".[17]

---

[15] Gottfried, *After Liberalism*, xi. See also O'Meara, *New Culture, New Right*, 77–124; Sunic, *Against Democracy*, 125–197; Ruuben Kaalep and August Meister, *Rebirth of Europe: The Ethnofuturist Manifesto* (London: Arktos, 2020), 28–35.

[16] For a critical analysis of Claremont's move towards the radical Right, see Laura K. Field, 'What the Hell Happened to the Claremont Institute?', *The Bulwark* (13 July 2021).

[17] John Fonte, 'What the Right Must Learn from Trump', *The American Mind* (10 April 2019). Fonte makes yet another nod to Gramsci: 'Under the all-consuming concept of "diversity", mainstream liberalism enforces ethnic and gender group rights and

In the face of this onslaught, Fonte concludes in tones remarkably reminiscent of Sam Francis that since liberalism is 'firmly entrenched in American civic life the conservativism of the future ... needs to be more "disruptive". We are not defending the status quo. Therefore, moderate policies and a restrained "conservative disposition" are not an adequate mind-set for the task ahead.'

In the eyes of another influential proponent of this critique, John Marini, the legislative and executive branches of government have increasingly been usurped by the bureaucratic rationality and power of administration: of rule by experts and officials who claim to speak in the name of an objective, disinterested public good.[18] He holds that 'the bureaucracies have developed the instinct for self-preservation at all costs. They do not, however, defend themselves on the basis of self-interest. Rather, they see themselves as defenders of institutional rationality, as a part of the social intelligence that establishes the legitimacy of rule within the administrative state.'[19] He continues,

> America is in the midst of a great crisis in terms of its economy, its chaotic civil society, its political corruption, and its inability to defend any kind of tradition – or way of life derived from that tradition – because of the transformation of its culture by the intellectual elites. This sweeping cultural transformation occurred almost completely outside the political process of mobilizing public opinion and political majorities. The

---

political correctness in the major institutions of civil society that the progressives have captured. Liberals under the banner of "diversity" are establishing what Italian Marxist Antonio Gramsci called "ideological-cultural hegemony".'

[18] Before becoming a professor at the University of Nevada-Reno, Marini was an assistant to Clarence Thomas prior to the latter's appointment to the Supreme Court. Thomas is now perhaps the most influential conservative on the court; see Jill Abramson, 'In the Ultimate Coup for the Right, It's Justice Thomas's Court Now', *Financial Times* (7 July 2022). A call for the courts to 'reign in' the administrative state is Peter J. Wallison, *Judicial Fortitude: The Last Chance to Reign in the Administrative State* (New York: Encounter Books, 2018).

[19] John Marini, 'Donald Trump and the American Crisis', *Claremont Review of Books* (22 July 2016). The themes are explored more extensively in his *Unmasking the Administrative State: The Crisis of American Politics in the Twenty-first Century*, Ken Masugi ed. (New York: Encounter Books, 2019).

American people themselves did not participate or consent to the wholesale undermining of their way of life, which government and the bureaucracy helped to facilitate by undermining those institutions of civil society that were dependent upon a public defense of the old morality.[20]

From this perspective, the prominence of liberal rights in modern politics is not just a deviation from conservative positions that assert the importance of tradition and substantive values or natural law. It is yet another avenue of managerial power and domination. These analyses highlight the extraordinary expansion of the modern language of rights and the power of liberal-dominated legal elites: disability rights, LGBTQ+ rights, the right to choose, the right to die, the right to health care, the right to work, the right to live free from discrimination, etc. In this open-ended framework, de Benoist protests, 'to respect the dignity of another human being is no longer to respect the respect which he conserves for himself for the moral law; it is today, more and more, to respect the choice that he has made, whatever this choice may be, in the realisation of his rights.'[21] The fusion of mass democracy with this conversion of a vast assortment of demands, desires, and interests into the language of rights has transformed liberal ethics into a dual mechanism for the affirmation of the unlimited right to individual hedonism on the one hand, and the determination and enforcement of acceptable or unacceptable rights through the limitless geographical expansion of managerial networks of power on the other. As de Benoist and Champetier declare in their millennial manifesto of the European New Right:

> In the process of globalisation, Western civilization is promoting the worldwide domination of a ruling class whose only claim to legitimacy resides in its abstract manipulations

---

[20] Marini, 'Donald Trump and the American Crisis'.
[21] Alain de Benoist, *Beyond Human Rights: Defending Freedoms* (London: Arktos, 2011), 6. De Benoist attributes this formulation to the conservative political theorist Pierre Manent.

(logico-symbolic) of the signs and values of the system already in place. Aspiring to uninterrupted growth of capital and to the permanent reign of social engineering, this New Class provides the manpower for the media, large national and multinational firms, and international organizations. This New Class produces and reproduces everywhere the same type of person: cold-blooded specialists, rationality detached from day-to-day realities. It also engenders abstract individualism, utilitarian beliefs, a superficial humanitarianism, indifference to history, an obvious lack of culture, isolation from the real world, the sacrifice of the real to the virtual, an inclination to corruption, nepotism and to buying votes.[22]

GLOBAL MANAGERIALISM

For the radical Right, globalisation is the product of the logic of liberal rule and power, of the interests and the utopia underpinning liberal modernity as an epoch. When its protagonists speak of the liberal world order in this ideological context, they do not mean the relatively thin view espoused by many liberals in the study of complex interdependence, global governance, or 'soft power' (which many on the radical Right would likely regard as New Class ideologies supporting that order rather than analysing it). Instead, fusing philosophy, history, and sociology in a diverse but identifiably resonant multi-level analysis, they refer to managerialism as a much deeper form of sociopolitical power that is not strictly inter-national in its mode of operation but *intrinsically* globalist.

Drawing on Max Weber's classic account, Gottfried argues that this is because 'administration ascribes to itself a rationality that

---

[22] De Benoist and Champetier, *Manifesto*, 29. In full rhetorical flow, Michael Anton, a former Trump official, suggests that the theory of the administrative state explains America's '"regime change", how we got from "there" – our founders' understanding of justice, morality, and politics – to "here": the tradition-and-history-destroying, common-good-denying, anarcho-tyrannical, pathologically altruistic dystopian oligarchy currently throttling the West.' Anton, 'Draining the Swamp'.

transcends cultural specificity. It is the rules of bureaucratic organization that seek, or are alleged, to provide the moral substance of a society thus governed, and those rules, as Weber notes, are seen to be coextensive with a universal science of management.'[23] What experts in the domestic realm call public administration thus has its global counterpart in the growth of expert-dominated international organisations, transnational legal orders, liberal rights-advocating NGOs, and a host of other actors populating contemporary world politics. As Pat Buchanan wrote while campaigning against NAFTA in the mid-1990s:

> Why does the Populist Right abhor NAFTA? Because NAFTA epitomizes all that repels us in the modern state. Though advertised as "free trade," it is anti-freedom, 1,200 pages of rules, regulations, laws, fines, commissions – plus side agreements – setting up no fewer than 49 new bureaucracies. Henry Kissinger is right: NAFTA is not really a trade treaty at all, but the architecture of the New World Order. Like Maastricht, it is part of a skeletal structure for world government. At its root is an abiding faith in the superior wisdom of a global managerial class – our would-be Lords of the Universe.[24]

In this analysis, the global expansion of this administrative will to power is mandated by the progressive universalism validating the normative premises of the managerial revolution, and by the endless opportunities that technological and biopolitical innovation offers to address a wide variety of increasingly global political and developmental challenges. Over the course of the twentieth century, this has facilitated the alignment of bureaucratic interests with those of a growing intellectual elite that has consolidated and expanded its influence under the umbrella of proliferating international agencies and the global authority invested in them. The Hungarian-American 'counter-revolutionary' Thomas Molnar noted these trends in the early 1960s:

---

[23] Gottfried, *After Liberalism*, 74.
[24] Patrick J. Buchanan, 'America First, NAFTA Never', *Washington Post* (7 November 1993).

Within a national community the obstacles to progress, as it is envisaged by the intellectuals, are difficult to overcome: tradition; the memory of previous conflicts; concrete interests represented by pressure groups; the weight of an entrenched bureaucracy and civil service – all of these factors narrow the field of action and frustrate the intellectuals' reforming zeal. It is then quite natural that they find a greater challenge in a situation where the means and ends of a problem are far from settled, where the problem itself has not even been formulated. The very fact that the "society of nations" is in a state of nature, that it is unregulated by a central and enforcing authority, helps the intellectuals to devise new means of dealing with its just-emerging problems.[25]

Put differently, the real driving forces behind economic and cultural globalisation are the functional dynamics of liberal managerialism itself. Global managerial liberalism targets 'traditional' social orders, states, ideas, and identities that oppose its expansion, eroding non-liberal societies and refashioning them in its image. As in domestic politics, the primary methods for dealing with this resistance are the soft powers of liberal global governance – claims of expert knowledge, therapeutic social and education policies, development, cultural stigmatisation, and legal activism – though recourse to violent coercion is also frequent, as the wars advocated and conducted by managerial liberal elites and states in the name of liberal democracy and human rights demonstrate.[26]

This interpretation provides the radical Right with a distinctive view of US hegemony. To Francis, for instance, the American managerial state is 'itself part of an interdependent global complex of other mass states and transnational structures, each of which contains mass

---

[25] Thomas Molnar, *The Two Faces of American Foreign Policy* (Indianapolis: Bobbs-Merill Co., 1962), 24.
[26] Paul Gottfried, 'America and the West: The Multiculturalist International', *Orbis* 45 (2002), 145–161; Francis, *Leviathan*; Alain de Benoist, *Carl Schmitt Today: Terrorism, 'Just War' and the State of Emergency* (London: Arktos, 2003); O'Meara, *New Culture, New Right*, 210–225.

populations, commands massive amounts of economic resources, spans massive distances and territories, and controls massive levels of lethal force.'[27] To be sure, some of these mass states occasionally disagree or come into conflict over material gains, prestige strategies, and fundamental cultural disagreements. Yet because their interactions are overseen by managerial elites through multiple channels, across many different issue areas, and at many levels of mass organisation (the military, diplomatic corps, foreign and trade ministries, multinational corporations, commercial bureaucracies, intelligence gathering agencies, transnational and regional organisations, and NGOs), the functional imperatives of these organisations, along with the interests of those who control them, eventually outgrow the territorial constraints of the sovereign state and become predatory on the idea and political rationality of the national interest.[28] As Francis argued in the early 1990s:

> The managerial state and its linked economic and cultural structures have succeeded in breaking down the regional variations, local and sectional autonomy, and institutional stability and independence of Middle Americans, and the regime now lurches happily toward a globalization that seeks to integrate all Americans (and all other peoples as well) into a planetary political, economic, demographic, and cultural order in which national identity will eventually disappear entirely. The homogenization of subnational social and regional differences through political centralization, urbanization and mobility, mass communications, and mass consumption and production means that the older, decentralised identities of particular social classes, sections, communities, and religious and ethnic groups no longer effectively mobilise Americans for political action. Identities as Southerners or Midwesterners, Catholic or Protestant, Anglo-Saxon Old Stock or European ethnic, small businessman or assembly-line worker, no longer seem to offer sufficient bonds or

[27] Francis, *Leviathan*, 471.
[28] Ibid., 471–473, 533.

common interests for serious political cooperation for any goal beyond immediate special interests.²⁹

Thus, whereas the embedded liberalism of the post-war period expanded free trade while providing individual states with the opportunity to develop public welfare provision and protect labour forces, post–Cold War liberalism unleashes the full power of managerial capitalism and culture to cut individuals loose from all communal bonds and traditional networks of support while releasing them from the responsibilities and restrictions that those networks impose. More recently, 'woke capitalism' has made this attack on culture and tradition even worse, and according to the 2024 Republican presidential hopeful Vivek Ramaswamy, risks empowering a small group of corporate elites to decide what is right for society at large.³⁰ The result is not an increase in cosmopolitan pluralism and diversity, but the creeping 'standardization of lifestyles, reduction of differences and particularities, conformity of attitudes and behaviours'.³¹ Politically, these homogenising trends make it almost impossible to construct durable identities that cohere over time and space, and which can effectively mobilise particular populations for collective action – in no small part because such identities are ruled out by liberalism as an unacceptable (even fascist) kind of essentialism or reaction. It is in this sense that radical Right polemics often speak of the 'soft totalitarianism' of late modern managerial liberalism. As Ruuben Kaalep and August Meister declare in their 'ethnofuturist manifesto' for the Baltic radical Right:

> Where liberalism talks of diversity, it really aims at erasing all distinctions. Where it talks of multiculturalism, it aims at

---

[29] Samuel T. Francis, 'Nationalism: Old and New', *Chronicles* (May 1992), 20. See also Greg Johnson, *Towards a New Nationalism* (San Francisco: Counter-Currents Publishing, 2018); Norman Lowell, *Aristocratic Manifesto for Imperium Europa* (London: Arktos, 2019), 61–68.

[30] Vivek Ramaswamy, 'The "Stakeholders" vs The People', *Wall Street Journal* (12 February 2020); see also Andrew Edgecliff-Johnson, 'The War on "Woke Capitalism"', *Financial Times* (27 May 2022).

[31] Alain de Benoist, 'Confronting Globalization', *Telos* 108 (1996), 133.

creating a global melting pot where no culture survives. Where liberalism talks of individual rights and happiness, it is building a mass society with a lack of personal creativity ... If there is a demand for something genuinely new, it either becomes part of the mass culture, compulsory for everyone – or if it cannot be reconciled with the essence of modernism, it becomes a threat and a violation of the party line of liberalism. In a way, the Western mass society has nearly achieved what any totalitarian system in the past could only dream of. It controls all choices and options. The mass of consumers lacks the means to even imagine an alternative to liberalism. The same cityscape, the same multiracial faces would greet us in New York, London, Mumbai or Hong Kong.[32]

In this analysis, the continuous growth and proliferation of international institutions since 1945 is cast as a powerful mechanism for the globalising expansion of managerial structures of identity and interests. Drawing on a variety of policy instruments designed to circumvent national democratic legislative processes, these institutions redistribute decision-making authority to a conglomerate of supranational bureaucrats, technical experts, and judges, who in turn open the legislative process to a globalised liberal network of organisations operating outside the bounds of democratic accountability. These include the International Criminal Court, which seeks to place itself over and above the UN Security Council to impose binding rules that will constrain the conduct of states; the World Trade Organisation, which creates mechanisms that allow for binding trade rules to be imposed without the consent of all member states; and national judges who often rely upon the decisions of foreign and international tribunals in their opinions and in their interpretations of domestic law. Under the guise of universality, morality, pluralism, and tolerance, liberal structures of

---

[32] Kaalep and Meister, *Rebirth of Europe*, 33–34.

global governance place such decisions in the hands of managerial elites who seek institutional power to enforce their decisions over national decision-making bodies in ways that subvert the authority of the sovereign territorial state system and empower immigrants and minorities vis-à-vis national majority cultures. In the words of Kaalep and Meister:

> The most advantageous world for the global elite is one where the highest value is the individual, but the individual himself is freed with the help of postmodernism from any meaning, significance and wider context, and finds himself isolated and vulnerable. Carl Jung once wrote that the mass state has no interest in strengthening mutual understanding between people – it strives towards atomisation and the physical isolation of individuals. The more isolated are individuals, the more consolidated becomes the state, and vice versa. The only thing that has changed is that the system has become more anonymous – it is not the state that contributes to the entropy of society, because the state itself is one of the objects of attack.[33]

This vision avers that the same 'Western and purely academic constructivism' informed the Eastern enlargement process after the end of the Cold War.[34] Instead of strengthening existing political structures, the EU hastily extended membership to countries poorly prepared for entry, while simultaneously pursuing what the British conservative philosopher Roger Scruton called the liberal 'de-Christianizing of Europe' through the European Parliament, the Fundamental Rights Agency, and other organisations charged with advocating at all legislative levels an expanding human rights agenda 'inherently hostile to the traditional family and the religion-based morality that shaped it'.[35]

---

[33] Kaalep and Meister, *Rebirth of Europe*, 29.
[34] Tomislav Sunić, 'L'Union Européenne est entrain de s'autodétruire', *Éléments* (8 May 2014). Our Translation.
[35] Roger Scruton, 'The Future of European Civilization: Lessons for America', *Heritage Foundation Report* (8 December 2015).

If successful, the result will be the increasing dissolution of the sovereign nation-states of Europe into an amorphous continental space without cultural coherence and sense of political determination. As Guillaume Faye argues in his reflections on the Brexit referendum, this was never the idea of European integration per se. Instead, it reflects the Atlanticist liberalism that has guided this project over the years:

> Initially, with a common agricultural policy and a philosophy of continental protectionism, the European Community was going in the right direction. But this has been completely abandoned in favour of unbridled free trade by the Commission and other institutions that have nothing but ineffective and undemocratic management. They are not built according to the needs of the peoples and nations of Europe, but to serve the interests of a privileged caste of eurocrats (technocratic and parliamentary) which paradoxically contains many Europhobes who abuse the system ... The idea of European integration was ruined by anti-European forces in reality. The refusal to admit the "Christian roots" of Europe is symbolic. Europe is desired without roots, open to all migratory invasions and without economic protection. The European Union was seen as a voluntary and objective way to destroy the historical and ethnic nations of Europe. All under the benevolent eye of Washington.[36]

According to this narrative, NATO's post-Cold War enlargement has charted a similar path in the security sector. Originally created to fight the Cold War, the alliance should have disappeared at the same time as the Soviet Union and the Warsaw Pact. Instead, it rapidly transformed itself from a military organisation into an international police force devoted to the defence and expansion of the so-called liberal zone of peace. By the end of the decade, this vastly expanded

---

[36] Guillaume Faye, 'Brexit: Quake or Squib?', *Radix Journal* (20 July 2016).

'global NATO'[37] had adopted a broad, interventionist security agenda that stressed the normative and institutional structures of states. Liberal state building and democratisation became the alliance's aims, often working in tandem with other international organisations such as the UN and NGOs.

For the radical Right, these transformations show that the NATO alliance has become the illegitimate and destructive agent of liberal managerialism and the New Class.[38] Writing on the website *American Greatness*, Angelo Codevilla[39] argues that NATO is not about the protection of sovereign states: it has become 'An Alliance to Protect the Ruling Class's Power and Prestige'. The alliance's embrace of 'progressive' universalism erodes national sovereignty and denies the particularist values of 'Western civilization' that it was created to protect. Instead, it is now yet another mechanism through which the transnational managerial elite projects its values and advances its interests to the detriment of the very peoples it is supposed to protect. 'This class', he declares, 'regards self-rule, the capacity of people in towns, regions, or nations to decide by vote how they shall live, as among the evils to be done away with. It treats as the enemy anything – thoughts, practices, institutions – that limit its own power and prestige. For their power and prestige, after all, are what it is allied to protect'.[40]

---

[37] Alain de Benoist, 'The Return of the Iron Curtain', *The Postil Magazine* (1 August 2022); 'Otan, Assimilation et Syrie', *Girodivite* (12 April 2021). See also Robert Steuckers, 'Géopolitique et avenir de l'Europe', *Geopolitika* (8 September 2022). Our translation.

[38] For an early post–Cold War diagnostic, see Thomas Molnar, *The Emerging Atlantic Culture* (New Brunswick: Transaction, 1994).

[39] An obituary by Daniel McCarthy, the editor of *Modern Age*, notes Codevilla's significance: 'In retrospect, he wasn't just prescient about the Trump movement … Codevilla helped bring it about by diagnosing it.' Quoted in Clay Risen, 'Angelo Codevilla, Whose Writings Anticipated Trumpism, Dies at 78', *New York Times* (30 October 2021). Codevilla's most extended treatment in this vein is *The Ruling Class: How They Corrupted America and What We Can Do about It* (New York: Beaufort Books, 2010).

[40] Angelo Codevilla, 'NATO Now Serves the Interests of the Transatlantic Ruling Class', *American Greatness* (15 July 2018). On the pro-Trump Claremont conservatives and foreign policy, see Matthew J. Peterson, 'Claremont vs. Foreign Policy Establishment', *The American Mind* (21 January 2019).

The radical Right is also fiercely critical of how this managerial 'biopolitics' has impacted countries and cultures in the Global South, where the expansion of managerial rationalities and networks under the guise of Cold War containment and later various modernisation and development programmes has eviscerated traditional cultures and modes of social organisation. Although they have varied over decades and geographical regions, such programmes have sought in one way or another to cultivate allegiances to an abstract conception of humanity at the expense of concrete kinship ties and ethnic, religious, national, and social identities. Concerted efforts to extend or export late-modern conceptions of liberal statehood to these societies, to modernise their military, health, education, and communication infrastructures, and to harmonise their business, banking, and accounting practices with those of Western managerial states are all regarded as part of the same process.

The result of this global expansion, however, was not the wholesale transformation of traditional societies as predicted by the high priests of modernisation theory and Western development agencies, but instead the creation of various hybrid types of authoritarian managerial regimes with few organic ties to the communities over which they rule.[41] The main consequences, according to the radical Right, were the destruction of the environment, the spread of vast urban slums, the proliferation of ethnic conflicts, civil wars, and religiously motivated terrorism. The subsequent securitisation of these failed modernisation experiments in turn provided the rationale for a major refunctioning of the Cold War managerial complex through organisations such as the UN, the EU, NATO, OSCE, and the proliferation of new globalist formulas: democratic enlargement, human security, poverty reduction, the climate crisis, and the war on terror that have all intensified anti-Western sentiments.

There are, following this logic, clear causal links between the failures of liberal globalist initiatives and what the radical Right

[41] Francis, *Leviathan*, 473–474.

perceives as a growing refugee crisis that exacerbates the longstanding problem of 'Third World' economic migration and threatens to irreversibly change the ethnic composition of populations in the North.[42] Guillaume Faye suggests that we understand this situation as some sort of 'Scramble for Africa' in reverse:

> Colonising migrations are pouring into the northern hemisphere like a backlash against colonisation and the demographic ageing of the North; the Nineteenth and Twentieth century opposition between Europe and North America, and – within the Eurasian continent – between "Westerners" (which did not always include Germans) and Slavs is coming to an end. Today's contrast – tomorrow's confrontation – is between North and South [...] We are witnessing the return of wide-scale invasions under a new guise. The phenomenon is far more serious today, as the "invaders" have preserved a formidable "home base": the countries they have left, the motherlands which are always solidly behind them and ready to defend them – and which secretly aspire to do so through force in the future. The modern egalitarian mindset is utterly powerless.[43]

The conspiratorial character of these polemics serves to rationalise a sense of disempowerment and impotence in the face of rapid sociocultural and economic change. The offensive rhetoric channelling this resentment expresses the desire for a politics that finds no legitimate outlet within existing domestic and international institutions. According to another influential narrative revived by the French novelist Renaud Camus, for example, the alleged 'replacement' of white European populations with non-European peoples is part of a wider process of de-spiritualisation, de-culturation, and economic

---

[42] Guillaume Faye, *Convergence of Catastrophes* (London: Arktos, 2004/2012); Francis, *Leviathan*, 471–474; Kaalep and Meister, *Rebirth of Europe*, 34; Alain de Benoist, 'Immigration: The Reserve Army of Capital', *Éléments* 141 (2011). See also Richard Arnold and Ekatarina Romanova, '"White World's Future": An Analysis of the Russian Far-Right', *Journal for the Study of Radicalism* 7:3 (2013), 79–107.

[43] Faye, *Archeofuturism*, 76.

neo-liberalisation designed to create more docile and completely malleable human populations without any racial, ethnic, sexual, geographic, or historical specificities.[44] Like Faye and Eric Zemmour (author of *Le Suicide Français*),[45] Camus contends that black and brown immigrants (many of them Muslims) are in the process of wiping out Europe's majority cultures in what amounts to a ruthless act of 'genocide by substitution'.[46] In this view, the 'great replacement' is not just a demographic theory or a xenophobic charge but a 'totalitarian system' competing with the totalitarianism of Islam for the mastery of the West.[47] This system is overseen by a global financial 'Davocracy' and a transnational 'cultural ruling class' empowered by the 'unprecedented development of the techniques of influence, suggestion and mind control' since the 1970s.[48] As Camus emphasises:

> Governments – and not only governments: the press, the media, intellectuals, judges – are not only coping with this sad conjuncture, as mere collaborators would. They have created it, either because they think it is unavoidable, or because they have construed it as an instrument serving their own interest. And most likely they think it is right because they feel that it is both unavoidable and in their interest. They are not collaborators, they are perpetrators (of the crime of ethnic substitution).[49]

Paleoconservatives have been disseminating similar ideas in the United States since at least the end of the Cold War, lamenting the open-border policies of a New Class that welcomes immigration as a

---

[44] Renaud Camus, *You Will Not Replace Us!* (Plieux: Chez L'Auteur, 2011/2018), 193.

[45] Eric Zemmour, *Le Suicide Français* (Paris: Albin Michel, 2014). Zemmour repeatedly endorsed Camus' great replacement theory during his 2022 French presidential election campaign. See Nice-Matin, 'Eric Zemmour toujours pas en campagne, enfin presque, mais pas encore', *Marianne* (4 August 2021).

[46] Camus, *You Will Not Replace Us*, 134. Camus appropriates the phrase from the Martinican poet and anti-colonial thinker Aimé Césaire.

[47] Ibid., 137.

[48] Ibid., 139–141. This echoes older, anti-Semitic, and conspiratorial themes, allowing a wide range of ideological affinities to coalesce.

[49] Ibid., 64.

bonanza of 'new opportunities for managing civil rights, ethnic conflicts, education, health, housing, welfare, social therapy, and assimilation itself'.[50] More recently, advocates of the North American New Right, such as Greg Johnson, have gone yet further, promoting an explicit ethnonationalism and the notion of a 'white genocide' through immigration.[51] In this view, conservative efforts to confront and reverse these demographic trends are constantly blocked by a concerted managerial campaign to build a global constitutional order that will supersede the decision-making process of all states in a wide variety of areas, including human rights, free movement of labour, the environment, health, and political-military affairs.[52]

The centre of these anti-immigration, frequently racist worldviews is undoubtedly in Europe and the United States, but radical Right ideologues and activists in the non-West share similar interpretations of the devastating effects of global managerialism on local traditions and cultures. In Japan, a number of thinkers have married their critique of America with the destructiveness of liberal managerialism.[53] According to them, the hallmark of American

[50] Samuel T. Francis, 'The New Underclass', in *Revolution from the Middle* (Rockford, IL: Middle American Press, 1997), 31. See also Pat Buchanan, *The Death of the West: How Dying Population and Immigrant Invasions Imperil Our Country and Civilization* (Spokane, WA: Griffin, 2002); Jared Taylor ed., *The Real American Dilemma: Race, Immigration and the Future of America* (Oakton, VA: New Century Books, 1998); Norman Lowell, *Imperium Europa: The Book That Changed the World* (Baldwin, KS: Imperium Books, 2009); Kaalep and Meister, *Rebirth of Europe*, 34–45; De Benoist, 'Immigration'.

[51] Greg Johnson, *White Identity Politics* (San Francisco: Counter-Currents Publishing, 2020).

[52] Radical Right polemics here converge with an expanding body of conservative 'sovereigntist' literature in the United States, Europe, and beyond. See, for instance, John Bolton, 'Should We Take Global Governance Seriously?', *Chicago Journal of International Law* 1:2 (2000), 205–221; Jeremy Rabkin, *Law without Nations: Why Constitutional Government Requires Sovereign States* (Princeton: Princeton University Press, 2007); John Fonte, *Sovereignty or Submission* (New York: Encounter Books, 2012); An overview is Michael Goodhart and Stacy Bondanella Taninchev, 'The New Sovereigntist Challenge for Global Governance: Democracy without Sovereignty', *International Studies Quarterly* 55:4 (2012), 1047–1068.

[53] See Keishi Saeki, *Gendai Nihon no Ideorogī: Gurōbarizumu to Kokka Ishiki* [Contemporary Japanese Ideology: Globalism and State Consciousness] (Tokyo: Kodansha, 1998); Hidetsugu Yagi, *Han 'Jinken' Sengen* [Declaring against 'Human Rights'] (Tokyo: Chikuma Shobo, 2001). Our translation.

hegemony has been the deconstruction of political institutions and traditional social networks, and the surreptitious implementation of liberal managerial structures and – crucially – liberal values. In this view, the post-World War II reconstruction of Japan as a liberal democracy was effectively a 'national experiment in forcible Americanisation'. As a foreign form of political organisation, liberal democracy required an artificial implementation of norms and traditions by discrediting those which had developed organically from the nation's long cultural history. In the words of Susumu Nishibe, 'Japan's status as a vassal state to the United States is underpinned not only by the relationship of power based in the latter's military might, but also on obeying the victors [of World War II] in the matter of values.'[54] Thus, the implementation of liberal and cosmopolitan values allows for continued American domination over Japan – and the non-Western world more broadly. Inherited by a class of traitorous national managerial elites, this foreign domination is self-perpetuating.

The radical Right's anti-managerialism also finds powerful resonances as anti-Westernism and anti-colonialism in many parts of the Global South. While rarely explicitly allied with radical conservative views in the North, the widespread view that liberal modernity and western interventionism reproduce inequality and long-standing historical hierarchies in the international system can nevertheless produce discursive equivalences and ideological alignments between populations in the Global South and radical Right agendas.[55] Deepak Nair has shown how right-wing populism in Indonesia, Cambodia, and the Philippines was facilitated by anti-colonial sentiments that served as the glue between ideologically

---

[54] Susumu Nishibe, *Bunmei no Teki Minshushugi: Kiki no Seijitetsugaku* [Democracy's Threat to Civilization: A Political Philosophy of Crisis] (Tokyo: Jiji Press, 2011), 224. Our translation.

[55] Rebecca Adler-Nissen and Ayşe Zarakol, 'Struggles for Recognition: The Liberal International Order and the Merger of Its Discontents', *International Organization* 75:3 (2021), 611–634.

disparate groups.⁵⁶ Another telling example of the global alliances facilitated by anti-Westernism is the Franco-Beninese, Pan-African writer and activist Kemi Seba who advocates a radical racial separatism or *ethno-differentialisme* that parallels the European radical Right's identitarian, anti-immigration discourses. Seba's Supra-Negritude stands for 'total and real separatism in relation to the Western world', politically, economically, spiritually, and psychologically.⁵⁷ This stance has endeared him to many of Europe's leading radical conservative thinkers and prominent ultranationalists, including Alain Soral who runs the webzine *Egalité et Réconciliation*, as well as Alexander Dugin, who has described Seba as 'a hope for all the forces of multipolar resistance'.⁵⁸ Seba also made common cause with the populist Italian Five Star Movement, joining the Italians in blaming French imperialism for the on-going migration crisis. Explaining his support for Russia in the war with Ukraine, Seba argued that:

> What is happening now in Ukraine will affect the whole world and not only Africa, as the latter is already at war with globalism. This war is a struggle between the defenders of globalism and those who defend multipolarity. Therefore, the war between Ukraine and Russia is really a confrontation between those who want to "westernize" humanity against those who want to protect the identity of the various peoples of the world. Vladimir Putin's fight against NATO and the West will affect Africa as well as other continents. The West not only wants to destroy Vladimir Putin but also Africa, Latin America and the Middle East, as the goal of globalism is to destabilize all continents equally.⁵⁹

---

⁵⁶ Deepak Nair, 'Populists in the Shadow of Great Power Competition: Duterte, Sukarno, and Sihanouk in Comparative Perspective', *European Journal of International Relations* 29:3 (2023), 723–750.
⁵⁷ Kemi Seba, *Supra-négritude: Autodétermination, antivictimisation, virilité du peuple* (Paris: Fiat-Lux editions, 2013), 189. Our translation.
⁵⁸ Rita Abrahamsen, 'Internationalists, Sovereigntists, Nativists: Contending Visions of World Order in Pan-Africanism', *Review of International Studies* 46:1 (2020), 56–74.
⁵⁹ Kemi Seba, 'Russia is at War with Globalism', *Geopolitika* (24 March 2022). The website is associated with Dugin.

As we show in Chapter 5, many groups and activists in the South have also found common ground with the radical Right's defence of the traditional family against the advancement of feminist and gender policies. Opposition to the relentless spread of liberal family values by so-called femocrats in international organisations such as the UN and WHO has united various normative and epistemic communities that are at other times antagonistic to each other and has given rise to powerful North–South coalitions where actors in the South are key proponents of radical Right critiques of global managerialism.[60]

CONSTRUCTING THE ENEMY

One could be forgiven for reading the radical Right's polemical analyses of global liberal managerialism as the latest offering of a longstanding tradition of reactionary pessimism and cultural despair.[61] And in many ways, it is just that. But they also depict the conditions of crisis and decadence as an opportunity for the re-assertion of a more 'authentic' conservative agency that can harness the social forces available to reverse the situation. This is where historical and analytic narratives of liberal orders are turned to practical use.

In ways that often resonate with the dialectical theses of the radical Left, radical Right analyses suggest that the globalising processes of liberal managerialism create the conditions for its own overcoming. Generally speaking, they identify at least two main weaknesses in the incumbent regime, both within states and internationally. First, managerial liberalism's hedonistic ethics, relativist values, and therapeutic social practices tend to fragment societies into ever more diverse groups, each advocating their own programmes and interests. This process inhibits collective action and weakens the progressive

---

[60] See Clifford Bob, *The Global Right Wing and the Clash of World Politics* (Cambridge: Cambridge University Press, 2012); Anne Marie Goetz, 'The New Competition in Multilateral Norm-Setting: Transnational Feminists and the Illiberal Backlash', *Daedalus* 149:1 (2020), 160–179.

[61] For a good overview of this tradition, see Arthur Herman, *The Idea of Decline in Western History* (New York: Free Press 2007).

state's ability to enact its promises through appeals to collective solidarity and national identity and unity. The resulting sense of failure is reflected in the general disbelief towards Enlightenment narratives of progress that sociologists have come to associate with our contemporary condition of postmodernity. Since the end of the Cold War and the collapse of the Soviet Bloc, the anomie and heightened anxiety that comes with the state's declining ability to act as the principal guarantor of existence under accelerating conditions of globalisation has been matched by a growing disconnect between the exercise of power and the ethical purpose of that power. As de Benoist and Champetier argue:

> The New Class finds itself again confronted with a whole series of conflicts (between capital and labor, equality and freedom, the public and the private) which it had attempted to avoid for over half a century. Likewise, its ineffectiveness, its wastefulness, and its counter-productivity appear more and more evident. The system tends to close in upon itself, while the public feels indifferent toward or angry at a managerial elite which does not even speak the same language as they do. As regards every major social issue, the gulf widens between the rulers who repeat the usual technocratic discourse and those governed who experience, in their day to day lives, the consequences of all this. All the while the media draw attention away from the real world towards one of mere representation. At the highest levels of society, we find technocratic double talk, sanctimonious babble, and the comfort of capital yield; at the bottom of the social ladder, the pains of day-to-day life, an incessant search for meaning, and the desire for shared values.[62]

A second source of instability stems from liberal managerialism's relentless attacks on the economic and social positions of those who refuse to adapt to the forces and demands of globalisation. In North

---

[62] De Benoist and Champetier, *Manifesto*, 29–30.

America and Europe, this represents large semi-skilled and geographically immobile populations for whom the more fluid and relativistic ethos of liberal modernity is irreconcilable with the traditional values they continue to cherish. These are the 'left behinds', those still tied to locality, who experience migration or cultural cosmopolitanism as a threat, as well as the 'basket of deplorables'[63] who hold onto tradition, to their inherited communities and prejudices, even as they are being eroded by globalisation. The 'left behinds' are systematically disparaged as backward, bigoted, dependent, and in need (if they are lucky) of re-skilling by a New Class elite that can afford to sustain progressive views because their affluence and privileges shield them from having to compete and share spaces, schools, and job markets with the minorities they seek to empower. As Francis put it in the US context when he was campaigning for Pat Buchanan during the 1990s among predominantly white, working, and middle-class constituencies:

> these Americans find that their jobs are insecure, their savings stripped of value, their neighborhoods and schools and homes unsafe, their elected leaders indifferent and often crooked, their moral beliefs and religious professions and social codes under perpetual attack even from their own government, their children taught to despise what they believe, their very identity and heritage as a people threatened, and their future – political, economic, cultural, racial, national, and personal – uncertain. They find that no matter which party or candidate they support, no matter what the candidates and parties promise, nothing substantially changes, except for the worse. Although they do the labor that sustains the managerial system, pay the taxes that support it, fight the wars its leaders devise, raise the families and try to pass on the beliefs and habits that enable the regime and the country to exist and survive, what they receive from the

---

[63] As Hillary Clinton infamously described them during her 2016 US Presidential campaign.

regime is never commensurate with what they give it ... They are at once the real victims of the regime and the core or nucleus of American civilization, the Real America, the American Nation.[64]

Radical Rightists attribute the under-representation of these large, culturally conservative segments of the population in large part to the misalignment of their interests with those of centre-right parties. In North America as in Europe, this misalignment is regarded as a symptom of the degeneration of mainstream conservative movements and ideologies. Since the end of the Cold War, this mainstream has fully embraced the administrative state and the consumerist culture of neoliberal capitalism. It has also supported the missionary wars instigated by the liberal Left and the misnamed 'neo' conservatives (who were actually liberal globalists masquerading as conservatives), while dismissing traditional conservative positions as political liabilities.[65] In the eyes of the radical Right, however, the financial crisis of 2008 and the catastrophic failures of the war on terror in the wider Middle East have significantly undermined the prospects of these mainstream managerial constellations of power and interests – not least because economic sectors affected by globalisation and population movement have now gone beyond declining industries to include once protected New Class professions threatened by offshoring and automation. As Buchanan explained in 2016 when asked why Trump had succeeded where he had repeatedly failed during the 1990s:

> What's different today is that the returns are in, the results are known. Everyone sees clearly now the de-industrialization of America, the cost in blood and treasure from decade-long wars

[64] Francis, 'Nationalism', 19–20.
[65] See Paul Gottfried and Richard Spencer eds., *The Great Purge: The Deformation of the Conservative Movement* (Washington, DC: Washington Summit Publishers, 2015); Samuel T. Francis, *Beautiful Losers: Essays on the Failure of American Conservatism* (Columbia: University of Missouri Press, 1994); Johnson, *Towards a New Nationalism*; Kaalep and Meister, *Rebirth of Europe*, 45–49. See also Alexander Dugin, *The Fourth Political Theory* (London: Arktos 2012).

in Afghanistan and Iraq, and the pervasive presence of illegal immigrants. What I saw at the San Diego border 25 years ago, everyone sees now on cable TV. And not just a few communities but almost every community is experiencing the social impact. The anger and alienation that were building then have reached critical mass now … Not to put too fine a point on it, the revolution is at hand.[66]

These developments over the past three decades are seen as creating numerous opportunities for fundamentally revised conservative projects based on the revitalisation of ethnicity, class, gender, race, and nation. These alternatives are populist in the sense that they seek to mobilise the cultural resentment and further the economic interests of the social forces portrayed as the primary victims of the dominant global liberal regime. Radical conservatives and other aligned actors outside of Europe and the United States also make powerful use of this logic, allowing them to appeal to sentiments of postcolonial critique and even appropriate its rhetoric.[67] Marginalisation and exclusion is cast as the authentic incubator of revived cultural traditions which can confront the foreign nature of global managerialism. According to the Japanese thinker Keishi Saeki, this is because these

> liberal values are founded on principles and historical context that cannot be separated from a Christian worldview that is particular to Western culture. At its foundation, each society is distinct from others. As western values are imported and implemented into a society, there is an equal and opposite reaction to seek out cultural distinction, and those fundamental characteristics that make that society unique are recognised as its "traditions". Japan is archetypal in this regard, but this dualistic process takes place across the non-Western world. Where there is

[66] Quoted in Chris Cilliza, 'Pat Buchanan Says Donald Trump is the Future of the Republican Party', *Washington Post* (12 January 2016).
[67] Chenchen Zhang, 'Postcolonial Nationalism and the Global Right', *Geoforum* 144 (2023), 1–5.

a reception of foreign Western values, there will inevitably be a rediscovery and reconstruction of a society's organic, traditional culture.[68]

In South Africa and Zimbabwe, the revitalisation of discourses of ethnicity, race, and nation finds its articulation in a resurgence of populist ideologies of nativism and Afro-radicalism.[69] While many of these formations would ardently deny any association with radical conservative ideas, their embrace of nativism (including their mobilisation of narrow xenophobic and frequently racist discourses) mobilises equivalent tropes that blame their positions on the dominant global liberal regime, be it its multiculturalism or imperial domination. In South Africa, for example, the (Black) nativism of political parties such as the Economic Freedom Fighters and Black First Land First is somewhat ironically mirrored in the (white) ethno-nationalism articulated by conservative Afrikaner groups, notably the activist group AfriForum and the political party FreedomFront+.

The aim of such populist discourses is not only to represent and give a voice to disaffected populations but also to socially construct and turn 'silent majorities' into reflexively antagonistic agents of political change. The enemy in this framework is not an abstract system or logic of capital: it is the concrete figure of the New Class liberal managerial elites and the client groups they support and that in turn support them – be they at home or in international institutions. By identifying the contradictions of the global managerial order with the concrete agency of the liberal enemy in this manner,

---

[68] Keishi Saeki, *Rinri toshite no Nashonarizumu: Gurōbarizumu no Kyomu wo Koete* [Nationalism as Ethics: Beyond the Nihilism of Globalism] (Tokyo: NTT Publishing, 2005), 180–181. Our translation.

[69] Sabelo J. Ndlovu-Gatsheni, 'Africa for Africans or Africa for "Natives" Only? "New Nationalism" and Nativism in Zimbabwe and South Africa', *Africa Spectrum* 44:1 (2009), 61–78; Abrahamsen, 'Internationalists, Sovereigntists, Nativists'. In the words of Achille Mbembe, the idea of nativism 'is that the encounter between Africa and the West resulted in a deep wound: a wound that cannot heal until the ex-colonised rediscover their own being and their own past'. Achille Mbembe, 'On the Power of the False', *Public Culture* 14:3 (2002), 629–641, 635.

radical Right discourses give political rationality to the sense of alienation and resentment among those perceived to be most hurt by the global networks of power. They also help create the very agents ('the people') capable of overthrowing the hegemonic order by giving them a transnational common cause, or a shared enemy. As Orbán proclaimed at the CPAC conference in 2022:

> progressives are threatening the whole of Western civilization, and the true danger is not from without but from within. You, Dear American Friends, are confronted with this in the United States, while we are confronted with it in the European Union. We are dealing with the same people: faceless, ideologically trained bureaucrats sitting in Washington DC and Brussels. Progressive liberals, neo-Marxists intoxicated by the dream of wokeness, those in the pay of George Soros, the advocates of the open society. They want to abolish the Western way of life that you and we love so much.[70]

While Orbán mobilises the threat to Western civilisation, the strength of this framing of the global managerial order is that it can support a wide range of agendas (as in the anti-Semitism associated with the attack on Soros), while simultaneously mobilising a set of transnationally resonating cultural strategies. It allows for hostility towards both certain kinds of capital and the managerial state, each of which is seen as supporting the other. It also helps to foment disdain and resentment by 'the people' towards both globalist elites and the 'undeserving underclass', migrants, and other subordinate or marginalised groups that benefit from the patronage of their New Class supporters. As Faye declared to a receptive Moscow audience:

> The endogenous and thus primary causes of this evil are internal spiritual pathologies of European peoples: ethno-masochism (hatred of oneself) and xenophilia (love of the foreign) which lead to cynical or naive collaboration with the enemy, mercantile

---

[70] Orbán, 'Speech at CPAC'.

materialism and unbridled individualism, egalitarianism, the inversion of values, the loss of memory of traditions as well as the future, emasculation and confusion of sexual roles, moral melancholy and morbidity dissimulated under a factitious and simulated optimism, loss of the aesthetic sense, etc.[71]

Whether it is the New Class 'woke' corporate executive, the 'lamestream' or 'fake news' media, the undeserving outsider, or the insidious intellectual, the moment of antagonism prompted by the identification of the enemy introduces a strong element of radicalism into public debates. It also involves an explicit turn to myth and emotional mobilisation. As Francis wrote in the US context during the early 1990s, the aim of this conservative populism is to destroy the old myth of America as an abstract 'philosophical proposition about the equality of all mankind (and which therefore includes all mankind)', and replace it with a new (yet old) hegemonic myth of the United States as a particular historical community of fate that will exclude those who cannot or will not assimilate into it:

> This is the real meaning of "America First". America must be first not only among other nations but first also among the other (individual or class or sectional) interests of its people. Unless a Middle-American nationalism (or any other socio-political movement) can achieve such cultural hegemony through the formulation of an accepted public myth, its political power and economic resources will remain dependent on the cultural power of its adversaries and eventually will succumb to their manipulation as it takes its cues on goals and tactics from its opponents.[72]

This politics of enmity enables a wide range of counter-hegemonic strategies depending on the region and the more immediate political

---

[71] Guillaume Faye, 'The Geopolitics of Ethnopolitics: The New Concept of "Eurosiberia"', Paper Presented at the International Conference on 'The Future of the White World', Moscow, 8–10 June 2006. counter-currents.com/2010/08/faye-on-eurosiberia/ (accessed 1 November 2023).
[72] Francis, 'Nationalism', 22.

goals of its protagonists. Yet in practically all geographical contexts, the politics of enmity is conveyed through a provocative and performative rhetoric of transgression and excess designed to subvert liberal norms of appropriate conduct and leadership. At the same time, these transgressive postures are justified by radical Right intellectuals and politicians on the grounds that the liberal elites do not actually live by their own professed standards of appropriate conduct and have in fact committed the worst transgressions of all by trampling on free speech and decoupling democracy from the jurisdiction of the modern nation-state.

The aim of these strategies is to radicalise the terms of public debates, polarise the electorate, and render centrist political parties irrelevant. Arguably, the radical Right's most significant challenge to contemporary politics and international affairs in this respect does not lie in the specifics of its policy positions, but rather in the ways in which it seeks to reconfigure political life as an all-consuming conflict between those who wish to deepen the infrastructures that grew out of the geopolitical transformations of the twentieth century and those who wish to dismantle these infrastructures to the profit of nativist and neo-traditionalist alternatives.[73] The stakes in this politics are not only the substantive transformations achieved since the 1950s on questions of race, gender, human rights, and welfare but also the discursive field within which conventional conceptions of Left and Right are being disarticulated and re-articulated into new relationships of friendship and enmity over the meaning and future of the nation-state, globalisation, and the idea of 'the West' and other distinct civilisations. As former Trump advisor Steve Bannon explained to an Italian audience during a tour of Europe in 2018:

> There will always be ideas, parties and politicians of the Left and the Right, but these categories are beginning to lose their meaning. "Left against Right" is simply a means to divide

[73] Paul Gottfried, 'Explaining Trump', in *Revisions and Dissents: Essays* (Dekalb: Northern Illinois University Press, 2017), 140.

communities within themselves. The real struggle in the future will be one between the privileged and the dispossessed; between peoples and political classes; between nationalists and globalists; between those who hold traditional values and those who dismiss those values as garbage ... Our system of global government was instituted after the Second World War on the basis of certain rules, and imposed through a mixture of central planning, political apathy and lack of trust in the working class. Their rights were progressively wiped away because technocrats believed that there were no other options – alternative possibilities were not seriously considered. Now, this is all changing.[74]

CONCLUSION

The radical Right's characterisation of its agenda as straddling the Left/Right divide cannot be reduced to a mere restatement of historical fascism. The first wave of fascist movements that swept across Europe in the 1920s and 1930s were avowedly committed to militarism, imperial conquest, and violent extra- and anti-parliamentary activism in ways that contemporary radical conservatism generally is not. The metapolitical focus of today's radical Right ideologues also distinguishes its visions and activities from the delusional conspiracy theories of QAnon and other like-minded groups who stormed the US Capitol in January 2021. Yet by associating practically all the ills of late modern life with the concrete agency of the New Class and its client groups, radical Right critiques of globalisation do lend themselves perfectly well to this sort of violent conspiratorial politics. Managerialism is not a conspiratorial theory, however it can easily shade towards views that are, and it provides an ideological core around which adjacent positions can coalesce.

[74] Steve Bannon, 'Soros est l'ennemi de tous les nationalismes: Entretien avec Steve Bannon', *Les Non-Alignés* (8 July 2018). Our translation.

The attack on global managerialism and the New Class, as we have shown, provides for a powerful rhetoric of enmity that can appeal to diverse constituencies. Importantly, however, for the radical Right, democratic self-determination is not primarily valued as an effort to remove obstacles to equal access to economic and cultural resources (as it often is for the Left), but as a mechanism to defend the privileges of the majority culture and foster cultural homogeneity against the differentiated civil society of postmodern liberalism. In common with many other reactions against globalisation, their strategy hinges on an essentialist interpretation of culture as being either 'lost' or 'under threat', and ultimately sustains the conclusion that the eradication of another 'incompatible' or 'hostile' culture from a given territory is imperative for the survival of one's own. Here, the political realism tasked with mediating estranged relations in more classical conservative frameworks gives way to a crusading 'clash of civilisations' style of politics that remains sufficiently adaptable to allow various movements to make common cause across conventional Left/Right divides, as aspects of anti-globalisation politics and the Brexit debates may well illustrate. Alexander Dugin, one of the leading radical Right affiliates in Russia, has long been arguing for such an alliance against the managerial liberalism of the West:

> Another question is the structure of a possible anti-globalist and anti-imperialist front and its participants. I think we should include in it all forces that struggle against the West, the United States, against liberal democracy, and against modernity and post-modernity. The common enemy is the necessary instance for all kinds of political alliances. This means Muslims and Christians, Russians and Chinese, both Leftists and Rightists, the Hindus and Jews who challenge the present state of affairs, globalization and American imperialism. They are thus all virtually friends and allies ... That is the basis for a new alliance. All who share a negative analysis of globalization, Westernization and postmodernization should coordinate their effort in the

creation of a new strategy of resistance to the omnipresent evil. And we can find common allies even within the United States as well, among those who choose the path of Tradition over the present decadence.[75]

Dugin's ideas are far from universally shared on the radical Right. However, they provide an illustration of the pervasiveness of the radical Right's philosophy, its politics of enmity, and the widespread dissemination of its perspectives. Inspired by their understanding of Gramsci, the radical Right has embarked on a full-scale war of position to overturn the cultural dominance of the liberal managerial elite. This counter-hegemonic struggle is the topic of the next chapter.

---

[75] Dugin, *The Fourth Political Theory*, 194.

4 The War of Position
Towards a Right Common Sense

The radical Right's study of Gramsci has not been confined to the level of theory and philosophy: it has also been diligently pursued as practice. Armed with a specific understanding of the deep cultural and social foundations of the liberal hegemonic order, radical conservatives have embarked on what Gramsci calls a war of position, a patient counter-hegemonic struggle to change the predominant common sense and produce organic intellectuals who can critique the existing order and provide alternatives to it.

The most visible and audible part of this strategy has been their transgressive and often offensive use of digital communication and social media. As one pseudonymised right-wing blogger put it nearly a decade ago: 'If you are alive in 2015 and you don't understand the power of the interwebz, you're an idiot ... The left won by seizing control of media and academia ... With the internet they lost control of the narrative.'[1] There is no doubt that digital media is central to the rise and globalisation of right-wing ideas and movements, as captured in a series of insightful academic analyses of right-wing echo chambers, outrage capitalism, rabbit holes, and targeted data mobilisation and manipulation.[2] But the radical Right's war of position cannot be reduced to social media and the dark web alone. It is also fought on the more traditional intellectual battlefields of

---

[1] 'Meow Blitz' in Andrew Marantz, *Antisocial: How Online Extremists Broke America* (New York: Picador, 2019), 6.

[2] For a small sample, see Christoper Wylie, *Mindf*ck* (New York: Random House, 2019); Jamie E. Settle, *Frenemies: How Social Media Polarizes America* (Cambridge: Cambridge University Press, 2018); Patricia Ann Simpson and Helga Druxes, eds., *Digital Media Strategies of the Far Right in Europe and the United States* (Lanham: Lexington Books, 2015); and Ralph Schroeder, 'Digital Media and the Entrenchment of Right Wing Populist Agendas', *Social Media + Society* 5:4 (2019), 1–11.

academic publishing, universities, and policy think tanks. Most of these initiatives inhabit or mimic more conventional organisations and forms of behaviour, thus giving radicals a less transgressive, or more acceptable face. The Right has of course always made such investments, seeking to influence party politics, electoral outcomes, and government policies.[3] The recent expansion of radical conservative engagement with academia and public policy institutes is nevertheless remarkable and indicative of a concerted effort gradually to change the intellectual landscape across social classes and between nations, or in Gramscian terms, our *senso comune*. Marion Maréchal explained this recognisably metapolitical strategy succinctly in her speech at the 2018 CPAC:

> Our fight cannot take place in elections. We need to convey our ideas through the media, culture and education to stop the domination of liberals and socialists. We have to train the leaders of tomorrow, those who have the courage, the determination, and the skills to defend the interests of their people … [and to displace] our nomadic, globalized, deracinated liberal system.[4]

This is not only a programmatic statement for the future but also an apt description of the present. New educational institutions, policy institutes, publishing houses, and journals have mushroomed in recent years, giving Maréchal and her allies a political platform with a much thicker organisational density than that captured by a focus on social media alone. Although the digital revolution is inseparable from the rise and visibility of the radical Right, the more established technologies and modes of communication and education are equally crucial to its long-term struggle for domination.

---

[3] In the American context, see Kim Phillips-Fein, *Invisible Hands: The Businessmen's Crusade against the New Deal* (New York: Norton, 2010); Jane Mayer, *Dark Money: The Hidden History of the Billionaires behind the Rise of the Radical Right* (New York: Doubleday, 2016).

[4] Quoted in Gary Potter, 'The New Catholic "Far" Right in France, Part II', Catholicism.org (23 January 2019).

This chapter focuses on two important, yet somewhat overlooked fronts in the contemporary battle of ideas. One is the emergence of a publishing industry that serves to make both old and new right-wing texts available and accessible to a global audience. The other is the birth and expansion of right-wing educational institutions dedicated specifically to educating a new elite, imbued with the values, sensibilities, and skills required for the long-term war of position. Our discussion does not aspire to provide a completely comprehensive picture of these activities. Instead, our aim is more modest and illustrative, seeking to demonstrate the importance the radical Right itself assigns to the less overtly transgressive, more long-term intellectual struggle for hegemony. In doing so, we are mindful of the risk of over-intellectualising the Right. This is not our intention, but it is equally important to avoid the opposite error of seeing support for the radical Right only as a product of social dislocation, alienation, resentment, or irrationality supercharged by digital media.

In tracing these various publication and education initiatives, we are not suggesting that the radical Right's counter-revolution is centrally coordinated or has a unified intellectual and political agenda. While radical Right ideologues have a clear understanding of metapolitics, the temptation to imbue today's various initiatives with a common directionality and central organisation must be avoided. There is no overall puppet master or central war room from where the war of position is directed. Instead, there are multiple, disparate activities that sometimes connect and intersect, at other times differ and collide. As such, the counter-revolution has both strategically directed and spontaneous and uncoordinated elements. Many struggles remain at the level of reactions against the existing order and are therefore likely to be ineffective. Nevertheless, as Gramsci argued, a successful war of position can contribute to the formation of insurrectionist movements against the dominant order without being the product of central control or direction. Indeed, we suggest that a proliferation of diverse and fluid movements and initiatives can produce effects despite, and even because of, their disparate and even mutually antagonistic natures. In this sense, the radical Right's counter-revolution may be greater than the sum of its parts.

PUBLISH OR PERISH: THE MAKING OF A RIGHT PUBLISHING INDUSTRY

Given their emphasis on metapolitics, it is hardly surprising that the radical Right is interested in education and the production and propagation of ideas. This is by no means a new conservative preoccupation. During the Cold War, a wide range of right-wing transnational networks focused on combatting communism, including its overtly and covertly 'cultural' dimensions.[5] The recent flourishing of new and revived publishing houses, journals, podcasts, and online magazines explicitly dedicated to the creation of a counter-hegemonic intellectual culture is nevertheless remarkable. Often founded by ideological entrepreneurs, these ventures seek to provide intellectual respectability, political inspiration, and points of connection for globally dispersed individuals and movements.

Prime within this expanding ecosystem of publishing houses is Arktos, which since its launch has published 'more than 170 titles in sixteen languages and circulated them globally'.[6] As the website puts it, Arktos has been 'making anti-globalism global since 2009'.[7]

---

[5] See, for example, Ignacio Arauju and Ernesto Bohoslavsky, 'The Circuits of Anti-Communist Repression between Asia and Latin America during the Second Cold War: Paraguay and the World Anti-Communist League', *Estudios Interdisciplinarios de America Latin y Caribe* 31:1 (2020), 105–122; Stéphanie Roulin, Giles Scott-Smith and Lu van Dongen, eds., *Transnational Anti-Communism and the Cold War* (London: Palgrave, 2014); Giles Scott-Smith, *Western Anti-Communism and the Interdoc Network: Cold War Internationale* (London: Palgrave, 2021); Giles Scott-Smith and Charlotte A. Lerg, eds., *Campaigning Culture and the Global Cold War: The Journals of the Congress for Cultural Freedom* (London: Palgrave Macmillan, 2017); Frances Stonor Saunders, *The Cultural Cold War: The CIA and the World of Arts and Letters* (New York: New York Press, 2001); Marla Stone and Giuliana Chamedis, 'Naming the Enemy: Anti-Communism in Transnational Perspective', *Journal of Contemporary History* 53:1 (2018), 4–11; Joonseok Yang and Young Chui Cho, 'Subaltern South Korea's Anti-Communist Asia Cooperation in the Mid-1950s', *Asian Perspectives* 44:2 (2020), 255–277.

[6] 'About Arktos', Arktos.com (accessed 12 July 2022).

[7] Arktos.com (accessed 29 February 2024).

It is far from alone. In the US, Counter-Currents has spearheaded the development and dissemination of a set of ideas described as the North American New Right, while the Claremont Institute and the more academically focused Encounter Books have also stepped up their publishing activities in the borderland between the right wing of conventional conservatism and the radical Right. The net result is that right-wing books and ideas are no longer hidden away in dusty library basements, but readily available with a click of the button, or if in Paris, at *La Nouvelle Librairie*, a right-wing bookshop centrally located in the highly intellectual Quartier Latin. The shop's website sums up the ethos that animates all these publishing efforts: 'The Latin Quarter is no longer a ZAD for us, a zone to be defended. It has been deserted for too long. It is a ZAR, a zone to be recaptured. The New Bookstore is part of this Reconquista. It is an outpost of the cultural fight which must shine well beyond its borders thanks to its online store.'[8]

The founder and CEO of Arktos, Daniel Friberg, occupies a central position within the radical Right publishing revolution. Described as 'the foremost strategist and implementer' of 'metapolitics in action', it is not too much of an exaggeration to say that through Arktos Friberg has single-handedly waged a global war of position against the liberal common sense.[9] While the press website claims that it 'does not seek to propagate any specific ideology, system of beliefs or viewpoint' but instead offers 'original and challenging alternatives to our prevailing culture', there is no doubt that Arktos' publishing falls squarely within the right-wing spectrum. As a youth, Friberg was involved with the Swedish neo-Right but describes how he discovered the French *Nouvelle Droite* and subsequently abandoned 'old Right' militancy in favour of the metapolitical struggle

---

[8] Nouvelle Librairie, 'Qui sommes nous?', nouvelle-librairie.com/qui-sommes-nous (accessed 6 March 2023). Our translation.

[9] Friberg perceptively suggests that 'metapolitics works best when people don't know you're shaping the way they think', quoted in Benjamin Teitelbaum, 'Daniel Friberg and Metapolitics in Action', in Mark Sedgwick, ed., *Key Thinkers on the Radical Right* (Oxford: Oxford University Press, 2019), 260.

of ideas.[10] Uninterested in party politics, Friberg seeks to effect change at a deeper level of ideas, values, and culture. A first step in this direction was Arktos' translation and publication of the leading *Nouvelle Droite* thinkers, including Alain de Benoist, Guillaume Faye, and Dominique Venner, thus helping to introduce these ideas to English-speaking audiences.[11] In 2011, for example, Arktos reissued Tomislav Sunic's *Against Democracy and Equality*, billed as the first ever English-language book on the European New Right. The following year the publisher issued a collection of essays by Sunic's mentor Paul Gottfried, the American paleoconservative critic of neoconservatism and the rule of experts. Entitled *War and Democracy*, the volume highlights many of Gottfried's key preoccupations, including the dangers of the administrative state and the imperialist fallacy of democracy promotion.

Reaching beyond Europe and North America, Arktos has embraced the Russian right-wing theorist Alexander Dugin, translating and publishing several of his works, including his 2021 book *The Great Awakening vs. The Great Reset*, a rabid attack on all things liberal. These volumes are accompanied by a series of podcasts, YouTube interviews, and online essays popularising Dugin's critique of the West and his vision of a multipolar illiberal world. Arktos has also published Friberg's own book *The Real Right Returns: A Handbook for the True Opposition*, which according to the website has been translated into fourteen languages. The book explains the metapolitics of the Right and includes a metapolitical dictionary and practical tips for anyone wishing to join the 'true opposition'.[12]

Another key feature of Arktos' publishing strategy is the reissuing of right-wing classics, most prominently the works of the Italian Julius Evola and the German Oswald Spengler. Reflecting

---

[10] Ibid., 265.

[11] Interestingly, this process began through the previously leftist, critical theory-inspired journal *Telos* in the 1990s.

[12] Friberg is also the Swedish translator of Michael O'Meara's popular book *New Culture, New Right*.

Arktos' interest in philosophy, metaphysics, and tradition, its publication list features no less than eight Evola titles, including *The Metaphysics of Power*, *The Metaphysics of War*, and *A Handbook for Right-Wing Youth*. The latter is also issued in German. Spengler's massive and (in)famous two-volume study *The Decline of the West*, originally published in 1918 and 1922, was re-launched by Arktos in 2021, and his *Man and Technics* has been published in English, German, Swedish, and as an audiobook. Two other Spengler titles, *Jahre der Entscheidung* (*Hour of Decision*) and *Preussentum und Sozialismus* (*Prussianism and Socialism*), are available in German and Swedish. The objective of this strategy is clearly to (re)construct a philosophic corpus and historical lineage for today's radical Right, providing it both with an intellectual genealogy and scholarly legitimacy. In this representation, the politics of the radical Right is not merely the protest politics of the street and the skinheads but also of the serious thinker. As such, Arktos' library is also intended as a source of inspiration for today's conservatives.

Arktos' main fellow traveller, the San Francisco–based Counter-Currents, has pursued a similar metapolitical strategy, publishing both right-wing classics and new, emerging political thinkers. Founded by Greg Johnson and Michael Polignano in 2010, Counter-Currents also takes direct inspiration from the *Nouvelle Droite* and brands itself as the North American New Right, though it is often identified with white nationalism. Initially it sought to 'educate Americans about the ideas of the French Groupement de recherche et d'études pour la civilization européenne ... and related European thinkers and intellectual movements, primarily in France, Germany and Italy.'[13] To this end, Counter-Currents has translated and published numerous texts by de Benoist, Faye, and Venner, while at the same time developing and promoting American right-wing ideas and ideology.

---

[13] Southern Poverty Law Center, 'Greg Johnson', www.splcenter.org/fighting-hate/extremist-files/individual/greg-johnson (accessed 6 March 2023).

Greg Johnson, the driving force behind this project, is a prolific writer with a PhD in Philosophy from The Catholic University of America in Washington. In an essay that stands as something of a manifesto, Johnson seeks to distinguish the North American New Right from both the Old Right and the European New Right. In this schema, the Old Right refers to Fascism, National Socialism, totalitarianism, terrorism, imperialism, and genocide, which Johnson claims to denounce. He acknowledges the deep intellectual debt to the European New Right but maintains that the North American New Right by necessity differs in three main ways: First, because the US has been a melting pot of identities and races, the North Americans are 'forced to stress the deeper roots of common European identity, including racial identity.' Second, because 'the United States is the citadel of Jewish power in the world today, the North American New Right must deal straightforwardly with the Jewish Question.' Third, 'the North American New Right cultivates a much more frank and direct critical engagement with Fascism and National Socialism.'[14] Put differently, the North American New Right is an explicitly white supremacist, anti-Semitic project, promoting white nationalism and the belief that racial and cultural diversity within a society inevitably creates conflict. It is not, however, an expansionist project in the imperialist cast of previous right-wing movements. Instead, it purports to advocate a pluralist world: all peoples should have their own homelands, a goal to be achieved not through the militant politics of the Old Right but through the seemingly less violent means of 'changing people's consciousness, i.e., by persuading enough people in positions of influence that everyone has a stake in ethnonationalism.' While ethnopluralist, this position is not egalitarian and instead overtly prioritises racial majority cultures and 'white survival'.[15]

To this end, Counter-Currents has published some eighty books, many of them by Johnson himself. These include *The White Nationalist Manifesto* and *White Identity Politics* where Johnson

---

[14] Greg Johnson, 'New Right vs Old Right', Counter-Currents (12 May 2012).
[15] *Ibid.*

sets out his ideas of a white genocide and defends the need for white identity politics. Since its publication in 2018, the first book has been translated into Italian and Spanish and is one of Counter-Currents' best-sellers. In 2019, it was banned from Amazon along with fifteen other Counter-Currents titles, but its sequel remains available from the world's largest bookseller. Counter-Currents has also published a three-volume collection by Francis Parker Yockey, the controversial American lawyer, fascist, and pan-European ideologist who sided with the Nazis during the Second World War. This includes Yockey's most well-known study *Imperium: The Philosophy of History and Politics*, originally published in 1948. Dedicated to 'the hero' Adolf Hitler, this 600-page, Spengler-inspired book calls for a pan-European imperial order governed by 'absolute politics'.[16]

While the majority of Counter-Currents releases are focused on politics, there is also a seemingly light-hearted cultural stream, focused on art, music, film, and popular culture. This includes a series of white nationalist guides to the movies, written by Johnson under his pen-name Trevor Lynch. In other titles, James Bond and Batman become right-wing, anti-liberal heroes, spiritually virile in a manner that would have pleased Evola. Children's entertainment is also subjected to right-wing analysis: *My Nationalist Pony*, by Buttercup Dew, provides a white nationalist reading of the popular children's cartoon series 'My Little Pony: Friendship is Magic'. Billed as a 'masterpiece of culture-jamming', the book finds deep right-wing insights and truths among the unicorns, ponies, and dragons inhabiting the kingdom of Equestria.

Alongside contemporary culture and aesthetic theory, there is a deliberate attempt to forge a radical Right aesthetics by foregrounding Right-wing artists, such as Richard Wagner, Wyndham Lewis, and T. S. Eliot.[17] There are also novels and poems, sometimes marketed as 'weird fiction', as well as more mystical, metaphysical,

---

[16] On Yockey, see Kevin Coogan, *Dreamer of the Day: Francis Parker Yockey and the Post-war Fascist International* (New York: Autonomedia, 2000).

[17] See, for example, Kerry R. Bolton, *More Artists of the Right* (San Francisco: Counter-Currents, 2017).

and philosophical explorations. Titles such as *Mysticism after Modernism* and *Reactionary Modernism* lay claims to the Right's modernist heritage, suggesting that modernism and the Right are not incompatible and seeking a revival of traditional spirituality.[18] In this sense, Counter-Currents epitomises the radical Right's embrace of the postmodern and the avant-garde; the world's intrinsic lack of coherence, opening room for a renewed focus on the mythological, the tragic, the transgressive, and the emotional aspects of Western culture.

The past decade, particularly since the election of Donald Trump, has also seen the revitalisation and emergence of intellectual outlets that straddle and, perhaps in important ways, blur the boundaries between what used to be the right wing of mainstream conservatism and the radical Right. Regnery Publishing, founded in 1947 and a long-time presence on the rightward edge of American conservatism, has stepped up its output and claims to have 'led the modern resurgence of conservative publishing over the past couple of decades.'[19] The original publisher of conservative classics such as Russell Kirk's *The Conservative Mind* and William F. Buckley's *God and Man at Yale*, Regnery's recent authors amount to a 'who's who' of right-wing activists and politicians, including Donald J. Trump, Ann Coulter, and Dinesh D'Souza.[20] Another important example is the revived Encounter Books, which takes its name from Encounter magazine, an Anglo-American Cold War literary journal founded in 1953 by the poet Stephen Spender and the journalist (and later neoconservative doyen) Irving Kristol.[21] Today Encounter Books claims

---

[18] James J. O'Meara, *Mysticism after Modernism: Crowley, Evola, Neville, Watts, Colin Wilson, and Other Populist Gurus* (Melbourne: Manticore Press, 2020); Jonathan Bowden, *Reactionary Modernism* (San Francisco: Counter-Currents, 2022).

[19] Regnery, 'About Regnery Publishing', www.regnery.com/our-story/ (accessed 6 March 2023).

[20] Regnery, 'New Releases', www.regnery.com/books/new-releases/ (accessed 6 March 2023).

[21] For Encounter Magazine's connections with the Congress for Cultural Freedom (which Burnham was also involved in) and through it to funding from the CIA during the Cold War, see Saunders, *The Cultural Cold War*.

to continue 'to advance its love of liberty and the cultural achievements of the West against a rising tide of collectivist sentiment and the soft totalitarianism of intellectual conformity.'[22]

Unlike Counter-Currents and Arktos, most of Encounter Books' authors are tenured academics or associated with well-known think tanks, such as the Heritage Foundation and the Cato Institute. Here, managerialist and New Class themes often come to the fore. For example, the book topping its list of bestsellers at the time of writing is *Black Rednecks and White Liberals* by Thomas Sowell, a well-known Black conservative and fellow at the Hoover Institution at Stanford University. Sowell argues against what he sees as a dysfunctional African American 'ghetto culture' identity that has been promoted and valorised by white liberals, or what we could call the New Class.[23] Another bestseller is *Bad News: How Woke Media Is Undermining Democracy*, written by Newsweek's deputy opinion editor Batya Ungar-Sargon. The book's argument that 'the moral panic around race, encouraged by today's elite newsrooms, does little more than consolidate the power of liberal elites and protect their economic interests' fits comfortably within the managerialist sociology outlined in Chapter 3.[24]

Encounter Books is also the publisher of John Marini's *Unmasking the Administrative State*, one of the most influential critiques of managerialism in contemporary America. Arguing against the 'tyranny of unbounded anti-constitutional bureaucracy',[25] Marini is Senior Fellow at the Claremont Institute in California, another think tank that has undergone a much-noted right-wing shift in recent years. Founded in 1979 by four students of Harry Jaffa, the godfather of so-called West Coast Straussianism, Claremont is now

---

[22] Encounter Books, 'About', www.encounterbooks.com/about/ (accessed 18 July 2022).
[23] Thomas Sowell, *Black Rednecks and White Liberals* (New York: Encounter Books, 2009).
[24] Batya Ungar-Sargon, *Bad News: How Woke Media Is Undermining Democracy* (New York: Encounter Books, 2021).
[25] John Marini, *Unmasking the Administrative State: The Crisis of American Politics in the Twenty-First Century* (New York: Encounter Books, 2019).

dedicated to 'recovering the American idea' and fighting what it calls 'woke' culture and 'woke' capitalism.[26] It also offers fellowships to working sheriffs, some of the most important administrative actors in the US system, inviting them to rethink questions of justice and law enforcement from an explicitly conservative perspective.[27]

Originally at the forefront of attempting to give intellectual cachet and respectability to Trumpism, Claremont also moved closer to Florida Governor Ron DeSantis, once Trump's chief rival for the 2024 Republican presidential nomination. When the institute presented DeSantis with a 'statesmanship award' at its 2021 gala, the governor gave a keynote address in which he invoked the wisdom of Angelo Codevilla, a Claremont graduate and a household name among so-called militant IR scholars: 'Biden's failures need to end up being the swan song for what the late Angelo Codevilla called the "ruling class" in this country. He saw this probably before anybody, but he was right on the money. This ruling class is a toxic combination of managerial incompetence and cultural radicalism.'[28] In early 2023, Claremont opened a new office in Tallahassee, Florida, signalling its desire to calibrate its relationship with Trump and DeSantis.[29]

At the time of writing, the Institute's senior fellows are an all-male line-up of twenty-four scholars with PhDs and associations with

---

[26] See Claremont Institute, 'Mission and Overview', www.claremont.org/page/claremonts-mission/ (accessed 19 July 2022); John Ganz, 'The Week in Fascism: On Claremont and Tucker', https://johnganz.substack.com/p/the-week-in-fascism (28 March 2021); Laura K. Field, 'What the Hell Happened to the Claremont Institute?', *The Bulwark* (13 July 2021); Amanda Marcotte, 'How a Far-Right Think Tank Made Everything "Woke"', *Salon* (17 March 2023); Katherine Stewart, 'The Claremont Institute: The Anti-Democracy Think Tank', *The New Republic* (10 August 2023).

[27] Claremont Institute, 'Sheriffs Fellowship', www.claremont.org/page/sheriffs-fellowship/ (accessed 24 February 2023). For an analysis of the 300-page packet of readings prepared for the class of 2022, see Jessica Pishko, 'Here's the Secret "Sheriff Fellowship" Curriculum from the Country's Most Prominent MAGA Think Tank', *Slate* (21 September 2022).

[28] Quoted in Cameron Joseph, 'Trump's Favorite Extreme Think Tank Is Jumping Ship for DeSantis', *Vice News* (27 March 2023).

[29] *Ibid.*; See also Michelle Goldberg, 'DeSantis Allies Plot the Hostile Takeover of a Liberal College', *New York Times* (9 January 2023).

universities such as Chicago, Stanford, Loyola, UC Davis, as well as Hillsdale College, a small but influential Christian liberal arts college in Michigan to which we will return shortly. Claremont senior fellows often publish books with Encounter and contribute regularly to the Institute's flagship journal, *The Claremont Review of Books* (CRB), which is edited by Charles Kessler, a political scientist with a PhD in Government from Harvard University. The CRB's increasing radicalism first became evident with the publication of Michael Anton's now infamous essay 'The Flight 93 Election', which urged voters to elect Trump in a desperate effort to save America – charge the cockpit or die, just like the passengers on Flight 93 on September 11, 2001.[30] In the aftermath of President Trump's defeat in 2020, the Claremont web-magazine *The American Mind* was an active promoter of the 'stolen election' narrative.[31] In clear Gramscian-style, the magazine's 'Salvos' section is billed as a 'counter-revolution.' In words that could easily have been those of Sam Francis three decades earlier, one contributor argues that 'Conservatism is no longer enough' because America is no longer America but inhabited by 'citizen-aliens' who do not 'believe in, live by, or even like the principles, traditions, and ideals that until recently defined America as a nation and as a people.' As such, 'there is almost nothing left to conserve' and instead it is 'all hands on deck as we enter the counter-revolutionary moment' towards 'a recovery, or even a refounding, of America.' To achieve this counter-revolution, the essay's recommendation is to 'read some books'.[32]

Prime Minister Orbán' offered the same advice for political success: 'Read every day. A book a day keeps the defeat away', he told the CPAC Conference in May 2022. He continued:

---

[30] Anton went on to work in the Trump Whitehouse and remains a prominent figure.
[31] See, for example, the essay 'The Fight Is Now: From the Editors', *The American Mind* (5 November 2020).
[32] Glenn Ellmers, '"Conservatism" Is No Longer Enough', *The American Mind* (24 March 2021). In February 2021, the Claremont Institute launched its Center for the American Way of Life in Washington DC, dedicated to a reinvigorated and restored conservatism and to reclaiming America's institutions.

I know that this sounds strange. I am not an academic myself, but the fact is that no invention has yet surpassed the book as a vehicle for understanding and conveying ideas. The world is becoming increasingly complex, and we need to dedicate time to understanding it. I, for instance, set aside one whole day every week for reading. Reading also helps us to understand what our opponents think and where their thinking is flawed.[33]

It is difficult to judge and ascertain the influence and effect of these diverse publishing endeavours, especially in the short term. It is of course possible that the books, magazines, and fancy websites reach only a small fringe, preaching primarily to the already converted. It is certainly the case that a relatively small number of authors produce the majority of content, review each other's books and sometimes publish under more than one name. Care must therefore be taken in ascribing too much significance to the radical Right's recent intellectual production, keeping in mind that those involved have an interest in inflating their reach and numbers. Appearances can be deceptive – and that may be precisely the point. The very existence of professional websites, books, and podcasts can give the impression of importance and gravity, as well as international and political organisation. It is also a strategy for claiming legitimacy and intellectual credibility; the mere presence of books signals that the radical Right is a project of the mind, not of shadowy protest politics. One curious, but perhaps telling, outcome is an emerging 'iconography of books and other emblems of learnedness' on right-wing social media platforms where more and more profile photos are taken in libraries or in front of packed bookshelves.[34]

The possibility of smoke and mirrors aside, reputable sources indicate that the Counter-Currents website attracted over 2.2 million unique visitors in the three-month period from March to May

---

[33] 'Speech by Prime Minister Viktor Orbán at the opening of CPAC Hungary', Website for the Office of the Prime Minister (19 May 2022) miniszterelnok.hu/speech-by-prime-minister-viktor-orban-at-the-opening-of-cpac-hungary/ (accessed 26 March 2023).

[34] Benjamin Teitelbaum, *Lions of the North: Sounds of the New Nordic Radical Nationalism* (New York: Oxford University Press, 2017), 57–58.

2022, while Arktos had over 105,000 visitors in the same period.[35] More importantly for our argument, these various publishing activities testify to the radical Right's firm belief that political change requires a prior change of public discourse and debate. By bringing right-wing thinkers and ideas into the limelight, they seek to normalise their presence in everyday life. While the Right might be vitriolic in their critique of intellectuals, they simultaneous seek to produce and reclaim their own philosophers and thinkers and support their own 'organic intellectuals'. The re-publication of formerly forgotten and discredited thinkers such as Spengler and Evola is not only an effort to rehabilitate their ideas but also to re-write intellectual history from an explicitly radical conservative perspective, reclaiming it from the academic liberal and left-wing mainstream. In doing so, the radicals are constructing a long disciplinary history for themselves, an academic lineage of credibility and respectability. In this telling, the fascism of the past is acknowledged, albeit to varying degrees, but it is not allowed to become the only legacy of the Right. Instead, the message is that there are important intellectual contributions to be gleaned from thinkers who have been incorrectly assigned to the intellectual dustbin by the liberal Left and the academic establishment. As part of the counter-hegemonic struggle, their ideas need to be brought to the attention of new, contemporary audiences.

Culturally, these publication strategies also evince an ambition to reclaim the sphere of creativity for the Right. As one review of Counter-Currents' book *More Artists of the Right* argues, 'Marxist and socialist ideologies are too easily assumed to be the natural badges of modern artists', whereas in fact 'many important poets, novelists, and thinkers of the 20th century were profoundly rightist in their political views.'[36] The purpose is thus to construct a

---

[35] Data from Similarweb.com (accessed 14 July 2022). Most visitors are from the US, but interestingly 13.56 per cent of Counter-Currents traffic is from Iran.

[36] Dr Joseph S. Salemi, online endorsement of Kerry Bolton's book *Artists of the Right: Resisting Decadence*, counter-currents.com/books/artists-of-the-right-resisting-decadence/ (accessed 11 July 2022).

'counter-canon to show that, no matter what your teachers told you, the great minds of the 20th century were culturally, politically and spiritually on the Right.'[37] By highlighting likeminded artists, poets, and musicians, these publishing houses are seeking not only to correct the impression of the Right as uncultured knuckleheads but also to capture the cultural high ground from the Left and create a sense of pride in their own artistic heritage. Importantly, the publishing industry also provides a platform for contemporary right-wing creativity that would otherwise struggle to find a public outlet. This includes novels and poetry, often branded as representing the aesthetic vanguard and cutting edge of popular culture. As such, there is a strong recognition of the power of popular culture to inspire thought and action and the need to fill the artistic space with appropriate ideological material.

One effect of the expanding and evolving industry of radical Right publishing and online commentary is the normalisation, and even banalisation, of right-wing perspectives and opinions. In addition to books and magazines, websites such as Counter-Currents, Arktos, and Claremont release daily commentaries on contemporary affairs, and little by little right-wing interpretations and framings of political, social, and cultural issues seep into mainstream thinking – on both the Right and the Left.[38] Right-wing intellectuals and publications are also more readily accepted in the public sphere. In France, for example, GRECE's monthly publication *Eléments* is now sold nationwide at most newsstands, and Alain de Benoist, previously an outcast in the mainstream media, is regularly interviewed in French newspapers, radio, and TV.[39] The counter-revolution in publishing, we can safely conclude, is not only well underway but is already showing results.

[37] James J. O'Meara, online endorsement of Bolton, *Artists of the Right:* counter-currents.com/books/artists-of-the-right-resisting-decadence/ (accessed 11 July 2022).
[38] See Kenan Malik, 'It's Not Just the Far Right That Should Worry Us. It's Their Ideas Seeping into the Mainstream', *The Observer* (3 July 2022).
[39] See Jean-Yves Camus, 'The French Right 52 Years On: Alive and Kicking as Ever', Centre for Analysis of the Radical Right (30 April 2020).

TRAINING THE NEW ILLIBERAL GLOBAL ELITE

Educational institutions have long been a major preoccupation of conservatives of all stripes.[40] Today, the radical Right's criticism of universities centres on the teaching of progressive ideas variously categorised as 'wokeism', 'critical race theory', and 'decolonisation of the curriculum', which they allege stifle free speech through 'political correctness', 'gender ideology', and 'cancel culture' – some of the many reasons given for restrictions on curricula and other attacks on higher education in the US, the UK, Brazil, Turkey, India, and elsewhere.[41] At the same time, universities are attacked for fostering a cadre of de-territorialised, technocratic experts. In one of the most bitter and well-documented struggles, the Central European University (CEU) was chased from Budapest by a government that disparaged 'the George Soros University' and its open society, liberal 'globalist' teaching that allegedly poisoned the Hungarian body politic. All these themes are ubiquitous, and they function in parallel with the broader critique of liberal power as a combination of cultural relativism and abstract expertise.

This disdain for contemporary university life, however, has not prevented the Right from investing in universities of the right kind. This too has a long history. Already in 1951, the newly graduated William F. Buckley published *God and Man at Yale*, calling on conservative trustees, alumni, and donors to withhold funding to his alma mater and like-minded universities to force what he regarded as anti-Christian, anti-capitalist professors to change the curriculum.[42] Jane

---

[40] For the UK case, see Evan Smith, *No Platform: A History of Anti-Fascism, Universities and the Limits of Free Speech* (London: Routledge, 2020); for the US, Mayer, *Dark Money*.

[41] Alexander D. Barder, Isaac Kamola, and Aida A. Hozic, 'The Attacks on Higher Education in Florida Are Part of a Global Crisis' *Le Monde* (20 May 2023); Ishan Ashutosh, 'The Transnational Routes of White and Hindu Nationalisms', *Ethnic and Racial Studies* 45,2 (2022), 319–339.

[42] William F. Buckley, *God and Man at Yale: The Superstitions of 'Academic Freedom'* (Chicago: Regnery, 1951/2021). Published during the height of McCarthyism, the book is today considered a conservative classic and was reissued with foreword by Michael Knowles in 2021, seventy years after its original release.

Mayer and others have documented how the influx of secretive, or 'dark', money into US politics sustains a network of right-wing think tanks and institutes, as well as programmes and fellowships supporting right-wing education at elite and non-elite universities.[43] In the past, these initiatives stayed largely within the confines of 'establishment' conservatism, but in recent decades, they, like conservativism in general, show the influence of increasingly radical agendas.

This is plainly evident at Hillsdale College in rural Michigan, a private, conservative liberal arts college that traces its history back to 1844 and describes itself as 'a trustee of modern man's intellectual and spiritual inheritance from the Judeo-Christian faith and Greco-Roman culture.' This commitment is now gaining new lustre, thanks in large part to the increasingly strong links with the right-wing of the Republican Party. The relationship is symbiotic and mutually beneficial: the party receives a veneer of intellectual credibility and committed youth supporters; the college nationwide prominence, which in turn translates into more applicants and more donations. Hillsdale's long-standing president Larry Arnn, a Churchill Studies afficionado and former president of the Claremont Institute, was at the forefront of endorsing Trump's 2016 presidential candidacy. This immediately gained Hillsdale a reputation as 'a feeder school for the Trump administration' and 'the college that wants to take over Washington', a reference to the many alumni that subsequently held prominent positions under Trump.[44] The family

---

[43] These were originally conceptualised as 'beachheads' or incubators for future conservative leaders and power holders. Mayer, *Dark Money*; see also Ralph Wilson and Isaac Kamola, *Free Speech and Koch Money: Manufacturing a Campus Culture War* (London: Pluto, 2022). On the spread of this model to the UK, see Peter Geoghegan, *Democracy for Sale: Dark Money and Dirty Politics* (London: Head of Zeus, 2020). In the twentieth century, the need to train a conservative elite was bolstered by the elite sociology developed by thinkers such as Michels, Mosco, and Pareto and lauded by Burnham in his study *The Machiavellians: Defenders of Freedom* (New York: John Day, 1943). On the wider historical context of elite sociology, see Zeev Sternhell, *Neither Right, Nor Left: Fascist Ideology in France* (Princeton: Princeton University Press, 1995).

[44] Sam Tanenhaus, 'I'm Tired of America Wasting Our Blood and Treasure: The Strange Ascent of Betsy Devos and Erik Prince', *Vanity Fair* (6 September 2018); Alice Lloyd, 'The College That Wants to Take over Washington', *Politico Magazine* (12 May 2018).

of Betsy DeVos, Trump's secretary of education, has bankrolled the religious Right in the US and is also a major financial donor to Hillsdale. Her brother Erik Prince, founder of the private military company Blackwater and prominent Trump supporter implicated in the investigations into Russian meddling in the 2016 elections, is a Hillsdale alumnus. The pipeline between Hillsdale and the Trump administration also ran the other way: When Michael Anton, author of 'The Flight 93 Election', left his position in the White House he joined the Kirby Center, the school's Washington outpost. In 2019, Hillsdale boosted its prominence in Washington yet further by opening The Steve and Amy van Andel Graduate School of Government. Its MA programme is designed for young professionals such as government staffers, lawmakers, journalists, media professionals, speechwriters, lawyers, think tank analysts, as well as domestic and foreign policy experts.

The connections between Hillsdale and the Trump administration did not end with the 2020 election defeat. In the final days of his presidency, Trump set up the so-called 1776 Commission, a direct counter to the *New York Times Magazine*'s 1619 Project. The latter sought to centre slavery and the contributions of Black people in American history, and the former to create an avowedly traditional, patriotic curriculum. The chair of the 1776 Commission was none other than Hillsdale's Larry Arnn, and despite being disbanded by President Biden, the Commission continued to meet and released its report in January 2021. Echoing the critique of the managerial state, the report maintains that 'progressivism' has undermined the principles of the Declaration of Independence and that 'progressives' have 'created what amounts to a fourth branch of government called at times the bureaucracy or the administrative state. This shadow government never faces elections and today operates largely without checks and balances.'[45] In the administrative state, teachers function

---

[45] The 1776 Commission, *The 1776 Report*, trumpwhitehouse.archives.gov/wp-content/uploads/2021/01/The-Presidents-Advisory-1776-Commission-Final-Report.pdf (accessed 6 March 2023), 13.

as 'conveyor belts' pouring progressive ideas into students' heads.⁴⁶ Nevertheless, the solution is also to be found in education: 'This great project of national renewal depends upon true education – not merely training in particular skills, but the formation of citizens.' Patriotic education teaches 'the truth about America': 'At home, in school, at the workplace, and in the world, it is the people – and only the people – who have the power to stand up for America and defend our way of life.'⁴⁷

Across the US, a number of Republican governors have long been keen to give curriculum development over to Arnn and his activists. This is why the report of the 1776 Commission may matter less than the subsequent release of Hillsdale's '1776 Curriculum' – nearly 2,400 pages of teaching material made available online, free of charge, to K-12 schools. Inspired by the work of the Commission, this curriculum is meant to roll back the anti-American, progressive (or 'woke') education, advancing the 'truth' that 'America is an exceptionally good country'.⁴⁸ Hillsdale has also launched its own charter K-12 school project, which according to its website, includes over fifty member schools with more than 14,500 students in the 2020–2021 school year.⁴⁹ Crucially, Hillsdale's intervention coincides with the right-wing parents' rights movement, and a time when the number of home-schooled students in the US has reached 4 million. For Republican politicians, this constitutes a major opportunity. As Florida education commissioner Richard Corcoran, a close aide to Governor Ron DeSantis, told a Hillsdale audience: 'The war will be

---

⁴⁶ Larry Arnn, in an interview with Mark Levin, 'Life, Liberty & Levin', *Fox News* (18 March 2018).
⁴⁷ The 1776 Commission, 16.
⁴⁸ Kathleen O'Toole, 'The Hillsdale 1776 Curriculum Was Made by Professors and Teachers – Not Bureaucrats, Not Activists, Not Journalists – Teachers', Hillsdale College K-12 Education Office, k12.hillsdale.edu/Curriculum/The-Hillsdale-1776-Curriculum/Dear-Teacher/ (accessed 6 March 2023).
⁴⁹ Kathryn Joyce, 'Coming to a School Near You: Stealth Religion and a Trumped-Up Version of American History', *Salon* (16 March 2022); see also Kathryn Joyce, 'The Far Right's National Plan for Schools: Plant Charters, Defund Public Education', *Salon* (17 March 2022).

won in education. If we can get education right – we can have kids be literate and then understand what it means to be a self-governing citizen in a self-governing country – we'll win it back.'[50]

Hillsdale has been touted as a 'model' for New College of Florida, a liberal arts college in Sarasota that Governor DeSantis wishes to transform into a public version of Hillsdale.[51] According to the governor's spokesperson, New College 'like so many colleges and universities in America ... has been completely captured by a political ideology that puts trendy, truth-relative concepts above learning.'[52] To rectify this, DeSantis in January 2023 appointed six new conservative members to the board of trustees, including Matthew Spalding, a professor and dean at Hillsdale College; Charles Kesler, a professor at Claremont McKenna College and a senior fellow at The Claremont Institute; and Christopher Rufo, a member of the Manhattan Institute and a well-known opponent of what he calls critical race theory and gender ideology.[53] Their mission, in the words of Rufo, is to 'design a new core curriculum from scratch' and 'encode it in a new academic master plan.' For both DeSantis and Rufo, the battle over education does not stop at the small Florida college. Instead, a reconstructed New College would serve as a model for conservatives to copy all over the country. As Rufo puts it, 'If we

---

[50] Quoted in Kathryn Joyce, 'Coming to a School Near You.' In many European countries, including Poland, Hungary, France, and Germany, radical Right parties are also targeting school curricula. In Germany, for example, Alternative for Germany (AfD) has pursued a disturbing attack on history and Holocaust teaching, arguing that schools should teach pride and patriotism; see Emily Schultheis, 'Teaching the Holocaust in Germany as a Resurgent Far Right Questions It', *The Atlantic* (10 April 2019). On the political initiatives reshaping the teaching of history in nationalist directions in India, see Ashutosh, 'The Transnational Routes', 328. On Japan, see Karin Narita, 'Travelling Theory and Its Consequences: José Ortega y Gasset and radical Conservativism in Post-Cold War Japan', *Millennium* 49:3 (2021), 556–576, 573–575.

[51] Ana Ceballos and Sommer Brugal, 'Conservative Hillsdale College Is Helping DeSantis Reshape Florida Education', *Tampa Bay Times* (5 July 2022).

[52] Zac Anderson, 'DeSantis Seeks to Transform Sarasota's New College with Conservative Board Takeover', *Herald-Tribune* (9 January 2023).

[53] Christopher Rufo, *America's Cultural Revolution: How the Radical Left Conquered Everything* (New York: Broadside Books, 2023).

can take this high-risk, high-reward gambit and turn it into a victory, we're going to see conservative state legislators starting to reconquer public institutions all over the United States.' The purpose is, he continues, to 'steal the strategies and the principles of the Gramscian left, and then to organize a kind of counterrevolutionary response to the long march through the institutions.'[54]

Others are more impatient, preferring instead to start their own universities from scratch. Although they generally deny being on the Right, these institutions reflect its critique of contemporary higher education. This is the case with the University of Austin, Texas (UATX), which is set to open its doors to full-time students in the fall of 2024. Not to be confused with the highly regarded University of Texas, UATX is privately funded and claims to be different due to its fearless pursuit of truth. 'Dare to think', its website encourages prospective students, who will reportedly pay no tuition until the university receives its accreditation.[55] Its summer programme is billed as 'Forbidden Courses', while a week-long political symposium is dedicated to Leo Strauss, again free of charge due to 'the generous support of our donors'.

In Europe too, the radical Right has not been content with infiltrating existing institutions and has instead founded its own, separate establishments, all of them closely connected to right-wing leaders and intellectuals and explicitly designed to train nationalist elites, bureaucrats, and diplomats.[56] Despite their overt nationalism, most of these schools are linked through transnational exchanges in what can be described as an effort to create a network of finishing schools for ultra-conservatives. Their founders are upfront about this goal, expressing their determination to train a nimble, global network of

---

[54] Quotes from Goldberg, 'DeSantis Allies Plot the Hostile Takeover of a Liberal College.'
[55] University of Austin, 'Homepage', www.uaustin.org (accessed 26 October 2023); Jemima Kelly, 'The Reopening of the America Mind', *Financial Times* (26 October 2023).
[56] Dorit Geva and Felipe G. Santos, 'Europe's Far-Right Educational Projects and Their Vision for the International Order', *International Affairs* 97:5 (2021), 1395–1414.

conservative elites who will successfully wage the war of position and eventually displace the liberal common sense. The rationale for this was captured by Orbán, in his address to the first CPAC in Budapest:

> For successful politics, one needs institutions and institutes. Whether they are think tanks, educational centers, talent workshops, foreign relations institutes, youth organizations or whatever, they should have a political aspect. Let us not forget: politicians come and go, but institutions stay with us for generations. They, the institutions, have the capacity to renew politics intellectually. New ideas, new thoughts and new people are needed again and again. If they run out, we will run out of ammunition, and our opponent will show no mercy in laying us low.[57]

The highest profile of these endeavours was also the most publicised failure. In 2016, ex-Trump campaign manager and short-lived White House staffer Steve Bannon secured a lease from the Italian Ministry of Culture on an 800-year-old Carthusian monastery, a short distance from Rome. The new educational institution – the Academy of the Judeo-Christian West – that Bannon and his allies hoped to create was to operate under the Dignitas Humanae Institute, directed by the British conservative Benjamin Harnwell. According to reports, Bannon was personally involved in drafting the Academy's curriculum, which included courses such as 'Cultural Marxism, Radical Jihad, and 'The C.C.P.'s Global Information Warfare', and sought to create political 'gladiators' and the next generation of activists.[58] In Harnwell's words, 'We're treating the West as a concept rather than a geographical entity. This is fundamentally a battle of ideas.'[59] In

---

[57] 'Speech by Prime Minister Viktor Orbán at the opening of CPAC Hungary.'
[58] Mark Hosenball, 'Steve Bannon Drafting Curriculum for Right-Wing Catholic Institute in Italy', *Reuters* (14 September 2018); see also Ben Munster, 'The Last Stand at Steve Bannon's "Gladiator School"', *The New Yorker* (24 May 2021).
[59] Quoted in Haley Ott, 'Steve Bannon Backs "Gladiator School" to Bolster Europe's Right Wing', *CBS News* (3 March 2019).

2019, after a series of protests and political controversies, the Ministry revoked the lease on the monastery, and despite legal attempts to overturn the decision, the revocation was upheld in March 2021 and the project collapsed.

The failure of the Academy was only one of a series of setbacks Bannon encountered in his attempt to build networks of radical conservative expertise between Europe and America.[60] These failures, however, should not blind us to the wider strategy they were part of – a strategy of counter-hegemonic institution-building that continues with greater success elsewhere. The first radical Right personality to meet Bannon in Italy was Lega Nord politician Armando Siri, who sponsors the Milan-based School for Political Education.[61] At the time of writing, over 2,500 students have taken part in its annual conference-like events, with the eighth edition scheduled in 2023. The school's events have featured several high-profile speakers, including former prime minister Silvio Berlusconi, several mayors, and Italian politicians. The school's motto is, roughly translated, 'I think, I know, I create.' In the words of Matteo Salvini, one of the School's key supporters: 'The goal is this: to stimulate debate and to train prepared and competent people who aspire to govern this country.'[62] To this effect, the School's website claims that over thirty-five of their former participants ran in the 2020 administrative and regional elections in Italy. Through its association with Formapolis, a non-profit social enterprise, the School also contributes to training for businesses and organisations, while a publishing branch ensures the circulation of Armando Siri's multiple books.

One of the most established and influential of the new European right-wing institutions of learning is undoubtedly Hungary's Ludovika University of Public Service (UPS), described by Dorit Geva

---

[60] His Brussels-based initiative, The Movement, similarly crumbled after receiving, at best, a lukewarm reception by the continent's radical Right.

[61] J. Lester Feder and Giuia Alagna, 'One of Steve Bannon's Top Allies in Italy Is under Investigation over Corruption', *BuzzFeed News* (20 April 2019).

[62] Matteo Salvini, quoted on the School's website, www.scuoladiformazionepolitica.it (accessed 6 March 2023). Our translation.

and Felipe Santos as 'a prime site for examining the ambitions of right-wing globalists who see themselves as playing a long game of working to transform globalist institutions from within.'[63] Founded in 2012 by Orbán's Fidesz government explicitly to educate a 'new generation of people for the operation of a good state',[64] Ludovika registers 5,000 students annually across four faculties and prides itself on maintaining close relationships with both the government and the Fidesz party. Students and future civil servants are invited to join the university both in the service of the Hungarian nation 'as the vocation of the homeland' and in support of 'the construction of the Europe of nations.'[65] Among its degree offerings is an MA in International Relations, with a curriculum developed in cooperation with the Ministry of Foreign Affairs and Trade and specialisations in International Economic Relations, Regional and Civilisational Studies, and European Studies. The MA in International Public Service Relations is taught in English in order to accommodate foreign students and seeks to educate future experts for international and EU institutions, as well as national public administrations. The university also offers three PhD programmes in Public Administration Sciences, Military Sciences, and in Law Enforcement. In addition to its degrees, the University organises a free six-month training course called the 'Europe of Nations Career Programme', designed to equip Hungarian diplomats and EU professionals with critical knowledge of Hungary's circumstances and EU institutions, while the College of Visegrad+ aims to inform students about Central Europe.

Deeply committed to Christian and European values (rendered in distinctly non-liberal terms), Ludovika has an ambitious internationalisation strategy. It has academic partnerships with thirty-four countries, and by 2025, it aims to involve all professors

---

[63] Geva and Santos, 'Europe's Far-Right Educational Projects', 1403.
[64] Quoted in *Ibid*.
[65] 'Mission, Vision, Strategy', Ludovika – University of Public Service, https://en.uni-nke.hu/about-ludovika-ups/mission-vision-strategy (accessed 6 March 2023).

and every third student in international mobility.[66] In September 2020, it established the Budapest Fellowship Program for young American scholars and professionals. In cooperation with the Hungary Foundation and the Mathias Corvinus Collegium (MCC), these are full-time, fully funded ten-month fellowships designed to nurture future bridge-builders between the two countries and further their understanding of Central and Eastern Europe.[67] On the surface, the various courses offered by Ludovika operate as conventional academic programmes, with ample opportunities for study and networking. What distinguishes them is the explicit commitment to Christian values and the strong emphasis on specific visions of European and especially Hungarian history, culture, and institutions. This is not an institution dedicated to producing radical activists, much less neo-fascist streetfighters. It carries forward the more subtle, but arguably more substantial, political project of refashioning academic common sense and its relationship to expertise. The principles of global liberal progressivism are not its touchstone; they are its target.

The same applies to the Danube Institute and the MCC, two other key institutions in Budapest's expanding ecosystem of right-wing centres and think tanks. The former was established in 2013 by the Batthyány Lajos Foundation, which appears to receive substantial funding from the Orbán government. Originally dedicated to spreading conservative ideas (including neoliberal economics), it has subsequently added explicit commitments to the nation-state and patriotism to its agenda. The Institute hosts an extensive programme of events and conferences, focusing on topics such as 'The ABC of Critical Race Theory' (featuring Christopher Rufo), the importance of the family in Western

---

[66] 'The University of a Secure Future, 2020–2025', Ludovika – University of Public Service, en.uni-nke.hu/document/en-uni-nke-hu/Institutional%20Development%20Plan%202020-2025%20UPS.pdf (accessed 6 March 2023).

[67] 'Budapest Fellowship Program', Hungary Foundation (accessed 6 March 2023). www.hungaryfoundation.org/budapest-fellowship-program/; for a personal account, see Bence X. Szechenyi, 'Victor Orbán's Pet University Is All about Propaganda – I Know, I Was There', *The Guardian* (11 September 2023).

political thought, and the contemporary relevance of Alexander Dugin's political ideology. Its list of speakers and visiting fellows features prominent radical Right figures, including Michael Anton, Frank Furedi (discussed later in this section), and Nigel Biggar, an emeritus Oxford professor of moral and pastoral theology whose work highlights the positive aspects of British colonialism. The Institute also pursues an active research and publication strategy and is a partner in the slickly produced magazine *Hungarian Conservative*, which seeks to counter 'progressivism in order to create a sustainable future not only for the sake of Hungary but for the preservation of Western heritage'.[68] Among its international partners is Policy Exchange, the influential UK think tank that provides a home for radical Right academics such as Eric Kaufman and Matthew Goodwin.[69]

However impressive the activities of the Danube Institute, they pale in comparison with those of the MCC, an elite, privately owned training institution. Founded in 1996, the Collegium has massively expanded its activities after receiving billions in funding from the Orbán government in the 2020s.[70] Aiming to prepare a 'patriotic generation' that can confidently represent Hungary in global competition and participate in national and international decision-making, the Collegium runs a wide range of education and training programmes with 7,000 students in 24 cities. Its headquarters in Budapest is a frequent host to the luminaries of the global radical Right, including Jordan Peterson, Tucker Carlson, Christopher Rufo, Yoram Hazony, and Marion Maréchal, to mention but a few. In 2022, the MCC opened its Brussels outpost, a think tank and education centre designed 'to shake up European debate and discussion' and 'acquaint and influence European policy makers with its distinct approach towards the political, socio-economic and cultural issues

---

[68] *Hungarian Conservative* 2:4 (2022), back cover page.
[69] The Danube Institute, https://danubeinstitute.hu (accessed 6 March 2023); *Hungarian Conservative* 2:4 (2022).
[70] Valerie Hopkins, 'Campus in Hungary Is Flagship of Orban's Bid to Create a Conservative Elite', *New York Times* (28 June 2021).

of our time'.[71] According to the Executive Director Frank Furedi (a Hungarian-Canadian sociology professor and former leader of the UK's Revolutionary Communist Party now flying the flag of national conservatism), Brussels is 'groaning under the weight of political complacency and bureaucracy' and needs an 'alternative' in the form of a think tank that will 'bring together those who are worried about Europe's increasingly polarized cultural landscape'.[72] In Furedi's view, 'Hungary is hated by the West's culture warriors for the simple reason that it dares to question their post-traditionalist, identity-politics-fuelled world view.'[73] By taking the ideological fight to Brussels, the MCC hopes not only to disrupt this comfortable consensus of the pro-European establishment but also, as Orbán's Political Director Balázs Orbán puts it, to make Hungary 'an intellectual powerhouse'.[74] As part of its internationalisation effort, the MCC in May 2023 acquired a stake in Modul University Vienna, Austria's largest private university.

In France, the Lyon-based Institute of Social Sciences, Economics, and Politics (ISSEP) has proved an important addition to the right-wing educational landscape. Its founder and Director is none other than Marion Maréchal, the former National Front politician and niece of the *Rassemblement National*'s leader Marine Le Pen. Maréchal figures prominently on the School's website. So does the Institute's ambition to train the leaders of tomorrow, with the slogan 'choose to lead!' visually enticing website visitors through its doors and into the library. ISSEP's values of Excellence, Engagement, Ethics, and *Enracinement* (rootedness) echo the radical Right's opposition to liberalism's bland, valueless world without moral order and cultural, racialised boundaries: 'We share with our students a taste

---

[71] MCC Brussels, 'New Forum Launched to Shake Up European Debate and Discussion', https://brussels.mcc.hu/news/mcc-brussels-a-new-forum-launched-to-shake-up-european-debate-and-discussion (accessed 8 May 2023).
[72] Frank Furedi, 'Brussels Needs a Hungarian Think Tank', *Politico* (1 November 2022).
[73] Ibid.
[74] Wilhelmine Preussen, 'Victor Orbán Funded Think Tank Vows to Shake up Brussels', *Politico* (1 November 2022).

of their history and civilisational heritage. We enable them to learn from the lessons and riches of the past through a solid general knowledge (*culture générale*) and encourage them to adopt a long-term view of their actions.'[75]

Often dubbed the *Sciences Po en Droite*, ISSEP offers master's degrees in Political Science and Project Management, and since 2018 has taught over 300 students.[76] Students can choose to major in the history of political ideas, geopolitics, constitutional law, general history, or economics and monetary policy, with minors available in philosophy, the philosophy of law, electoral analysis, and defence analysis. In addition to the focus on geopolitics, an extensive curriculum is dedicated to the quintessential aspects of French culture, including courses in oenology, dancing, and protocol, with the objective of teaching the French 'way of life'. The School also offers a ten-month continuing education programme in Leadership and Political Science, which alongside more conventional courses on international relations and economics includes sections dedicated to election campaigning, media training, and 'Europe and Secularism.' In August 2023, five years after the inauguration of ISSEP in Lyon, Maréchal announced the opening of a branch in Paris.

ISSEP professors and instructors have close links with other universities, with the EU, and the business world, as well as with right-wing parties such as *Rassemblement National*.[77] Similarly, the ISSEP's sister organisation in Madrid has strong ties to the Spanish Vox party, with the Vox Foundation granting fellowships to ISSEP students and some of the party's most influential ideologues featuring among the school's frequent visitors.[78] The anti-managerial, anti-liberal globalism of the radical Right is clearly articulated by the all-white, male

---

[75] ISSEP, 'Présentation', www.issep.fr/presentation/ (accessed 6 March 2023). Our translation.
[76] BAC+4 and BAC+5.
[77] ISSEP's partner universities are St Petersburg University, Holy Spirit University of Kaslik in Lebanon, and Collegium Intermarium in Poland.
[78] Laura Galaup, 'El instituto de Maréchal Le Pen y Vox comparten entornos para formar a la futura élite de la extrema derecha', *El Diario* (29 August 2021).

line-up of professors in both Lyon and Madrid. At Lyon, for example, Matthieu Baumier's recent book entitled *Voyage au bout des ruines libérales–libertaires* (*Journey to the End of the Liberal–Libertarian Ruins*) bemoans the globalist threat to national cultures and criticises the 'globalist elites' for having developed a world without limits, which endangers the French way of life and threatens its 'deculturation'.[79] The academic director of ISSEP in Madrid, Miguel Ángel Quintana Paz argues that the Left is leading a culture war that undermines the politically neutral spaces of democratic societies, including the family and places of worship. The Left, he contends, is conducting a 'blitzkrieg against our culture', and the Right needs to enter the culture wars in order to protect everything from becoming politicised.[80]

Another of ISSEP's partner institutions is Poland's Collegium Intermarium, a Catholic university founded in 2021 by the Education for Values Foundation and the ultra-conservative think tank Ordo Iuris Institute for Legal Culture. Dedicated to educating a new generation of conservative lawyers, the Collegium maintains close links with Poland's conservative-nationalist Law and Justice Party (PiS), with two ministers of the PiS government at the time attending its opening ceremony.[81] According to its website, the Collegium 'was established as an answer to the crisis of academic life. At a time when the sense of order, purpose, and meaning is fading away, our university has a fixed point of reference – unchanging ideas of Truth, Good, and Beauty.'[82] Jerzy Kwasniewski, the Warsaw lawyer who heads Ordo Iuris, described the Collegium as a counterweight to existing institutions. The Collegium, he suggested, will be 'a space of free academic inquiry at a time of perceived censorship in

---

[79] Matthieu Baumier, *Voyage au bout des ruines libérales–libertaires* (Paris: P-G. de Roux, 2019).

[80] Miguel Ángel Quintana Paz, '¿Qué queremos decir cuando decimos que estamos en una guerra cultural?', *The Objective* (5 December 2019). Our translation.

[81] Claudia Ciobanu, 'Ordo Iuris: The Ultra-Conservative Organisation Transforming Poland', *Balkan Insight* (22 June 2021).

[82] Collegium Intermarium, 'Mission and Values', collegiumintermarium.org/en/our-mission (accessed 1 November 2023).

traditional academic settings', referring specifically to the targeting and silencing of conservative thinkers.[83] It espouses 'the classical values of European civilization: Roman legal culture, philosophy of ancient Greece, and Christian ethics' and is dedicated to furthering cooperation within the 'Intermarium area', a geopolitical construct we address in Chapter 5.

In familiar tones, the Collegium began the 2021/2022 academic year with a conference on 'the place of truth in an age of cancel culture', where one of the speakers was Marion Maréchal. Primarily a law school, the main programme is a five-year, full-time degree in law, while at the postgraduate level, students can choose 'Classical Europe: Politics – Culture – Art of Debate', a course designed to provide them with the conditions for learning about, reflecting upon, and embracing the European tradition. Alternatively, the Collegium offers a course for local level officials and politicians wishing to learn how better to conduct effective pro-family policies. The latter underlines the link with Ordo Iuris, which is well known for its strong opposition to abortion and same-sex marriage in Poland and beyond.[84] Indeed, the anti-abortion, pro-family agenda unites all of these various radical Right educational establishments, and many of their instructors have previous experience as active political opponents of progressive gender policies.[85]

In addition to these formal educational establishments, numerous think tanks have significantly increased their education and

---

[83] Vanessa Gera, 'Warsaw University Aims to Shape Future Conservative Lawyers', *AP News* (28 May 2021).

[84] Ordo Iuris defines itself as a 'legal training center' that fights against the 'various radical ideologies that aggressively question the existing social order' and seek to 'destroy its very foundation'. Ordo Iuris, 'Who We Are', en.ordoiuris.pl/who-we-are (accessed 6 March 2023).

[85] At the ISSEP Madrid branch, this includes the former Spanish Minister of Internal Affairs Jamie Amjor Oreja, who was among the founders of 'One of Us', a European citizens' initiative that united many ultra-Catholic groups to demand that the EU ban or limit abortion. Guillaume Drago, who teaches law courses at ISSEP, is the president of the Christian-inspired think tank Institute famille et république, which mounted a legal challenge to same-sex marriage and continues to propose legal reforms to reverse the law.

training activities. As *The Economist* has documented, the radical Right has expanded its 'Washington army' in preparation for power.[86] This includes the think tank American Moment, launched in February 2021 to identify and train young national conservatives for careers in Washington. The Charlemagne Institute, a non-profit publisher and educational organisation, was established in 2018 with a mission to restore the principles and traditions 'upon which Western Civilization was founded.'[87] The name of the Institute refers to the first Holy Roman Emperor, whose ascension is credited with ending the Dark Ages and giving way to a unified, enlightened, and Christian West. Charlemagne's lieutenant was Alcuin, who according to the organisation's website 'led the charge to bring about a renaissance in learning and wisdom'. Through the Alcuin Internship programme, the Institute seeks to replicate this transformation by training 'young aspiring journalists for lives of service and the long-march through the institutions' and thus fight back against the 'the vast promotion of postmodernism, globalism, and cultural Marxism' in education, media, business, and government.[88]

There are also various online right-wing educational initiatives, one of the most recent being the Peterson Academy, spearheaded by the Canadian psychologist Jordan Peterson and his daughter. Set to open its virtual doors in November 2023, the Academy promises to teach students 'how to think not what to think'.[89] The most successful example of conservative online education, however, can be found in Brazil, where the late Olavo de Carvalho, widely regarded as the architect of former President Jair Bolsonaro's right-wing vision, launched his online philosophy courses in 2009. While lacking formal education, the intellectual maverick exercised tremendous

---

[86] 'Trumpism's New Washington Army', *The Economist* (9 July 2022), 21.
[87] The Charlemagne Institute, 'What Is Charlemagne Institute? Who We Are', charlemagneinstitute.org/about/ (accessed 6 March 2023).
[88] The Charlemagne Institute, 'The Alcuin Internship', charlemagneinstitute.org/the-alcuin-internship/ (accessed 26 July 2022).
[89] Peterson Academy, https://petersonacademy.com (accessed 27 October 2023). See also Kelly, 'The Reopening of the America Mind'.

influence on Brazil's political elite through his voluminous writing and online activities. Having diagnosed Brazil's problem as 'leftist dominance' of the media and universities, Carvalho – in classic Gramscian style – set out to build a conservative political vanguard and movement. In an ambitious self-depiction of his Gramsci-inspired mission, Carvalho declared: 'my influence on Brazil's culture is infinitely bigger than anything the government is doing. I am changing Brazil's cultural history. Governments go away; the culture stays.'[90] By the time of his death in January 2022, more than 5,000 people had attended his classes, including several members of Bolsonaro's cabinet. Abraham Weintraub, Bolsonaro's controversial Minister of Education, was a 'graduate' of Carvalho, translating his teaching into practice by combating 'cultural Marxism' and slashing funding for federal universities by 30 per cent.[91] Bolsonaro's equally controversial Minister of Foreign Affairs, Ernesto Araújo, was also a convert to Carvalho's philosophy and was appointed on his recommendation. Filipe Martins, Bolsonaro's Advisor on International Affairs, similarly endorsed Carvalho's theories and saw globalisation as a project advanced by 'cosmopolitan and stateless' bureaucrats.[92] Together, Araújo and Martins oversaw attempts to shift Brazil's foreign policy away from multilateralism and towards anti-globalism and sovereigntism.[93] Carvalho's effort to foster inter-regional exchange of conservative ideas led to the short-lived Inter-American Institute for Philosophy, Government and Social Thought, where among others Paul Gottfried was a distinguished senior fellow.[94]

---

[90] Letícia Duarte, 'Meet the Intellectual Founder of Brazil's Far Right', *The Atlantic* (28 December 2018).

[91] Ibid.; Michelle Abidor, 'The Gramsci of the Brazilian Right', *Dissent* (Summer 2020). The latter article describes Carvalho as 'obsessed with Gramsci'.

[92] Quoted in Guilherme Stolle Paixão e Casarões and Déborah Barros Leal Farias, 'Brazilian Foreign Policy under Jair Bolsonaro: Far-Right Populism and the Rejection of the Liberal International Order', *Cambridge Review of International Affairs* 35:5 (2022),741–761, 752.

[93] Ibid.

[94] See the Inter-American Institute website on archive.org: theinteramerican.org/dr-paul-gottfried-commentary/.

In sum, the radical Right's critique of mainstream universities and expertise is a critique of the specific form of liberal elite rule, not of elites *per se*.[95] As such, this is not a straightforward populist opposition between the elites and the people. Instead, as we argued in Chapter 3, it is a populism grounded in opposition to specific (liberal) elites. Their goal is to educate a new elite; the next generation of leaders, public intellectuals, diplomats, and civil servants, schooled in their vision of the world and more accepting of the protection of national sovereignty in issues of culture and values. It is a classic Gramscian counter-hegemonic strategy, seeking to build a new historic bloc through patience and perseverance. Furthermore, some of these activities have at least a potential to blur Gramsci's line between war of movement and war of position. Claremont's Sheriffs Fellowship may look insubstantial – a week in California to attend 'over twenty intensive daily seminars and relaxed evening symposia' on topics such as 'The New Left & the Roots of Radical Leftist Ideology'[96] – but given the power and influence of sheriffs, their ideological inclinations are of considerable potential significance. Finally, most of the institutions and practices analysed here are designed to strengthen and extend the transnational networks of conservative elites around the world. Indeed, one of the stated aims behind the creation of the Lyon-based institute is 'to build alliances with like-minded schools throughout Europe, the United States, Russia and China'.[97] Their aim is to replace the liberal, 'woke', managerial, globalist elite with a Right elite, schooled in the critique of managerialism and critical of the over-reach of international institutions and liberal power. As such, these schools are nationalist in

---

[95] In fact, some – many neo-monarchist, neo-Cameralists, and techno-utopians, for instance – are radically and unapologetically elitist, and often anti-democratic as well. Although we do not deal with these more marginal positions, they show the diversity and the tensions on the radical Right.

[96] Claremont Institute, 'Sheriffs Fellowship', www.claremont.org/page/sheriffs-fellowship/ (accessed 24 February 2023).

[97] Adeline Sire, 'Le Pen's Niece Opens Grad School to Train New Generation of French Far-Right Leaders.' *Public Radio International* (4 January 2019).

their outlook, but they are not anti-internationalist per se. Instead, they seek to educate leaders who will be pro-capitalist but also protect sovereignty, traditional culture, and the virtuous working class against the economic and cultural predations of global liberal managerialism.

CONCLUSION

Much of the literature on the radical Right has focused on their innovative and effective use of social media. While these analyses are crucial to an understanding of the global rise of the Right, they are also incomplete. The counter-hegemonic struggle is simultaneously digital and analogue, offensive and polite, shocking and mundane – just as it is simultaneously national and global. As we have shown in this chapter, alongside its claims to philosophical innovation and use of transgressive rhetorics, the radical Right is also actively and strategically pursuing more traditional, mainstream routes towards a new common sense. These efforts are not coordinated or unified and theorising these disparate and constantly evolving initiatives is challenging. The temptation to see them as coherent and connected must therefore be avoided. But, as we argued in the introductory chapter, multiplicity is in part the radical Right's strength. Their commonality – and potential future unity – emerges from diverse positions and demands articulated in ways that allow its participants to see themselves as engaged in analogically similar struggles. Successful politics, in other words, involves constructing, propagating, and adapting core conceptual oppositions that allow divergent groups to recognise themselves as part of the same fight. It also involves efforts to gain greater visibility and acceptability for your core ideas, normalising and mainstreaming them one step at a time.

Successful formation of such global networks and transnational social forces is not guaranteed. Far from it. Yet, there is no doubt that hard metapolitical work is well underway, with an actual globe-spanning coalition of conservatives waging what Gramsci calls a 'war of attrition, trench warfare' against existing common sense. Such war, by definition, takes decades and requires considerable economic and cultural resources, as well as organisational structures and strategies. Should it succeed in these endeavours, the radical Right would be in an even stronger position to impact not only domestic, but also international politics. Accordingly, we devote Chapter 5 to the radical Right's possible implications for the future of geopolitics and the liberal world order.

5 The Right World

For almost a decade, the crisis of the liberal international order (LIO) has been a dominant theme in world politics. In these discussions, the rise of the radical Right is commonly, and accurately, seen as both a cause and a symptom of the crisis, with the LIO charged with providing the disruptive conditions of possibility for political movements dedicated to its demise. This relationship is generally traced to three sources. The first is the hollowing out or retreat of Keynesian 'embedded liberalism' and its replacement by the powerful forces of neoliberal globalisation that themselves fell into increasing disarray following the 2008 financial crisis. The result was significant socioeconomic dislocation in both the developed world and the Global South, including the decline of traditional industries, relative working-class prosperity, and social safety nets.[1] Second, neoliberal trade and financial policies weakened domestic political institutions and representation, and governments had less leverage over social support and economic policy, or less desire to exercise it. Supposedly non-ideological 'post-politics' – epitomised by the 'Third Way' approaches of the Centre Left – supplanted previous divisions between Left and Right, ushering in an era of technocratic management and the belief that 'There Is No Alternative' to neoliberal globalisation. As part of this process, political parties became professional vote-winning machines and their mass membership bases collapsed, leaving a political 'void' where substantial

---

[1] Edward Luce, *The Retreat of Western Liberalism* (New York: Atlantic Monthly Press, 2017); Dani Rodrik, 'Why Does Globalization Fuel Populism? Economics, Culture, and the Rise of Right-Wing Populism', *Annual Review of Economics* 13:1 (2021), 133–170; Erik Swyngedouw, 'Illiberalism and the Democratic Paradox: The Infernal Dialectic of Neoliberal Emancipation', *European Journal of Social Theory* 25:1 (2021), 53–74.

parts of the public in democratic states felt increasingly powerless, unrepresented, and alienated – and susceptible to 'anti-elite' political movements.[2] Finally, the rise of illiberal powers, particularly Russia and China, provided direct challenges to the dominance of liberal states, institutions, and ideas, as well as ideological and material support and a range of 'exit options' for states and movements wishing to distance or extricate themselves from the LIO.[3] This enabled radical Right movements and parties positioned within the traditional heartland of the LIO to build new alliances and find ideological common-ground with powerful illiberal states, joining forces in their pursuit of a less liberal world order.

This final chapter builds on these insights and examines the possible impact of the radical Right's counter-hegemonic struggles on the future and stability of the LIO, as well as their own visions of a re-imagined world order. While we agree that the hierarchical, unequal nature of the LIO is a condition of possibility of the global Right, we argue that the radical Right has built powerful transversal global alliances based on a logic and discourse of difference and diversity rather than claims to liberal, Western superiority. This demand for recognition of diversity is linked to powerful visions of civilisations and multipolarity, which in turn has enabled a new geopolitics characterised by the complex entanglements of illiberal states such as China and Russia, radical Right forces, and states and people in the Global South. While the agendas of these actors frequently vary greatly, they are unified in their opposition to Western dominance of the LIO and their desire for recognition within a more multipolar world order. However, the radical Right's commitment to difference and multipolarity should not be confused with advocacy of equality. It is, in fact, the other face of their identitarian vision of domestic political order.

[2] A key early treatment is Peter Mair, *Ruling the Void: The Hollowing of Democracy* (London: Verso, 2013). On elite-mass differences in the post-2008 LIO, see Bentley Allan, Srdjan Vucetic, and Ted Hopf, 'The Distribution of Identity and the Future of International Order', *International Organization* 72:4 (2018), 839–869.

[3] Alexander Cooley and Daniel Nexon, *Exit from Hegemony* (Oxford: Oxford University Press, 2021).

RECOGNITION AND THE RIGHT

Some of the most innovative analyses of the crisis of the LIO have treated it not just as a result of economic disruptions or shifts in political and military power but also as an effect of the struggle for status recognition in international politics.[4] This perspective breaks with the dominant interpretation of the LIO as consisting of sovereign equals or states as 'like units' and draws on a growing body of research that challenges the relegation of hierarchy to a relic of past world orders. Theoretically and empirically diverse, this literature argues instead that overlapping hierarchies stratify and structure relations among states and a range of other actors. Perhaps most importantly, the survival and reproduction of hierarchies from the colonial past continue to influence the post-colonial present, as formal independence and legal sovereignty have failed to deliver equality in terms of material power, political influence, international law, symbolic status, or access to key positions of international decision-making. In short, the world order that emerged in the post-war period cannot be described in the conventional IR manner as consisting of 'like units' of sovereign states. It is more accurately characterised as a regional or Western order, marked by enduring inequalities between states that are ranked hierarchically according to their power and status.[5]

Hierarchy and inequality translate into differential recognition of states within the international system. As Rebecca Adler-Nissen and Ayşe Zarakol have convincingly argued, the struggle for recognition takes on particular importance within the LIO because it is premised on the promise to abolish hierarchy. Unlike previous international orders, the post-war order makes no legal distinctions

---

[4] Rebecca Adler-Nissen and Ayşe Zarakol, 'Struggles for Recognition: The Liberal International Order and the Merger of Its Discontents', *International Organization* 75:3 (2021), 611–634. For a review of the literature on hierarchy, see Janice Bially Mattern and Ayşe Zarakol, 'Hierarchies in World Politics', *International Organization* 70:3 (2016), 623–654.

[5] Bially Mattern and Zarakol, 'Hierarchies in World Politics'.

between 'savages' and 'barbarians', nor between 'civilised' and 'uncivilised'. Instead, it espouses equality based on legal sovereignty. Sovereignty, however, is a necessary, but insufficient, condition for recognition in the international system. As a long tradition of thinking following Hegel's original formulation in *The Phenomenology of Spirit* has argued, recognition is linked to a much more fundamental human need to be 'known, understood, and affirmed'.[6] Although, as Axel Honneth observes, transferring the category of recognition from individuals to states is far from seamless, there is by now a rich body of analysis showing that just as individuals need to have their identities recognised by others, so do groups and states.[7] Sovereign equality can thus be seen as an important but nonetheless 'thin' form of legal recognition; what states (and humans) crave is 'thick' recognition, not merely as universal subjects or sovereign states but also as substantive equals and for 'what makes them special and unique'.[8]

Recognition is central to identity formation, and like people, states tell stories about themselves, their identities and standing in the world, which in turn need to be confirmed and recognised by others.[9] Recognition is thus a social act through which an actor is 'constituted as a subject with legitimate social standing',[10] able to maintain a certain status and identity within a political community. Perfect recognition, however, is impossible, as others do not see us as we see ourselves, or in the way we would like to be seen. In the same way, states have expectations of how much recognition they deserve, and they feel snubbed when their expectations are unmet

---

[6] Adler-Nissen and Zarakol, 'Struggles for Recognition', 614.
[7] Axel Honneth, 'Recognition between States: On the Moral Substrate of International Relations', in Thomas Lindemann and Erik Ringmar, eds. *The International Politics of Recognition* (Boulder: Paradigm Publishers, 2012), 25–38; Michelle Murray, *The Struggle for Recognition in International Relations* (Oxford: Oxford University Press, 2018).
[8] Alexander Wendt, 'Why a World State Is Inevitable', *European Journal of International Relations* 9:4 (2003), 491–542, 511–12.
[9] Erik Ringmar, 'Introduction: The International Politics of Recognition', in Lindemann and Ringmar, *The International Politics of Recognition*, 3–24.
[10] Wendt, 'Why a World State Is Inevitable', 511.

or repeatedly dashed. There is, in other words, always a degree of misrecognition, and the struggle for recognition is therefore continuous rather than settled once and for all.[11]

In the eyes of many states and populations in both the Global North and the Global South, the LIO has failed to deliver the kind of thick recognition they feel entitled to, and the success of the radical Right, as well as the current crisis of the LIO, emerges in large part from the Right's ability to mobilise and merge the discontent of these different groups. In other words, the challenges to global institutions and multilateral cooperation originate not only from the failure of the LIO to deliver fully on the promise to remove existing social, political, and economic inequalities in the international system, but also from its continuing stigmatisation of certain states and populations due to their 'failure' to meet the universal standards set by liberal modernity and liberal states. As Adler-Nissen and Zarakol explain, states and populations in the semi-periphery frequently regard the LIO as Western-centric, hypocritical, and as a cover for the pursuit of Western interests.[12] At the same time, liberalism's efforts to reform previous racial, gender, religious, and other hierarchies in the core liberal states in the North have antagonised large constituencies who feel their previously secure, superior status is under threat, leading them to support populist, anti-liberal positions – a case in point being the 'traditional' working classes, those racialised as 'white' and cast as 'alienated' and 'left behind' by economic globalisation. In short, the LIO is being simultaneously undermined by recognition dynamics within its core and its semi-peripheral member states.

---

[11] Charlotte Epstein, Thomas Lindemann, and Ole Jacob Sending, 'Frustrated Sovereigns: The Agency That Makes the World Go Around', *Review of International Studies*, 44:5 (2018), 787–804; George Lawson and Ayşe Zarakol, 'Recognizing Injustice: The "Hypocrisy Charge" and the Future of the Liberal International Order', *International Affairs* 99:1 (2023), 201–217.

[12] Adler-Nissen and Zarakol, 'Struggles for Recognition', 615; Lawson and Zarakol, 'Recognizing Injustice'. On ideological contestations revolving around claims to civilization, see Gregorio Bettiza, Derek Bolton, and David Lewis, 'Civilizationism and Ideological Contestation in the Liberal International Order', *International Studies Review* 25:2 (2023), First View.

This perspective provides a powerful lens on the crisis of the LIO. But much as the LIO is a Western, hierarchical world order, the ability of the radical Right to build transversal global alliances does not necessarily rely on assertions of Western superiority, but on their embrace of diversity and civilisational difference. The sense of loss of superiority among the 'left behind' in core liberal states may help explain support for the radical Right in the North, but the global resonances of this project stem from quite different analogous claims to thick recognition from states and peoples outside the West.[13] The themes of recognition, stigmatisation, and liberal power have long been preoccupations of the radical Right, and as we demonstrated in Chapter 3, influential parts of its discourses diverge sharply from assumptions of Western, liberal modernity's civilisational superiority. Instead, they have developed a wide range of critical analyses of the power of liberal forms of recognition and strident rejections of it. As Alain de Benoist recently reiterated this long-standing view:

> the liberal system is the prisoner of a major contradiction: on the one hand, it is theoretically based on fundamental tolerance vis-à-vis all individual choices, which leads it to defend the idea of a necessary "neutrality" of the public authorities ... On the other hand, it wants at all costs to extend its individualistic values to the whole world to the detriment of any other system of values, which goes against its principle of tolerance. It is not content, for example, with affirming the universal and absolute superiority of liberal democracy. Instead, it intervenes to impose it everywhere in the world, by multiplying interference of all kinds, so that what was at the start a simple theoretical option becomes the alibi of the most brutal imperialism.[14]

This rejection of liberal universalism and its recognition power is linked to an alternative account of civilisation and world order that

---

[13] For an analysis of Pan-Africanism and recognition, see Rita Abrahamsen, 'Pan-Africanism, Recognition, and World Order' (forthcoming).

[14] Alain de Benoist, 'The Dawn of the Civilizational State', *Agon* (9 April 2023).

advocates differentialism: the idea that cultures or civilisations are incommensurably diverse and that none has a claim to universal validity or virtue. This position allows the radical Right to disavow the doctrines of racial or cultural superiority and imperialism associated with fascism and the Old Right. Perhaps even more importantly, it allows them to draw ideologically powerful equivalences between their positions and those of others who also see themselves as stigmatised and 'symbolically disempowered'[15] by the LIO. Transversal alliances can thus be built with actors in the Global South on the basis of their common commitment to differentialism (and, often, state sovereignty), validating shared claims for thick recognition of fundamental traditions and political–cultural differences and mobilising shared resentment towards liberalism's efforts to stigmatise and efface those traditions and differences. These equivalences can be extended quite easily to include wider articulations with anti-imperialist positions, where liberal colonialism (and neocolonialism) become joint targets of resentment and opposition.[16] The assumption of liberal superiority and denial of recognition is thus turned against liberalism by actors in both the North and the South, providing the bases for mutual hostility towards liberal universalism's managerialist agents in states, international institutions, and human rights NGOs.

THE RIGHT FAMILY: THE PERSONAL IS GEOPOLITICAL

The global campaign to defend and protect the 'natural family' from the onslaught of progressive liberalism is a striking example of such transversal alliances and their potential ability to undermine and change crucial aspects of the LIO. This alliance consists of a heterogenous, contingent assemblage of actors that variously

---

[15] Bettiza, Bolton, and Lewis, 'Civilizationism and Ideological Contestation'; see also Pablo de Orellana and Nicholas Michelsen, 'Reactionary Internationalism: The Philosophy of the New Right', *Review of International Studies* 45:5 (2019), 748–767.

[16] See Marlene Laruelle, 'Illiberalism: A Conceptual Introduction', *East European Politics* 38:2 (2022), 303–327, 313.

includes committed radical Right activists and politicians, Christian evangelicals, Russian Orthodox organisations, cultural traditionalists, and political entrepreneurs, to mention but a few. Like other global assemblages, it does not have a defined geographical centre or decision-making body, but as an alliance it functions together as a whole by virtue of the various actors' shared disdain for liberalism's failure to recognise the 'natural family'. The main battleground of these recognition struggles has been the United Nations, which is accused of having massively exceeded its original mandate by engaging in a form of ideological and cultural colonialism, promoting and pushing countries to adopt progressive values, sometimes in return for international assistance.

Importantly, for the members of this alliance family and gender policies are not accidental or peripheral to the LIO, nor merely the 'softer' side of the harsh world of international politics and diplomacy. Instead, family and gender policies are at the very heart of the making of world order, providing an access point for global liberalism to insert itself into the personal life of individuals, families, and nations. Put differently, the personal is not merely political, as in the feminist slogan. It is also geopolitical.

Created in the aftermath of the Second World War to prevent the recurrence of international aggression and help states resolve their disputes without resort to conflict, the UN today is a bureaucratic behemoth that from the radical Right's perspective increasingly interferes in affairs that should properly be left to domestic leaders and their citizens. In other words, the UN is not only overstepping its bounds, but it is doing so in a manner that is erasing the cultural distinctiveness of the world's nations. The Universal Declaration of Human Rights, adopted by the UN General Assembly in 1948, is often seen as the main tool of this destruction. While not legally binding, the Declaration advances a distinctly liberal vision of a good and just society. In the decades since its adoption, it has 'been transformed into a web of commitments from governments about how they should behave within their own borders'.[17] Article 16 of the Human Rights Declaration states that 'The family is the natural and fundamental group unit of society.' Within the UN system, 'natural' in this statement has come to be interpreted in an inclusive manner, bestowing acceptance and legitimacy on diverse forms of families, be they the heterosexual nuclear family, the extended family, the single-sex family, or any version thereof. By the same token, the Declaration has provided the basis for interpreting abortion and same-sex marriage as human rights under international law.

In response, the radical Right has mounted a concerted global counter-hegemonic struggle to promote a different normative international order with their vision of the 'natural family' and the sovereign national state as its foundational units. One important initiative in this campaign is the Geneva Consensus Declaration on Promoting Women's Health and Strengthening the Family. Launched in 2020 by Brazil, Egypt, Hungary, Indonesia, Uganda, and the United States, the Consensus is a direct and explicit attack on prevailing interpretations of the Universal Declaration of Human Rights, seeking to undermine it as a basis for the defence of abortion and same-sex marriage as human rights under international law. Instead, it reinterprets human rights as 'better health for women' and celebrates women as 'indomitable, fearless, and inspiring, as the very heart and core of civilization'.[18] In this discourse, 'better health for women' means a denial of the right to abortion. It also implies a rejection of the rights of LGBTQ+ people to equality and marriage, and a defence of the sovereign rights of states to make their own laws on these issues, absent external pressure.

Launched in the dying days of the Trump administration and spearheaded by Secretary of State Mike Pompeo, it is tempting dismiss the Consensus as an irrelevant relic of a bygone era. The Biden

---

[17] David Bosco, 'For the UN the Rise of Populism Reveals an Old Challenge', *The Wilson Quarterly* (Fall 2018).

[18] 'Together We Are Stronger', video for the launch of the Consensus, www.theiwh.org/geneva-consensus-declaration/ (accessed 5 November 2023).

administration quickly withdrew its support for the Consensus, as did Brazil after the defeat of President Bolsonaro. But the Consensus is far from dead, and neither is the radical Right's campaign against the UN's liberal family policies.[19] In fact, the Consensus is best understood as part of a broader project of 'antigenderism'.[20] It is one component of a multifaceted radical Right strategy against the UN's family policies, seeking to empower and justify UN member states in rejecting international human rights rulings on topics related to abortion, gender identity, and the rights of sexual minorities. To date, thirty-six countries have signed the Consensus, most of them authoritarian countries with poor or appalling records on human and women's rights. It is promoted within the UN by a growing network of conservative NGOs that maintain close and productive relations with the signatories to the Consensus, various state groups within the UN, as well as powerful conservative individuals and funders.[21]

In the words of Katharine Young, the Geneva Consensus can be seen as a form of 'human rights originalism', a new twist in the radical Right's weaponisation of human rights in the pursuit of illiberal causes.[22] Human rights originalism seeks to restructure the human rights discourse by reducing it to only two original texts – the US Declaration of Independence and the Universal Declaration of Human Rights – thus discounting the elaborate infrastructure of

---

[19] Lynn Morgan, 'Anti-Abortion Strategizing and the Afterlife of the Geneva Consensus Declaration', *Developing World Bioethics* 23:2 (2023), 185–195.

[20] Elżbieta Korolczuk and Agnieszka Graff, 'Gender as "Ebola from Brussels": The Anticolonial Frame and the Rise of Illiberal Populism', *Signs: Journal of Women in Culture and Society* 43:4 (2018), 797–821. As they explain, 'antigenderism' links gender conservatism and critiques of neo-liberalism and 'interpellates subjects as victims of a global conspiracy, manipulated by the neoliberal elites targeting their true nature as men, women, and children, as mothers and fathers', 813.

[21] Jelena Cupać and Irem Ebetürk, 'Backlash Advocacy and NGO Polarization over Women's Rights in the United Nations', *International Affairs* 97:4 (2021), 1183–1201; see also Cooley and Nexon, *Exit from Hegemony*, Ch. 6; and Clifford Bob, *Rights as Weapons: Instruments of Conflict, Tools of Power* (Princeton: Princeton University Press, 2019).

[22] Katharine G. Young, 'Human Rights Originalism', *Georgetown Law Journal*, 110 (2022), 1097–1169.

human rights that has developed subsequently.[23] The treaties and special procedures of the UN are rejected as the views and interpretations of liberal, managerial experts and elites within an unaccountable UN system. It thus allows the radical Right to maintain that they remain supportive of human rights – in their original form, not in their 'progressive' expansion to cover almost all aspects of human life. To this end, the Geneva Consensus is explicitly framed with reference to the Universal Declaration of Human Rights, employing the same language and formulations agreed to by all member states in the 1948, but claims to return to the original intentions and disregard more recent interpretations.[24] Article 16's statement that 'The family is the natural and fundamental group unit of society' thus becomes the subject of intense struggles over language and meaning, with the Right interpreting Article 16 to confirm that there can only be one family – 'the natural family' consisting of a mother, a father, and their children.

The Geneva Consensus is bolstered by an extensive network of conservative NGOs, aligned under the banner of the UN Family Rights Caucus, which claims to have organisational and individual members in over 160 countries. As Jelena Cupać and Irem Ebetürk show, these NGOs work with member states to counter progressive gender initiatives by inserting words and phrases such as the 'natural family' or 'protection of families' into UN documents and policies.[25] Similarly, they contest or block phrases such as 'sexual and reproductive health and rights', 'comprehensive sexual education', and 'women and girls in all their diversity'.[26] Often such formulations and reformulations are passed due to the support of member states

---

[23] The former plays powerfully within the US, the latter is most relevant globally.
[24] As the Trump administration's Secretary of State for Health and Human Services, Alex Azar, stated at the signing ceremony: 'The Declaration is much more than a statement of beliefs – it is a critical and useful tool to defend these principles across all United Nations bodies and at every multilateral setting, using language previously agreed to by member states of those bodies.'
[25] Cupać and Ebetürk, 'Backlash Advocacy', 1189.
[26] Ibid.

from the Global South, including the African Group of States, which the conservative NGO C-Fam praises for 'their relentless efforts to protect the family and children from this harmful policy prescription over the past 4 years'.[27]

The UN is not the only target of this campaign. Regional organisations and individual governments are regularly subjected to pressure and lobbying to reject liberal family policies and laws. In April 2023, for example, in the immediate aftermath of the Ugandan Parliament's approval of one of the world's harshest anti-homosexuality bills, a two-day inter-parliamentary conference on 'family values and sovereignty' was hastily convened in Entebbe. Organised by Ugandan parliamentarians, attended by parliamentarians from twenty-two African countries, and supported by several American conservative, anti-abortion NGOs, the conference was deliberately designed to counter the liberal international community's call for the Ugandan government to respect universal human rights. Thus, as liberals inside and outside Uganda were calling on President Yoweri Museveni not to sign into law a bill that would criminalise homosexuality and make certain acts of homosexuality punishable by death, the President himself opened the conference with a speech entitled 'Protecting National Sovereignty and the Institution of the Family: An African Imperative'. The First Lady, Janet Museveni, tweeted that she was concerned about the global forces threatening African families and about the foreign 'imposition of harmful practices like homosexuality'.[28]

The conference sought to unify African parliamentarians against 'cultural colonialism in African laws, policies and programs'. In the words of the Uganda MP Sarah Opendi, there is a growing

---

[27] Stefano Gennarini, 'Best Moments of the Year for Life and Family at the United Nations', *C-Fam* (29 December 2016).

[28] Julius Luwemba, 'Religious Leaders, African Legislators Parliamentarians Discuss Family Values', *New Vision* (1 April 2023); Additional reporting in *The Independent*, 'African Parliamentarians Call for Scrutiny of International Instruments on Family Values and Sovereignty' (4 April 2023); Janet Museveni, Twitter, 4 April 2023, https://twitter.com/JanetMuseveni/status/1643150905179602945 (accessed 5 May 2023).

threat to African family values, humanity, dignity, and sovereignty: 'Many African countries depend on foreign support to fund the education, health, agriculture and infrastructure sectors, amongst others. But this support is now being conditioned, and if not strongly tackled, will directly impact our African values'.[29] Accordingly, the Parliamentarians called on their respective governments to cease signing international instruments that bind their countries to such 'neo-colonialist' family policies without allowing legislators to scrutinise them.

The conference thus staged a geopolitical clash of values, pitting a transnational alliance of right-wing value conservatives against the progressive impositions of the LIO. It was also a demand for 'thick' recognition of sovereignty and cultural difference. The international sponsors of the conference included Family Watch International (FWI), an American NGO dedicated to fighting abortion and homosexuality that also chairs the UN Family Rights Caucus. FWI, alongside numerous other American religious NGOs such as World Congress of Families (WCF), have organised many similar family-friendly conferences and summits on the continent, as has the Russian Orthodox Church.[30] Such foreign influences aside, the emergence of these value-conservative, anti-LGBTQ+ sentiments and alliances cannot be understood simply as an extension of Western or Northern culture wars to Africa and the Global South, nor are Africa and the Global South simply pawns in a new geopolitical, cultural struggle. Just as there are many Africans who support liberal

---

[29] Luwemba, 'Religious Leaders'.
[30] Kapya Kaoma, 'Globalizing the Culture Wars: U.S. Conservatives, African Churches, and Homophobia', *Political Research Associates* (2009); Kristina Stoeckl, 'Traditional Values, Family, Homeschooling: The Role of Russia and the Russian Orthodox Church in Transnational Moral Conservative Networks and Their Efforts at Reshaping Human Rights', *International Journal of Constitutional Law* 21:1 (2023), 224–242; Kristina Stoeckl and Dimitry Uzlaner, *The Moralist International: Russia in the Global Culture Wars* (New York: Fordham University Press, 2022); Krissy Stroop, 'A Right-Wing International? Russian Social Conservatism, the U.S.-Based WCF, and the Global Culture Wars in Historical Context', *Political Research Associates* (2016).

rights, there are powerful domestic actors that mobilise and activate anti-liberal narratives to claim 'thick' recognition for their identities and to serve their own agendas, be they traditionalist, conservative, religious, or simply opportunistic.[31] These global and local actors are deeply intertwined and their identities and agendas profoundly relational.

The struggle against liberal family values epitomises the radical Right's ability to form transversal global coalitions. As we have argued throughout this book, uniformity, unanimity, or centralised organisation are not required to craft loosely shared but still salient and impactful political identities. There is no single actor orchestrating this counter-hegemonic struggle, and one looks in vain for a central war room where strategies are hatched and tactics agreed. Instead, the pro-family, anti-feminist coalition is geographically and organisationally dispersed, a multifaceted and flexible assemblage containing political parties, religious groups, individuals, and NGOs that coalesce, cohere, and cooperate on key issues and at key points, but that cannot be captured as a single coherent entity.

Importantly, these positions do not depend on assumptions or assertions of Western superiority in the manner of older Right or fascist views of racial or civilisational superiority. On the contrary, in these discourses the *denial or rejection* of Western, liberal superiority becomes a strategic resource in articulating or constructing global alliances demanding recognition of diversity and traditions. Whether one takes these claims of mutual respect at face value or not is in some ways less important than acknowledging the discursive equivalences and the strategic articulations and alliances they enable. Positioning themselves against the superiority of liberal progress and modern universalism, highly diverse actors and movements can come together, each claiming recognition for their diversity – and for their exclusivity.

[31] On the general question of African agency, see Olúfẹ́mi Táíwò, *Against Decolonization: Taking African Agency Seriously* (London: Hurst 2022).

MULTIPOLARITY AND RECOGNITION DIPLOMACY

The worldview of the radical Right is inextricably linked to sovereignty, civilisationalism, and multipolarity. This understanding of multipolarity differs in important ways from the conventional definition in most theories of international relations. For the latter, multipolarity indicates a situation where states as 'like units' of roughly equal coalitions form strategic balances of power. For the former, a multipolar world is defined by the incommensurability of civilisations and will be built around different civilisational states – that is, states such as China, Russia, Iran, India, the US, and other regional powers that see themselves as representing not just a particular nation or a historical group of nations but a distinct civilisation. In this vision, the political forces driving these transformations will have to collaborate in certain areas where they have common interests, such as protecting the environment and preventing a nuclear disaster. But postmodernity and the relative decline of the liberal West have freed world politics from ideological commitments to teleological accounts of a common globality, allowing each civilisational bloc to evolve according to its own epistemic, cultural, and spiritual system of belief.

Unlike Samuel Huntington and other influential IR scholars who developed similar views in the early 1990s, radical conservatives do not present these arguments as an inevitable, social scientific reality of the post–Cold War international order but as an ideological project to be realised. As Alexander Dugin emphasises, the key issue is not whether the existence of civilisations today 'is a demonstrated and weighty factor or a weak and turbulent hindrance on the path to the certain onset of unipolarity or West-centric globalisation'. The idea of civilisations as agents of international order is a response to the perceived exhaustion of the modern nation-state, not some sort of return to the pre-modern age. Civilisations 'are that which needs to be created. There is a cultural, sociological, historical, mental, psychological base for civilizations, and it is empirical. But the transition from civilization as a cultural and sociological given to civilization as a source of agency in a multipolar world requires *effort*.'[32]

In this interpretation, the historical decline of European civilisation is cast as a paradoxical consequence of the Westernisation of the world, which has dissolved the historical boundaries of Europe and relativised its contributions and accomplishments through emulation, assimilation, and absorption.[33] Accordingly, the post–Cold War civilisationalism of the radical Right is deployed not in a discourse of universal superiority, but in one of 'mutual respect' and 'anti-imperialism' – albeit with a routine caveat concerning the geopolitical dominance of civilisational states within their respective spheres of influence. In de Benoist's formulation: 'In the past, a universalist idea of Civilization, "the civilized world", has been the basis for colonialism. Civilizational states, however, don't defend Civilization in the abstract but their particular civilization, their distinctive culture'. Importantly, he insists that

> Civilizational states set against Western universalism a model according to which each civilizational group is considered to have a distinct identity, both in terms of cultural values and in political institutions, an identity that is not reducible to any universal model. These states do not simply want to pursue a sovereign policy without submitting to the dictates of supranational elites. They also seek to thwart any "globalist" project aimed at making the same principles prevail throughout the planet, because they are aware that the culture they embody is not identical to any other. Here we must bear in mind that no single culture can encompass all cultures; the notion of a "world culture" is a contradiction in terms.[34]

---

[32] Alexander Dugin, *The Theory of a Multipolar World* (London: Arktos Media, 2021), 58–59. For a conservative assessment of Russian and Chinese variations on multipolarity, see Jonathan Culbreath, 'Rival Theories of Multipolarity: Aleksander Dugin and Jiang Shigong', *The European Conservative* (3 January 2023).

[33] Julien Freund, *La Décadence: Histoire sociologique et philosophique d'une catégorie d'expérience humaine* (Paris: Sirey, 1984), 383.

[34] De Benoist, 'The Dawn of the Civilizational State'.

The equivalences between this approach to multipolarity and elements of Global South opposition to Western dominance of the LIO facilitate complex global entanglements between diverse actors, governments, and movements. They also intersect with Russian and Chinese efforts to build a multipolar international order and their rejection of Western universalism.[35] Although the radical Right in the North is often virulently alarmist about the 'China threat',[36] the convergence of these diverse oppositional stances is paradoxically a crucial part of the contemporary challenge to the LIO, defying geographical boundaries and mobilising powerful new identities and political allegiances. The radical Right is not necessarily driving these dynamics, nor is it directly present in all of them. Instead, it occupies a range of positions – cheerleading from the margins, providing ideological support, mobilising social organisations, and seeking to influence governments or political leaders. The net effect of these multiple circulations, however, is a transnational ideological ecosystem that is not simply hobbling the LIO but becoming part of a defining struggle over the emerging world order.

Like the radical Right's views of multipolarity and critique of global liberalism, China's and Russia's visions of a more multipolar world contain strong elements of civilisationalism. Officially, the two countries jointly committed themselves to 'the multipolarization of the world and the establishment of a new international order' as early as April 1997.[37] This position was repeated at the Putin – Xi summit in February 2022, less than three weeks before Russia's invasion of Ukraine, when their joint statement declared that the Western 'imposition' of universal human rights and other liberal values is misdirected

---

[35] Bettiza, Bolton, and Lewis, 'Civilizationalism and Ideological Contestation', 12.
[36] Steve Bannon, for example, was involved in relaunching the Cold War era 'Committee on the Present Danger' with a focus on China, and a range of voices on the radical Right systematically link this danger to liberal decadence that undermines patriotism, national culture, and security. See Wendy Wu, 'Cold War Is Back: Bannon Helps Revive the U.S. Committee to Target "Aggressive Totalitarian Foe" China', *Washington Post* (23 May 2019); Bobby Jindal, 'Forget China: This Is America's Greatest Challenge', *Fox News* (10 April 2023).
[37] Cooley and Nexon, *Exit from Hegemony*, 81.

because all 'countries have different histories, cultures, and national conditions, and each has the right to independently choose its development path.'[38] The civilisational theme was even more explicit in President Xi's speech at the Davos Forum in January 2021:

> Just as no two leaves in the world are identical, no [two] histories, cultures, or social systems are the same. Each country is unique with its own history, culture, and social system, and none is superior to the other ... Difference in itself isn't a cause for alarm. What does ring the alarm ... is the attempt to impose a hierarchy on civilizations or to force one's own history, culture, or social system upon others.[39]

This commitment mirrors Putin's civilisationist ideology in which 'liberal globalization means depersonalization and imposing Western model on the entire world', whereas Russia is seeking to unlock 'each civilization's potential in the interests of the entire world so that everyone will win'.[40] The world, in this view, is moving from globalisation to the emergence of civilisational platforms, and the Kremlin's mission is to help 'traditional societies' fight the West's 'decadent', 'globalist', 'unipolar', and 'colonial' ordering.[41]

These diverse civilisational discourses can be articulated into a powerfully multipolar vision of world order aimed explicitly against the LIO,[42] and both China and Russia are mobilising them in forms

---

[38] 'Joint Statement of the Russian Federation and the People's Republic of China on the International Relations Entering a New Era and the Global Sustainable Development', www.en.kremlin.ru (4 February 2022).

[39] Quoted in de Benoist, 'Civilizational State'; see also Nadège Rolland, 'China's Vision for a New World Order', in *NBR Special Report #83* (Seattle: National Bureau of Asian Research 2020).

[40] Alexey Drobinin, 'The Vision of a Multipolar World: The Civilizational Factor and Russia's Place in the World Order', *Russia in Global Affairs* (20 February 2023).

[41] Ivan U. Klyszcz, 'Messianic Multipolarity: Russia's Resurrected Africa Doctrine', *Riddle* (3 April 2023).

[42] Bettiza, Bolton, and Lewis correctly note: 'current global efforts to uphold "cultural diversity" or defend "civilizational identities" cannot be completely divorced from ideological political projects intended to reject and articulate alternatives to liberal universalism'. 'Civilizationism and Ideological Contestation', 5.

of recognition diplomacy that seek to establish common cause with a number of states and actors in the Global South on the basis of their shared rejection of Western dominance. Both have framed the LIO within the legacy of colonialism and neo-imperialism, seeking to build support based on their recognition of cultural and political difference in contrast to the LIO's imposition of liberal values and standards.

Russian diplomacy in Africa, for instance, has used these discourses extensively, effectively combining anti-liberal, anti-colonial, and multipolar positions to engage a range of African governments and seek their support for its invasion of Ukraine.[43] At the start of a multi-country tour of the continent in July 2022, Foreign Minister Sergei Lavrov wrote of Russia's role in the anti-colonial struggles and its lack of colonial legacy in Africa. He then continued:

> our country does not impose anything on anyone or tell others how to live. We treat with great respect the sovereignty of the States of Africa, and their inalienable right to determine the path of their development for themselves. We are firmly committed to the "African solutions to African problems" principle. Such an approach to developing inter-State ties dramatically differs from the "master – slave" logic imposed by former metropolitan countries, which reproduces the obsolete colonial model.[44]

Lavrov's recognition diplomacy explicitly contrasts Russia's respect for Africa's history and identity with the liberal West's disdain and supremacist impositions. This was clearly illustrated at the second Russia – Africa Parliamentary Conference, hosted by the State Duma in Moscow in March 2023 and attended by more than forty official African

---

[43] Jade McGlyn, 'Why Russia Markets Itself as an Anti-Colonial Power to Africans', *Foreign Policy* (8 February 2023); Witold Rodkiewicz, 'An Anti-Colonial Alliance with the Global South. The New 'Foreign Policy Concept of the Russian Federation', Center for Eastern Studies (7 April 2023).

[44] Russian Ministry of Foreign Affairs, 'Article by the Minister of Foreign Affairs of the Russian Federation Sergey Lavrov for the Egyptian newspaper Al-Ahram, the Congolese Dispatch de Brazzaville, the Ugandan New Vision, as well as the Ethiopian Ethiopia Herald, 22 July, 2022'.

parliamentary delegations. Dedicated to 'Russia – Africa in the multipolar world', the conference focused on the 'Neocolonialism of the West: How to Prevent the Repetition of History'. Addressing the conference, President Putin stated that 'Russia and African countries stood against neocolonial ideology imposed by foreign states', adding that Russia was 'convinced that Africa will become one of the leaders of the emerging new multipolar world order'. According to the Speaker of the Federation Council, Valentina Matvienko, 'The world is throwing off the remnants of the shackles of colonial dependence and moving towards real multipolarity, a more just world order. And it is hard, impossible to imagine the new world without Africa'. African parliamentarians for their part stressed the long-standing support of the USSR and Russia for African independence and sovereignty, the reliability of Russia as a friend, and the common interest in a multi-polar world order.[45]

Prior to this form of recognition diplomacy, most states in the Global South had few options but to participate in and seek to conform to the standards and demands stipulated by the LIO and the Western states that dominate it. The rise of powerful illiberal states and alternative models of world order not only provides possible 'exit options', allowing states in the Global South more flexibility and ability to pursue their own agendas. It also acts as a reminder that participation in the LIO can be half-hearted and should not be confused with acceptance or normative endorsement of its rules. In this way, the new exit options are simultaneously alternative routes to status recognition, meaning that small and middle powers can now seek status and recognition in the world by questioning the parameters of 'good international citizenship' as defined within the Western-led LIO.[46]

---

[45] Kester Kenn Klomegah, 'International Conference Strengthens Multifaceted Relations between Russia and Africa', *Modern Diplomacy* (21 March 2023).

[46] William Wohlforth, Benjamin De Carvalho, Halvard Leira, and Iver Neumann, 'Moral Authority and Status in International Relations: Good States and the Social Dimension of Status Seeking', *Review of International Studies*, 44:3 (2018), 526–546; Jelena Subotic and Srdjan Vucetic, 'Performing Solidarity: Whiteness and Status-Seeking in the Non-Aligned World', *Journal of International Relations and Development* 22:3 (2019), 722–743.

By way of illustration, consider the other three BRICS – Brazil, South Africa, and India. Prior to Bolsonaro's election, Brazil's foreign policy was characterised by a deep involvement in multilateral institutions and mechanisms of international cooperation in order to secure and expand its power on the global stage.[47] While critical of US dominance, and often arguing for reform of the LIO, Brazil's status was both dependent upon and enhanced by its support for the LIO. By contrast, by adopting an anti-globalist position, the Bolsonaro government achieved recognition and status on the illiberal global stage.[48] A similar, albeit more ambivalent, posture characterises South Africa's recent foreign policy, where the global rise of illiberal forces has empowered the anti-Western, anti-imperialist elements within the ruling ANC. The perceived pressure to support the West against Russia's aggression in Ukraine has stirred painful memories of a bipolar world order that reduced African countries to mere pawns in a game of superpower rivalry, and South Africa has increasingly positioned itself as a critic of the LIO and a defender of multi-polarity and non-alignment. India's claim to be a distinct civilisation has a long and rich history[49] that in recent years has increasingly intersected with radical right-wing Hinduism. Domestically this is pushing towards growing illiberalism, whereas internationally Prime Minister Modi has often aligned

---

[47] Guilherme Stolle Paixão e Casarões and Déborah Barros Leal Farias, 'Brazilian Foreign Policy under Jair Bolsonaro: Far-Right Populism and the Rejection of the Liberal International Order', *Cambridge Review of International Affairs*, 35:5 (2022), 741–761; See also Oliver Stuenkel and Matthew Taylor, eds. *Brazil on the Global Stage: Power, Ideas, and the Liberal International Order* (London: Palgrave, 2015).

[48] Charalampos Efstathopoulos, 'Southern Middle Powers and the Liberal International Order: The Options for Brazil and South Africa', *International Journal* 76:3 (2021), 384–403; J. Luis Rodriguez and Christy Thornton, 'The Liberal International Order and the Global South: A View from Latin America', *Cambridge Review of International Affairs* 35:5 (2022), 626–638.

[49] J. N. Dixit, *Across Borders: Fifty Years of India's Foreign Policy* (New Delhi: Picus Books, 1998), 17; see also Kanti Bajpai, 'India's Grand Strategy: Six Schools of Thought', in Kanti Bajpai, Saira Basit, and V. Krishnappa, eds., *India's Grand Strategy: History, Theory, Cases* (New Delhi: Routledge, 2014), 113–150.

himself with various right-wing governments and their demands for multipolarity.⁵⁰

The fact that both South Africa and India assertively defend their foreign policies as forms of non-alignment and continuations of anti-imperialist histories is another reminder that unity and agreement are not required for equivalences to have powerful effects. For example, the anti-imperialist elements that drive the ANC's foreign policy position themselves firmly on the political Left, locating their ideological roots in the anti-colonial and anti-apartheid struggles, as well as in the Third Worldism of the Bandung Conference and the Non-Aligned Movement. They thus recall an order based on international solidarity between former colonies, a Global South (or a Third World as it was then called) united not only in opposition to Western dominance but also to a militarised world divided between rival superpowers. The ability of China, and to a lesser extent Russia, to position themselves within this intellectual and political tradition helps account for the successes of Chinese and Russian diplomacy in many countries in the South, various misalignments and even antagonisms notwithstanding. This development generates fundamental instability for the LIO, in turn opening the exit door ever further in the direction of illiberal and post-liberal alternatives.

Civilisationalism and anti-Westernism likewise facilitate alliances between the radical Right, illiberal states, and more nativist movements commonly positioning themselves on the radical Left. The sovereigntist, anti-Western elements of Pan-Africanism, for example, have facilitated strong links between key figures of the French *Nouvelle Droite* and Pan-African activists like Kemi Seba, who subscribe to a civilisationalist discourse where Africa as

---

⁵⁰ See the Special Section on 'India as a "Civilizational State"', *International Affairs*, 99:2 (2023); Vaishna Ashok and Vineet Thomas, 'The Illiberal Turn in Indian Democracy: Shifting the Trajectory of India's Foreign Policy', *India Review* 22:4 (2023), 564–592; Asad Essa, *Hostile Homelands: The New Alliance between India and Israel* (London: Pluto Press, 2023).

a Black civilisation should be separate from the West and Western imperialism.[51] Seba and his NGO *Urgences Panafricanistes* have also made common cause with radical conservatives in Russia, and Seba has long been personally acquainted with radical Right Russian intellectuals such as Dugin, who plays a prominent role in ideological debates in Russia. Seba, in turn, has been fomenting anti-French sentiments in West Africa, where the withdrawal of French troops and support has frequently been followed by the entry of Russian influence and soldiers from the Wagner Group (later renamed the Africa Corps). According to leaked documents, Seba's activities have received extensive funding and support from Russia,[52] as have other anti-imperialist 'influencers' who often style themselves as being on the radical anti-colonial Left.[53] Similarly, Moscow has continued its long-standing support for radical Right actors in Europe, seeking to mobilise their support in the Ukraine conflict, and even trying to use its anti-colonial and anti-liberal discourses to foster supportive alliances between radical Right and Left forces in Germany and elsewhere. While such alliances reflect a mix of misinformation, propaganda, and dirty tricks, they are formed along a common opposition to the West, or put differently, grounded in a struggle for thick recognition of difference in which ideas and actors from the radical Right can play significant parts.

Seeing these ideologically 'differentialist' dimensions and their place in the radical Right's transnational entanglements provides a fuller vision of its impact on contemporary world politics than can be captured by focusing only on traditional right-wing

---

[51] Rita Abrahamsen, 'Internationalists, Sovereigntists, Nativists: Contending Visions of World Order in Pan-Africanism', *Review of International Studies* 46:1 (2020), 54–74.

[52] Benjamin Roger, 'Russia: How Yevgeny Prigozhin Funded Kemi Seba to Serve His Own African Ambitions', *The Africa Report* (11 April 2023).

[53] Again, according to leaked US intelligence reports, see Catherine Belton, Souad Mekhennet, and Shane Harris, 'Kremlin Tries to Build Antiwar Coalition in Germany, Documents Show', *Washington Post* (April 21 2023). On the longer history of such ties, see Anton Shekhtovsov, *Russia and the Western Far Right* (London: Routledge, 2018).

claims to Western superiority. Certainly, the formulations of the future multipolar world differ considerably among anti-liberal states and social movements, and radical Right actors are rarely among its most important figures. But they are neither absent, nor irrelevant. Indeed, the potential and actual articulations between the radical Right on one hand and a range of actors across the political, geopolitical, and ideological landscape on the other have already started to structure new types of transnational networks and assemblages. Pierre Bourdieu provided a typically dense but acute account of the practical dynamics (and theoretical challenges) at work in these kinds of processes. In his words, the 'principle of minimum coherence' connecting such practices

> cannot be anything other than analogical practice founded on the transfer of schemes, which takes place on the basis of acquired equivalences facilitating the substitutability and substitution of one behaviour for another and making it possible through a kind of practical generalization, to master all problems of similar form capable of arising in new situations. This economical use of polysemy, fuzzy logic, vagueness, approximation, and this art of sequencing practices linked by a more or less observable "family likeness" is ... [the operation of forms of] ... practical logic which, though our theories do not allow for them, we often indulge in, especially in the political order, when, for example, we put into play vague sets of imprecise metaphors and approximate metaphors – liberalism, liberation, liberalization, flexibility, free enterprise, deregulation, etc.[54]

Bourdieu's insights capture both the complex dynamics and analogical relations operating in the inter-societal spaces such as those that constitute the global Right in its struggle against the LIO. We turn now to a second crucial aspect of its relationship to world order: the future of the West.

[54] Pierre Bourdieu, *Pascalian Meditations* (Stanford: Stanford University Press, 2000), 57.

CIVILISATIONAL GEOPOLITICS

The radical Right's vision of civilisational multipolarity has significant implications for their visions of the future of the West and its key institutions, most importantly NATO and the EU. These issues have been brought starkly into view by the war in Ukraine, which has fractured some of the comfortable assumptions previously held about Russia's relationship to the West. For those positioned closest to the *Nouvelle Droite*, the war is about more than age-old strategic rivalries in the Eurasian heartland and threats to the territorial integrity of a sovereign nation-state. More than anything, they see the war as a proxy struggle between US-lead global liberal managerialism and its alternative: a post-postmodern, multipolar world free from liberal universalism and managerial domination. As de Benoist argues:

> This is a war that goes far beyond Ukraine, since it is a war of the worlds – a war for or against liberal hegemony, a war of civilizational states against rootless universalism, of peoples concerned with their historical continuity against "open societies", of the forces of rootedness against the forces of dissolution, of continental powers against "maritime democracies" (United States, Great Britain, Australia, Canada). A war of global significance. A war for world power ... This means that the appeals to "Western solidarity" of Joseph Robinette Biden, the living dead man in the White House, leave us cold – for the excellent reason that we are not Westerners, but Europeans.[55]

These views reflect an engagement with a long tradition of geopolitical thought often forgotten within more mainstream IR. Building on a distinctive interpretation developed in different ways by a previous generation of radical conservatives, this account portrays the Cold War as a division of the world between two variants of the same nihilistic techno-economic and organisational worldview. Despite their enmity, both superpowers saw an autonomous Europe

---

[55] De Benoist, 'The Return of the Iron Curtain'.

occupying what the British geopolitician Halford MacKinder called the 'Inner Crescent' as geopolitically unacceptable. Both in their different ways sought to usurp European sovereignty and prevent Europe from pursuing its own civilisational project by compelling its leaders to accept strategic and ideological positions inimical to the reproduction of distinctively European identities and interests, a situation Guillaume Faye during the 1980s called the 'Américo-Soviétique condominium'.[56]

For these radical Rightists, the idea that NATO secured 'the West' was a fallacy. In reality, it defended the 'Americano-sphere' – a zone of managerial occupation constantly adapting to the demands of neoliberal capitalism, not a distinct civilisational entity.[57] The anti-communist hysteria of the post-war Right 'helped justify the Americanization of Europe, recuperating, in effect, the anti-liberal forces for the sake of US interests' rather than representing a true conservative position.[58] While Soviet imperialism had to be confronted, the American incarnation of liberal modernity was ultimately seen to pose a greater threat, if only because it relied on much more insidious and complex liberal mechanisms of control.[59]

Many on the *Nouvelle Droite* across Western Europe have long argued for a withdrawal from NATO and the development of an autonomous European defence alliance breaking Europe's dependency on

---

[56] Guillaume Faye, *Nouveau discours à la nation européene* (Paris: Albatros, 1985), 19–20, 37, 73; Robert de Herte, 'Ni des esclaves, ni de robots', *Éléments* 34 (1980), 2–6; Guillaume Faye, 'Pour en finir avec la civilization occidentale', *Éléments* 34 (1980), 7–10. See also Mark Bassin, '"Everything Is Revealed in Maps": The European Far Right and the Legacy of Classical Geopolitics during the Cold War', *Geopolitics* 28:5 (2023), 13.

[57] Guillaume Faye, *Le système à tuer les peoples* (Paris: Copernic, 1981); Jean Thiriart, 'L'Empire Euro-Soviétique de Vladivostock à Dublin', in Christian Bouchet ed., *L'Empire Euro-Soviétique de Vladivostock à Dublin* (Nantes: Arg Magna, [1981] 2018), 51–86.

[58] O'Meara, *New Culture, New Right*, 212–213.

[59] Alain de Benoist, 'L'ennemi principal', *Éléments* 41 (1982), 37–40; Henri Gerfaut, 'Une certaine idée de l'Europe', *Éléments* 53 (1985), 29–32; Robert Steuckers, 'Sécurité et Défense en Europe', in *Le défi de Disneyland: Actes du XXe colloque national de la revue "Éléments"* (Paris: Le Labyrinthe, 1987), 17–29; Fréderic Julien, *Les Etats-Unis contre l'Europe: L'impossible alliance* (Paris: Le Labyrinthe, 1987).

the United States.⁶⁰ In this view, NATO has been hugely detrimental to the cultural, socioeconomic fabric of a distinctive European civilisation and reflects a profound geopolitical misapprehension where NATO has 'served as an alibi to those who refuse to imagine an autonomous European defence. It cultivates the 'Atlanticist' illusion that European interests and American interests are the same, which makes no sense from a geopolitical perspective.'⁶¹ The alternative lies in geopolitical models organised around the technological, natural, and industrial resources of Germany and *Mitteleuropa* and geared towards an eventual strategic rapprochement with Russia.⁶²

While this 'Europeanist' position still finds support on the radical Right, it has been largely supplanted by a civilisationalist discourse centred on the nature and future of the West. Proponents of this view are equally critical towards the post–Cold War evolution of NATO. They concede that during the Cold War, the alliance was a necessary evil, justified by the fight against communism. However, they do not view the fight against communism as being in the name of the universal values of democracy and market capitalism, but rather as a confrontation with the arch enemy of the 'Western religious heritage, of historic nationalities, and metaphysical as well as political freedoms'.⁶³ While some argue that NATO should have

---

⁶⁰ Although they start from very different positions, radical Right politicians converge with a series of liberal actors in the desire for an autonomous European defence. For example, while actors such as President Macron support an autonomous Europe to defend and promote liberal values, the radical Right regards European autonomy as a form of protection against liberal globalists. See Alexandra Gheciu, 'Remembering France's Glory, Securing Europe in the Age of Trump', *European Journal of International Security* 5:1 (2020), 25–45.

⁶¹ Alain de Benoist, 'Otan, Assimilation et Syrie', *Girodivite* (12 April 2021); see also Robert Steuckers, 'Géopolitique et avenir de l'Europe', *Geopolitika* (8 September 2022). Our translation.

⁶² Alain de Benoist, 'Vous Avez-dit "Mitteleuropa"?', *Éléments* 65 (1989), 21–23; Thiriart, 'L'Empire Euro-Soviétique'; Robert Steuckers 'La Russie, L'Europe et L'Occident', *Orientation* 4 (1983), 11–17; Guillaume Faye, 'The Geopolitics of Ethnopolitics: The New Concept of "Eurosiberia"', Presentation at the International Conference on 'The Future of the White World', Moscow, 8–10 June 2006. *Counter Currents*.

⁶³ Paul Gottfried and Thomas Fleming, *The Conservative Movement* (Boston: Twayne, 1988), xiii.

been disbanded after the end of the Cold War, most now stress the need for its radical reform and a return to shared, Atlanticist foundations in Judeo-Christian civilisation and national sovereignty.[64] Although this view differs from the 'Europeanist' position outlined earlier, both are articulated in a discourse of opposition to 'global NATO', which is portrayed as existing for the sole purpose of furthering managerial liberalism and dealing with the instability that it itself creates. What is needed is a new, streamlined form of interstate defence cooperation based on shared civilisational interests and more narrowly focused on guaranteeing the national security of its member states.[65]

In this context, the 'war against woke' is portrayed as a vital security issue. If the West is to survive, it needs to recover its sense of historical distinctiveness and pride in its past accomplishments. These are values – indeed entire collective identities – that the radical Right portrays as under relentless assault by progressive Left and liberal forces, forces that must be defeated in what is now an existential struggle for survival in an era of renewed Great Power competition and challenges to the West's global position. This fusion of national and civilisational security is widespread on the radical Right. Its 'existential' status was given prominence by President Trump in his oft-noted declaration in Warsaw on July 6, 2017:

> We have to remember that our defense is not just a commitment of money, it is a commitment of will ... The fundamental question of our time is whether the West has the will to survive. Do we have the confidence in our values to defend them at any cost? Do we

---

[64] Vibeke Schou Tjalve, 'Judeo-Christian Democracy and the Transatlantic Right: Travels of a Contested Civilizational Imaginary', *New Perspectives* 29:4 (2021), 332–348.

[65] 'Beyond NATO', *Radix Journal* (28 October 2016); Patrick J. Buchanan, 'U.S. Policy: Cheer Ukrainians On – and Keep Us Out!', *Chronicles* (8 March 2022). Figures associated with the Claremont Institute and the National Conservative movement also develop these themes, see Michael Anton, 'America and the Liberal International Order', *American Affairs* 1 (2017), 113–125; Michael Anton and Wayne Allensworth, 'Come Home, America', *Chronicles* (1 May 2022).

have enough respect for our citizens to protect our borders? Do we have the desire and the courage to preserve our civilization in the face of those who would subvert and destroy it?[66]

While Trump's speech was greeted with consternation in the political mainstream, such sentiments are commonplace on the radical Right, where the culture wars and the prospect of real wars meld in powerful fusions of identity and geopolitics. As two participants in these struggles put it: 'The woke onslaught is a war on the West itself' where 'anti-colonialists at home are allied – inadvertently no doubt – with illiberal regimes abroad'.[67] In a multipolar world, only strong civilisations with compatible component national states will prosper.

This civilisational understanding of multipolarity has similar implications for the radical Right's approach to the European Union. Just as NATO and the UN have become instruments of the globalist liberal elite, so the EU is seen as having vastly over-extended its original purpose and become part of the subjugation of a true European civilisation to the dictates of Atlanticist managerial power. Like 'global NATO', the European Union is an 'epiphenomenon of the American phenomenon' subject 'to the same ethnic and oligarchic mafias that dominate the US'. The EU will never be a geopolitical subject in its own right: 'It will still speak English after the Brits self-deport themselves. Anglo-Americanisation will continue. The EU stems from globalist ideology, bourgeois borderlessness, postwar effeteness, Last Manhood, not European *Wille zur Macht*.'[68]

---

[66] On Steve Bannon's influence on the speech, see Ivan Krastev, 'How Donald Trump Redefined "the West"', *New York Times* (11 July 2017). The speech was reportedly written mainly by Stephen Miller, who now runs America First Legal, an organisation dedicated to challenging left-of-centre policies in the US.

[67] Nigel Biggar and Doug Stokes, 'The Woke Onslaught Is a War on the West Itself', *Daily Telegraph* (6 June 2022); see also Thomas Spoehr, 'The Rise of Wokeness in the Military', Heritage Foundation (30 September 2022).

[68] The quotes are from Guillaume Durocher, 'An Uncertain Idea of Europe', *Radix Journal* (30 June 2016). See also Molnar, *The Atlantic Culture*; Marco Rubio, 'The Left's Civic Religion Is a Threat to National Security', *Washington Examiner* (20 June 2023).

Viewed from this perspective, if Europe is to survive as a civilisation it needs to engage in a deep, forward-looking spiritual and political renewal.[69] Visions of what this should look like vary greatly, but they tend to cluster around two broad narratives. The first continues more than half a century of radical Right ideas about re-organising the European space into various forms of federated structures and revivified conceptions of civilisations and empire.[70] Inspired by Schmittian notions of geopolitical 'great spaces' (*Großräume*),[71] the aim is to reverse the historical fracturing of European civilisation into centralising nation-states with their own cultures and to replace it with an 'ethno-pluralist order'. Unlike the EU, this new Europe would not suppress but affirm the substantive autonomy of its constituent cultures as Bretons, Bavarians, Celts, Venetians, Magyars, Laplanders, Pomeranians, Walloons, Basques, Thracians, and so on. A re-envisioned principle of subsidiarity would allow the renewal of intermediary structures and the cultivation of a shared constitutional myth of civilisational destiny. This 'Europe of a Hundred Flags' would facilitate association between its different groups, nations, and linguistic communities and allow its inhabitants to rediscover their common Indo-European origins.[72] Radical conservatives believe regionalist trends are to be strongly encouraged

---

[69] On how these civilisational views have already become influential within the EU, see Hans Kundani, *Eurowhiteness: Culture, Empire and Race in the European Project* (London: Hurst, 2023); Andrew Glencross, 'The EU and the Temptation to Become a Civilizational State', *European Foreign Affairs Review* 26:2 (2021), 331–350.

[70] In an extensive literature, see Julius Evola, 'Spiritual and Structural Presuppositions of the European Union' (1951), reprinted in *North American New Right*, 1 (2012), 14–25; Jordis von Lohausen, *Mut zur Macht. Denken in Kontinenten* (Berg Am See: Kurt Vowinckel, 1979); Jean Thiriart, *Europe: An Empire of 400 Millions* (London: Arktos 1964/2021); Robert Steuckers, *Europa: De l'Eurasie aux périphéries: une géopolitique continentale*, 3 vols. (Lille: Bios, 2017); Norman Lowell, *Imperium Europa* (London: Arktos 2019); Tamir Bar-On, 'Fascism to the Nouvelle Droite: The Dream of Pan-European Empire', *Journal of Contemporary European Studies* 16:3 (2008), 327–345.

[71] Carl Schmitt, 'The *Großraum* Order of International Law with a Ban on Intervention for Spatially Foreign Powers: A Contribution to the Concept of *Reich* in International Law (1939–1941)', in Timothy Nunan ed., *Carl Schmitt: Writings on War* (Cambridge: Polity Press, 2011).

[72] Alain de Benoist and Charles Champetier, 'Manifesto'; see also Alain de Benoist, *L'Empire intérieur* (Montpellier: Fata Morgana, 1995).

because regions and rural communities, like ethnic minorities, tend to be better at preserving 'authentic' traditional values and customs than metropolitan and cultural centres more directly connected to the Atlanticism of the West.[73]

This 'differentialist' model of federalism would regenerate regional cultures and local autonomies, producing a more organic form of participatory democracy linking ethnic kinship to qualitative civic participation.[74] This in turn would allow for a more organic and robust mechanism to address the problems associated with immigration. As Alberto Spektorowski emphasises in an insightful analysis of this neo-Medieval vision, the ethnic region championed by the European radical Right does not expel or keep foreigners out primarily or exclusively through draconian laws or parliamentary deliberation, 'but rather raises impenetrable cultural barriers against them. Although ethno-regional identity is not anti-liberal by definition, it provides the basis for the uprising of populist elites, which find a very easy path towards the mobilization of the masses through cultural myths.'[75] In this view, the marching orders for Europe's radical right-wing forces such as the French *Rassemblement National* and the Austrian Freedom Party are clear: abandon nostalgic attachments to the nationalism of the nation-state and instead foment a conservative revolution from within the EU, transforming it into a different kind of civilisational formation capable of exercising a meaningful degree of geopolitical sovereignty in the face of the strategic and techno-economic imperative our post-modern age.

The restrictive immigration policies and other transformations that this strategy is expected to generate would be supported internationally by collaborative pacts with the Global South to assist its

---

[73] Steuckers, 'Géopolitique et avenir de l'Europe'.
[74] De Benoist and Champetier, 'Manifesto', 236–237; Alain de Benoist, *The Problem of Democracy* (London: Arktos Media, [1985] 2021).
[75] Alberto Spektorowski, 'The New Right: Ethno-Regionalism, Ethno-Pluralism and the Emergence of a Neo-Fascist "Third Way"', *Journal of Political Ideologies* 8:1 (2003), 122.

nations and communities to develop according to their own economic paths, and in ways that reflect and preserve their respective cultural traditions and natural environment. This would put Europe at the heart of a common front against the institutions that have provided the necessary organisational support for the liberal managerial system of vassalage and aid dependency developed since 1945.[76] As with the long-advocated pivot towards Russia, building connections in the Global South will facilitate the construction of a multipolar world order organised in autarkic civilisational blocs capable of resisting each other's influence and evolving according to their own respective *'Weltanschauung'*: 'The main enemy of this pluriverse will be any civilization pretending to be universal and regarding itself entrusted with a redeeming mission ("Manifest Destiny") to impose its model on all others'.[77]

Though sharing their anti-liberal views, radical conservatives in Eastern and Central Europe tend to be sceptical of such Eurasianist visions, a scepticism that has only intensified since Russia's invasion of Ukraine. Indeed, instead of rejecting the EU completely, in recent years there has been a systematic radical Right effort to provide a blueprint for restructuring it. For instance, at the 2021 Madrid Summit organised by Spain's VOX Party, nine of Europe's leading radical Right politicians – including Hungary's Orbán and France's Marine Le Pen – agreed on a 'roadmap' for a 'patriotic Europe'.[78] The Summit attendees signed a document with nine specific commitments for the future, including fighting illegal migration, protecting traditional family values, and defending the sovereignty of member

---

[76] De Benoist and Champetier, 'Manifesto', 239. See also Alain de Benoist, *Europe, Tiers monde, même combat* (Paris: Juillard/L'Âge d'Homme, 1982).

[77] Alain de Benoist, 'The New Right: Forty Years After', in Sunic, *Against Democracy*, 28. These views have strong affinities with the Eurasian imperialism championed by Dugin and others in Russia. Dugin, *The Theory of a Multipolar World*, and Dugin, *Eurasian Mission* (London: Arktos, 2014). For further context, see Marlène Laruelle, *Russian Eurasianism: An Ideology of Empire* (Cambridge: Cambridge University Press, 2008).

[78] Fernando Heller, 'Far-Right Leaders Agree on "Roadmap" for Sovereign and Patriotic Europe', *Euractiv News* (31 January 2022).

states. The group held subsequent meetings in Warsaw and again in Madrid in 2022, where, despite frictions over their stance on Russia, they renewed their commitment to fight 'the globalist trend' and to defend the primacy of national constitutions over European law. In coming years, this is likely to translate into renewed attempts by the radical Right to change the direction of European integration, and to oppose attempts by the European Commission and other agencies representing managerial elites to pursue deeper integration in multiple areas.

Europe's radical Right parties have also taken steps to enhance coordination in the European Parliament, seeking to reshape the future of the EU enlargement process and gain more control over the boundaries of the EU. By coordinating their actions, they have been able to formulate a discursive coalition around a distinctive narrative that opposes further enlargement on cultural and religious grounds. The strengthening of radical Right representation in the European Parliament following the 2019 European elections, and the fact that they have acted in concert in contesting further EU enlargement, has put mainstream parties under increasing pressure to respond. This has not only resulted in a slowdown of accession negotiations but has also changed the dynamics of those negotiations in ways likely to have significant impacts on interactions between the EU and accession candidates.[79] Similarly, radical Right politicians have demonstrated their determination to pursue a long-term Gramscian counter-hegemonic strategy to challenge the liberal foundations and values of the EU.[80]

Elements of the Eastern and Central European nationalist radical Right also promotes the geopolitical idea of the *Intermarium*. Originally developed by Polish statesman and military leader Józef Piłsudski in

---

[79] See Marie-Ève Bélanger and Natasha Wunsch, 'From Cohesion to Contagion? Populist Radical Right Contestation of EU Enlargement', *JCMS: Journal of Common Market Studies* 60 (2022), 653–672.

[80] Dorothee Bohle, Béla Greskovits, and Marek Naczyk, 'The Gramscian Politics of Europe's Rule of Law Crisis', *Journal of European Public Policy* (2023), First View.

the early interwar period, the *Intermarium* (*Międzymorze*) proposed a (con)federative union of the 'lands between the seas', whereby 'the lands' initially meant Poland, Ukraine, Lithuania, and Belarus, but later a larger stretch of Eastern European territory from (at least) the Gulf of Finland in the north to (at least) the Adriatic in the south. For some geostrategists in Warsaw, the project was meant to emulate the Polish-Lithuanian Commonwealth (1569–1795), thus forming a counterweight to Russian and German imperialisms. The idea persisted after the Second World War and in fact outlived the Cold War, in part thanks to being promoted by the leading Polish émigré literary-political magazine in Paris, *Kultura* (1947–2000). More recently, the idea of *Intermarium* provided inspiration for the Three Seas Initiative, a diplomatic forum launched in 2015 by Polish President Andrzej Duda and Croatian President Kolinda Grabar-Kitarović. A club of thirteen member states – not counting Ukraine and Moldova as de facto members – the Initiative's aim is to improve economic development, transport, and energy infrastructure in the region.

For parts of the radical Right, however, the *Intermarium* remains a distinct geopolitical project to be realised on the bases of cultural–civilisational similarities between the nation-states of Central and Eastern Europe.[81] The idea is to build a revitalised 'Europe of Nations' in the area between the Baltic Sea, the Adriatic Sea, and the Black Sea, where Europe's Christian heritage is said to live on and where the cultural and ecological resources for the restoration of the sovereign ethno-state can still be found 'unpolluted by feminism, genderism, multiculturalism and anti-racism'.[82] This, as Kaalep and Meister's manifesto for the Baltic New Right puts it, is

---

[81] Matthew Kott, 'A Far Right Hijack of Intermarium', *New Eastern Europe* (26 May 2017). For further context, see Robert Ištok, Irina Kozárová, and Anna Polačková, 'The Intermarium as a Polish Geopolitical Concept in History and in the Present', *Geopolitics* 26:1 (2018), 314–341, and Gordana Grgić, 'The Changing Dynamics of Regionalism in Central and Eastern Europe: The Case of the Three Seas Initiative', *Geopolitics* 28:1 (2021), 216–238.

[82] Marian Piłka, 'Wielka Strategia', Geopolityka.net (23 November 2018); Paweł Lisicki, 'Polski bastion wolności', *Do Rzeczy* (4 September 2017). Our translation.

the one place in Europe 'where the unbroken, centuries-long line of a healthy national development has been able to survive in the consciousness of the people ... It has survived the communist years and shows the promise of surviving even more vicious strains of the same ideology'.[83] In this view, re-centring the European project around the historical and cultural experience of the *Intermarium* would bring an 'element of balance' to the continent.[84] It would allow the countries of Central and Eastern Europe to resist Russia's Eurasian expansionism and to exit the liberal domination of the EU to become equal partners in 'a much more effective and friendly interstate structure' for economic and security cooperation.[85]

While the various European actors and movements have different visions of the future of Europe, the West, and world order, they connected through a common civilisational geopolitics hostile to global liberalism. The ideological strength of this civilisational framework is that it cuts across the conventional distinctions between the domestic and the international in ways that can support a wide range of anti-globalist agendas. It can also mobilise a range of transnationally resonating cultural strategies that can either move beyond or combine with nationalism, or other new or existing forms of political hierarchies and divisions of the world.

CONCLUSION

As we were completing this book, three of us attended the National Conservatism UK conference in London.[86] In the domed, circular auditorium of an old church, a stone's throw from Parliament, we listened and watched as much of what we have written about in

---

[83] Kaalep and Meister, *Rebirth of Europe*, 87–88; also see Brubaker, 'Between Nationalism and Civilizationism'; Varga and Buzagány, 'The Two Faces of the "Global Right"'.
[84] Dariusz Matecki, 'Prof. Gil: Międzymorze szansą na wzmocnienie pozycji państw Europy Środkowej i Wschodniej', Prawicowyinternet.pl (8 July 2017). Our translation.
[85] Piotr Wójcik, 'Międzymorze nie jest ostoją chrześcijaństwa', *Dziennik Gazeta Prawna* (28 January 2018). Our translation.
[86] The conference took place from 15 to 17 May 2023. All quotations are from our notes, unless otherwise stated.

CONCLUSION 179

these pages played out on the stage in front of us. Academics, policy wonks and think tankers, influencers and interns from Israel, the US, Hungary, and Romania, as well as senior politicians from the governing UK Conservative Party spent three days discussing, debating, and engaging the culture wars, the dire threat of 'cultural Marxism', the perfidy of metropolitan elites and experts, and the dangers of globalist liberalism in all its forms. The traditional virtues and the need for drastic action were prominently on display. The conference received widespread media attention, generating jibes from its critics, cheers from its supporters, and a more general sense of consternation about the direction of conservatism in the UK and the wider world.[87] In short, it served both as a reminder and a confirmation of many of the themes and arguments we have made in the book.

NatCon UK illustrated and reinforced the diversity of the contemporary radical Right, a point we have emphasised throughout this study. Not everyone who attended could be described as belonging to the radical Right, just as not everyone could be described as a National Conservative. Many seemed simply to be, in the welcoming words of one of the organisers, 'NatCon curious'. In fact, much of the debate seemed to be about what it meant to be a National Conservative, with clear dividing lines emerging between free marketeers and protectionists, American culture warriors and British pragmatists, near-revolutionaries and relatively mild reformists. The divisions and jockeying for positions between the various factions of the UK Conservative party were also on full display, a dimension that naturally captured most of the media coverage of the event.

Such open displays of disagreement and division make it easy to miss the bigger story, and what is perhaps the main effect of an event like NatCon – the performance of unity, purpose, and direction – creating the perception that, as one speaker put it, 'something is happening in this room'. The very project of convening over 800

---

[87] See Peter Geoghegan, 'At NatCon London', *London Review of Books* 41:11 (2023).

conservatives of various stripes around the question of national conservatism is a powerful performance. It serves to create an impression of a unified movement on the rise. It emboldens and legitimises the ideas and personalities involved. Yoram Hazony, the chair of the Edmund Burke Foundation and the most significant intellectual energy behind the conference, began the event by cheerfully noting the extensive press coverage it had received even before the doors were opened. For some, including for Hazony himself, national conservatism is a specific ideological project, for others the cause is broader or only tangentially connected. As we have argued throughout this book, in this sense the radical Right is more than the sum of its parts. Yet as NatCon UK showed with striking clarity, a key part of its power arises from the ability to mobilise transnational and ideological equivalences that can unify diverse (national) constituencies and mobilise diverse supporters. They can agree to differ on specific issues but still converge on the broader ideological oppositions to liberal globalisation. In the words of ex-Trump Administration official and now Professor at Hillsdale College, Michael Anton, 'we are in the same leaky lifeboat together'.

The conference also confirmed our argument that the radical Right is unified – and defined by – its opposition to the global managerial class. Speaker after speaker railed at the betrayal by the globalist elite, and the manner in which liberalism has yielded a world governed by politically correct liberals, cold experts, and faceless bureaucrats in the UN, the EU, the IMF, the WHO, and so on. Corporate capitalism and the rootless global elite have waged a war on nations and national cultures. 'The ruling class does not rule as much as it occupies the nation', thundered Kevin Roberts, the President of the Heritage Foundation. The ex-radical Leftist, now Orbán supporter, Frank Furedi argued that in Brussels a new identity is celebrated every day – only national identity is despised. While none of the speakers outlined a full-scale, systematic international political sociology of global managerialism – this was after all not an academic conference – the event illustrated how opposition to liberal globalism is a central unifying feature of the radical Right. This is not only one of its core ideological claims but also a vital mobilising device and one of its strongest political calling cards. As we have shown, it has the ability to forge equivalences and transversal alliances, allowing different groups and populations to perceive the global elite as a common enemy. The NatCon conference was not itself representative of this diversity. Surprisingly young, the audience and the speakers contained a sprinkling of diversity in terms of ethnicity and religious symbols, and while many of the speakers were female, the conference was overwhelmingly a white, male, Christian affair. But the goal, as Hazony stated in the only published interview he gave surrounding the conference, is to 'build a coalition' of 'anti-Marxist liberals, Christians and nationalists'.[88]

The international gathering in London also underlined the importance the Right itself assigns to the counter-hegemonic struggle and the cultural sphere. This book has stressed the need to understand the radical Right as a longer-term struggle to change the common sense, or in a favourite phrase of the NatCon conference, to overturn the power and influence of the 'woke-industrial complex'. Universities were repeatedly singled out for special derision, held responsible for everything from European population decline, to cancel culture, and historical distortions of Europe's glorious past. The message was clear: the Right has for too long ceded the academic space to the Left. Now is the time to take it back and to engage in the battle of ideas. Praise was lavished on Florida Governor Ron DeSantis' educational policies as a model to be pursued. Others suggested infiltrating the universities by setting up smaller units and institutes within them to propagate 'real' conservative positions. As we argued earlier, for all its critique of the globalist elite, the radical Right is not

---

[88] David Rose, 'Yoram Hazony: "In Britain and in Israel, There Is No Stopping National Conservatism"', *The Jewish Chronicle* (18 May 2023). On the question of anti-Semitism, Hazony holds that: 'There is no antisemitism here. We are simply looking at unscrupulous leftist operatives who are willing to falsely accuse innocent men and women in order to drive conservative men and women out of politics.'

anti-elitist. Instead, it is engaged in a long-term counter-hegemonic strategy to create an elite in its own image, one that shares its values and is dedicated to creating a new common sense.

This leads to a final point. The NatCon conference, as well as myriad other intellectual and organisational initiatives surveyed in this book, reinforced our conviction that we underestimate the radical Right at our peril. In its counter-hegemonic, ideological discourses of civilisations and multipolarity, a new geopolitical imaginary is apparent, with different anti-LIO forces coalescing and working together. The ongoing transformation of the international system cannot be adequately explained only with reference to the West's relative decline, or conversely, to its claims of continuing superiority. Instead, we must acknowledge the feedback effects operating between, as well as within, nations, and the impacts of alliances forged through common disdain for Western dominance and the tyranny of liberal values and institutions. The multipolar, civilisational world order envisioned by these alliances and the radical Right is not anti-hierarchical and inclusive. It legitimises new differences and new forms of exclusion through its claims to difference and cultural diversity. It can both contain and conceal forms of racism, anti-Semitism, and hatred, while supporting new forms of essentialism and exclusionary identities. And it seeks a more sovereigntist vision of the world in which these exclusionary forces would be able to operate with fewer international constraints, be it in the Global North or the Global South.

Our suggestion is not that the radical Right will succeed, or already has succeeded, in transforming the world in its image. But the impact of these movements in recent years has been substantial, and it shows few signs of abating. As its proponents, strategists, intellectuals, and activists know, the global Right is a work in progress. For those who worry about its past successes and future potential, recognising its key elements and taking it seriously are essential steps in countering its impact.

Bibliography

1776 Commission. 'The 1776 Report'. Available at: trumpwhitehouse.archives.gov/wp-content/uploads/2021/01/The-Presidents-Advisory-1776-Commission-Final-Report.pdf (accessed 23 March 2023).

Abidor, Mitchell. 'The Gramsci of the Brazilian Right', *Dissent*, Summer 2020.

Abrahamsen, Rita. 'Internationalists, Sovereigntists, Nativists: Contending Visions of World Order in Pan-Africanism', *Review of International Studies* 46:1 (2020), 56–74.

Abrahamsen, Rita. 'Pan-Africanism, Recognition, and World Order' (forthcoming).

Abrahamsen, Rita, Jean-François Drolet, Alexandra Gheciu, Karin Narita, Srdjan Vucetic, and Michael C. Williams. 'Confronting the International Political Sociology of the New Right', *International Political Sociology* 14:1 (2020), 94–107.

Abramson, Jill. 'In the Ultimate Coup for the Right, It's Justice Thomas's Court Now', *Financial Times*, 7 July 2022.

Adenor, Jean-Loup. 'Eric Zemmour toujours pas en campagne, enfin presque, mais pas encore', *Marianne*, 4 August 2021.

Adler-Nissen, Rebecca, and Ayşe Zarakol. 'Struggles for Recognition: The Liberal International Order and the Merger of Its Discontents', *International Organization* 75:2 (2021), 611–634.

Ahmari, Sohrab, Jeffrey Blehar, and Patrick Deneen et al. 'Against the Dead Consensus', *First Things*, 21 March 2019.

Allan, Bentley, Srdjan Vucetic, and Ted Hopf. 'The Distribution of Identity and the Future of International Order', *International Organization* 72:4 (2018), 839–869.

Allen, Kye J. 'An Anarchical Society (of Fascist States): Theorizing Illiberal Solidarism', *Review of International Studies* 48:3 (2022), 583–603.

Andersen, Joakim. *Rising from the Ruins: The Right in the Twenty First Century*. London: Arktos, 2018.

Anderson, Perry. 'The Heirs of Gramsci', *New Left Review* 100 (2016), 71–97.

Anderson, Zac. 'DeSantis Seeks to Transform Sarasota's New College with Conservative Board Takeover', *Herald-Tribune*, 9 January 2023.

Anton, Michael. 'America and the Liberal International Order', *American Affairs* 1 (2017), 113–125.

Anton, Michael. 'Draining the Swamp', *Claremont Review of Books* 19:1 (Winter 2019).

Anton, Michael, and Wayne Allensworth. 'Come Home, America', *Chronicles*, 1 May 2022.

Arnn, Larry. Interview with Mark Levin, 'Life, Liberty & Levin', *Fox News*, 18 March 2018.

Arnold, Richard, and Ekatarina Romanova. '"White World's Future": An Analysis of the Russian Far-Right', *Journal for the Study of Radicalism* 7:3 (2013), 79–107.

Ashbee, Edward. 'Politics of Paleoconservatism', *Culture and Society* 37 (March/April 2000), 75–84.

Ashok, Vaishna, and Vineet Thomas. 'The Illiberal Turn in Indian Democracy: Shifting the Trajectory of India's Foreign Policy', *India Review* 22:4 (2023), 564–592.

Ashutosh, Ishan. 'The Transnational Routes of White and Hindu Nationalism', *Ethnic and Racial Studies* 45:2 (2022), 319–339.

Asladinis, Paris. 'Is Populism an Ideology? A Refutation and a New Perspective', *Political Studies* 64:1 (2016), 88–104.

Babic, Milan. 'Let's Talk about the Interregnum: Gramsci and the Crisis for the Liberal World Order', *International Affairs* 96:3 (2020), 767–786.

Bajpai, Kanti. 'India's Grand Strategy: Six Schools of Thought', in Kanti Bajpai, Saira Basit, and V. Krishnappa eds. *India's Grand Strategy: History, Theory, Cases*. New Delhi: Routledge, 2014.

Ballantyne, Tony, and Antoinette Burton. *Empires and the Reach of the Global 1870–1945*. Cambridge, MA: Belknap Press, 2012.

Banbury, Chris. 'Gramsci on Spontaneity, Organization and Leadership', *Counterfire*, 30 August 2012.

Bar-On, Tamir. 'Fascism to the Nouvelle Droite: The Dream of Pan-European Empire', *Journal of Contemporary European Studies* 16:3 (2008), 327–345.

Bar-On, Tamir. *Where Have All the Fascists Gone?* London: Routledge, 2016.

Barder, Alexander D., Isaac Kamola, and Aida A. Hozic. 'The Attacks on Higher Education in Florida Are Part of a Global Crisis', *Le Monde*, 20 May 2023.

Bassin, Mark. '"Everything Is Revealed in Maps": The European Far Right and the Legacy of Classical Geopolitics during the Cold War', *Geopolitics* 28:5 (2023), 1843–1867.

Bauman, Zygmunt. *Liquid Modernity*. Cambridge: Polity Press, 2000.

Baumier, Matthieu. *Voyage au Bout des Ruines Libérales–Libertaires*. Paris: P-G. de Roux, 2019.

Beauchamp, Zac. 'CPAC Goes to Israel', *Vox*, 23 July 2022.

Bélanger, Marie-Ève, and Natasha Wunsch. 'From Cohesion to Contagion? Populist Radical Right Contestation of EU Enlargement', *JCMS: Journal of Common Market Studies* 60 (2022), 653–672.

Belton, Catherine, Souad Mekhennet, and Shane Harris, 'Kremlin Tries to Build Antiwar Coalition in Germany, Documents Show', *Washington Post*, 21 April 2023.

Berle, Adolph, and Gardiner Means. *The Modern Corporation and Private Property*. New York: Harcourt, Brace, and World, 1932/1967.

Bettiza, Gregorio, Derek Bolton, and David Lewis. 'Civilizationism and Ideological Contestation in the Liberal International Order', *International Studies Review* 25:2 (2023), First View.

Bially Mattern, Janice, and Ayşe Zarakol. 'Hierarchies in World Politics', *International Organization* 70:3 (2016), 623–654.

Biggar, Nigel, and Doug Stokes. 'The Woke Onslaught Is a War on the West Itself', *Daily Telegraph*, 6 June 2022.

Bob, Clifford. *The Global Right Wing and the Clash of World Politics*. Cambridge: Cambridge University Press, 2012.

Bob, Clifford. *Rights as Weapons: Instruments of Conflict, Tools of Power*. Princeton: Princeton University Press, 2019.

Bohle, Dorothee, Béla Greskovits, and Marek Naczyk. 'The Gramscian Politics of Europe's Rule of Law Crisis', *Journal of European Public Policy* (2023), First View.

Bolton, John. 'Should We Take Global Governance Seriously?', *Chicago Journal of International Law* 1:2 (2000), 205–221.

Bolton, Kerry R. *More Artists of the Right*. San Francisco: Counter-Currents Publishing, 2017.

Bosco, David. 'For the UN the Rise of Populism Reveals an Old Challenge', *The Wilson Quarterly* (Fall 2018).

Boukala, Salomi. '"We Need to Talk about the Hegemony of the Left": The Normalization of Extreme Right Discourse in Greece', *Journal of Language and Politics* 20:3 (2021), 361–382.

Bourdieu, Pierre. *Outline of a Theory of Practice*. Cambridge: Cambridge University Press, 1977.

Bourdieu, Pierre. *Pascalian Meditations*. Stanford: Stanford University Press, 2000.

Bourdieu, Pierre. 'Participant Objectivation', *The Journal of the Royal Anthropological Institute* 9 (June 2003), 281–294.

Bowden, Jonathan. *Reactionary Modernism*. San Francisco: Counter-Currents Publishing, 2022.

Breitbart, Andrew. *Righteous Indignation: Excuse Me While I Save the World*. New York: Grand Central Publishing, 2011.

Brizzarelli, Marco. 'Podemos' Twofold Assault on Hegemony: The Possibilities of the Post-Modern Prince and the Perils of Passive Revolution', in Oscar Garcia, and Marco Brizzarelli eds. *Podemos and the New Political Cycle: Left-Wing Populism and Anti-Establishment Politics*. New York: Palgrave, 2017.

Brubaker, Rogers. 'Between Nationalism and Civilizationism: The European Populist Moment in Comparative Perspective', *Ethnic and Racial Studies* 40:8 (2017), 1191–1226.

Bruce-Briggs, Barry ed. *The New Class?* New Brunswick, NJ: Transaction Books, 1978.

Buchanan, Pat. 'America First – And Second and Third', *The National Interest* 19 (Spring 1990), 77–82.

Buchanan, Pat. 'America First, NAFTA Never', *Washington Post*, 7 November 1993.

Buchanan, Pat. *The Death of the West: How Dying Population and Immigrant Invasions Imperil Our Country and Civilization*. Spokane, WA: Griffin, 2002.

Buchanan, Pat. 'U.S. Policy: Cheer Ukrainians On – And Keep Us Out!', *Chronicles*, 8 March 2022.

Buckley, William F. *God and Man at Yale: The Superstitions of 'Academic Freedom'*. Chicago: Regnery, 1951/2021.

Burnham, James. *The Managerial Revolution: What Is Happening in the World*. New York: John Day, 1941.

Burnham, James. *The Machiavellians: Defenders of Freedom*. New York: John Day, 1943.

Burnham, James. *The Suicide of the West*. New York: John Day, 1964.

Burns, Nick. 'Latin America's "CPAC Right" Still Has Big Ambitions', *Americas Quarterly*, 15 November 2022.

Callison, William. 'Milei's Chainsaw', *Sidecar*, 5 October 2023.

Campos, Roderigo Duque Estrado. 'The International Turn in Far-Right Studies: A Critical Assessment', *Millennium* 51:3 (2023), 893–919.

Camus, Jean-Yves, and Nicolas Lebourg. *Far-Right Politics in Europe*. Cambridge, MA: Harvard University Press, 2017.

Camus, Jean-Yves. 'The French Right 52 Years On: Alive and Kicking as Ever'. Centre for Analysis of the Radical Right, 30 April 2020.

Camus, Renaud. *You Will Not Replace Us!* Plieux: Chez L'Auteur, 2011/2018.

Carofiglio, Vito, and Carmela Ferrandes. 'Les aventures de la droite française et les avatars de Gramsci', *Mots* 12 (1996), 191–203.

Casarões, Guilherme, and Déborah Barros Leal Farias. 'Brazilian Foreign Policy under Jair Bolsonaro: Far-Right Populism and the Rejection of the Liberal International Order', *Cambridge Review of International Affairs* 35:5 (2022), 741–761.

Ceballos, Ana, and Sommer Brugal. 'Conservative Hillsdale College Is Helping DeSantis Reshape Florida Education', *Tampa Bay Times*, 5 July 2022.

Chacko, Priya, and Kanishka Jayasuriya. 'Asia's Conservative Moment: Understanding the Rise of the Right', *Journal of Contemporary Asia* 48:4 (2018), 529–540.

Chakrabarti, Dipesh. *Provincializing Europe: Postcolonial Thought and Historical Difference*. Princeton: Princeton University Press, 2000.

Charlemagne Institute. 'The Alcuin Internship'. Available at: charlemagneinstitute.org/the-alcuin-internship/ (accessed 26 July 2022).

Charlemagne Institute. 'What Is Charlemagne Institute? Who We Are'. Available at: charlemagneinstitute.org/about/ (accessed 6 March 2023).

Cilliza, Chris. 'Pat Buchanan Says Donald Trump Is the Future of the Republican Party', *Washington Post*, 12 January 2016.

Ciobanu, Claudia. 'Ordo Iuris: The Ultra-Conservative Organisation Transforming Poland', *Balkan Insight*, 22 June 2021.

Claremont Institute. 'Mission and Overview'. Available at: www.claremont.org/page/claremonts-mission/ (accessed 19 July 2022).

Claremont Institute. 'Sheriffs Fellowship'. Available at: www.claremont.org/page/sheriffs-fellowship/ (accessed 24 February 2023).

Coaston, Jane. 'When Conservatives Turned into Radicals', *New York Times Magazine*, 31 October 2017.

Codevilla, Angelo. *The Ruling Class: How They Corrupted America and What We Can Do About It*. New York: Beaufort Books, 2010.

Codevilla, Angelo. 'The Rise of Political Correctness: From Marx to Gramsci to Trump', *Claremont Review of Books* 16:4 (Fall 2016).

Codevilla, Angelo. 'NATO Now Serves the Interests of the Transatlantic Ruling Class', *American Greatness*, 15 July 2018.

Collegium Intermarium. 'Our Mission'. Available at: collegiumintermarium.org/en/our-mission (accessed 1 November 2023).

Continetti, Matthew. *The Right: The One Hundred Year War for American Conservatism*. New York: Basic Books, 2022.

Coogan, Kevin. *Dreamer of the Day: Francis Parker Yockey and the Post-war Fascist International*. New York: Autonomedia, 2000.

Cooley, Alexander, and Daniel Nexon. *Exit from Hegemony: The Unravelling of the American Global Order*. New York: Oxford University Press, 2020.

Corbulo, Domitius. 'The Enlightenment from a New Right Perspective', in Greg Johnson ed. *North American New Right, vol. 2*. San Francisco: Counter-Currents Publishing, 2017.

CPAC Hungary. 'Homepage'. Available at: CPACHungary.com (accessed 1 April 2023).

Culbreath, Jonathan. 'Rival Theories of Multipolarity: Aleksandr Dugin and Jiang Shigong', *The European Conservative*, 3 January 2023.

Cupać, Jelena, and Irem Ebetürk. 'Backlash Advocacy and NGO Polarization over Women's Rights in the United Nations', *International Affairs* 97:4 (2021), 1183–1201.

Dahl, Göran. *Radical Conservatism and the Future of Politics*. London: SAGE Publications, 1999.

Danube Institute. 'Homepage'. Available at: danubeinstitute.hu (accessed 6 March 2023).

De Benoist, Alain. *View from the Right: A Critical Anthology of Contemporary Ideas*, 3 vols. London: Arktos, 1977/2017–19.

De Benoist, Alain. 'Ce que nous disons', *Le Monde*, 29 September 1979.

De Benoist, Alain. 'Le pouvoir culturel', in *Les Idées à l'Endroit*. Paris: Editions Libres-Hallier, 1979.

De Benoist, Alain. 'L'ennemi principal', *Éléments* 41 (1982).

De Benoist, Alain. *Europe, Tiers Monde, Même Combat*. Paris: Robert Laffont, 1986.

De Benoist, Alain. 'Vers l'indépendence. Pour une Europe souveraine et liberée de blocs', in *Le Défi de Disneyland. Actes du 20e Colloque National de la Revue Éléments*. Paris: Le Labyrinthe, 1987.

De Benoist, Alain. 'Une remise en cause salutaire des valeurs marchandes', *Éléments* 66 (September/October 1989).

De Benoist, Alain. 'Vous Avez-dit "Mitteleuropa"?', *Éléments* 65 (1989).

De Benoist, Alain. 'Europe: La question allemande', *Éléments* 65 (1989).

De Benoist, Alain. 'Tradition?', *Telos* 94 (1992), 82–88.

De Benoist, Alain. 'The Idea of Empire', *Telos* 98/99 (1993), 81–98.

De Benoist, Alain. 'Confronting Globalization', *Telos* 108 (1996), 117–137.

De Benoist, Alain. *Beyond Human Rights: Defending Freedoms*. London: Arktos, 2001.

De Benoist, Alain. *Carl Schmitt Today: Terrorism, 'Just War' and the State of Emergency*. London: Arktos, 2003.

De Benoist, Alain. 'On Identity', *Telos* 128 (2004), 9–64.

De Benoist, Alain. 'The European New Right Forty Years Later: Tomislav Sunic's Against Democracy and Equality', *The Occidental Quarterly* 9:1 (2009), 61–74.

De Benoist, Alain. *The Problem of Democracy*. London: Arktos, 2011.

De Benoist, Alain. 'Immigration: The Reserve Army of Capital', *Éléments* 141 (October 2011).

De Benoist, Alain. 'Otan, Assimilation et Syrie', *Girodivite*, 12 April 2021.

De Benoist, Alain. 'The Return of the Iron Curtain', *The Postil Magazine*, 1 August 2022.

De Benoist, Alain. 'The Dawn of the Civilizational State', *Agon*, 9 April 2023.

De Benoist, Alain, and Charles Champetier. 'Manifesto of the French New Right in Year 2000', *Telos* 115 (2000), 117–144.

De Benoist, Alain, and Charles Champetier. *Manifesto for a European Renaissance*. London: Arktos, 2012.

De Herte, Robert [De Benoist, Alain]. 'La "Revolution Conservatrice"', *Éléments* 20 (1977).

De Herte, Robert [De Benoist, Alain]. 'Ni des esclaves, ni de robots', *Éléments* 34 (1980).

De Orellana, Pablo, and Nicholas Michelsen. 'Reactionary Internationalism: The Philosophy of the New Right', *Review of International Studies* 45:5 (2019), 748–767.

Dent, Alec. 'The Right's Quiet Uncancelling of a Dead White Supremacist', *Vanity Fair*, 14 October 2022.

Dixit, Jyotindra Nath. *Across Borders: Fifty Years of India's Foreign Policy*. New Delhi: Picus Books, 1998.

Djilas, Milovan. *The New Class: An Analysis of the Communist System*. New York: Harcourt, Brace, Jovanovich, 1957.

Drobinin, Alexey. 'The Vision of a Multipolar World: The Civilizational Factor and Russia's Place in the World Order', *Russia in Global Affairs*, 20 February 2023.

Drolet, Jean-François, and Michael C. Williams. 'Radical Conservatism and Global Order: International Theory and the New Right', *International Theory* 10:3 (2018), 285–313.

Drolet, Jean-François, and Michael C. Williams. 'The View from MARS: US Paleoconservatism and Ideological Challenges to the Liberal World Order', *International Journal* 74:1 (2019), 15–31.

Drolet, Jean-François, and Michael C. Williams. 'America First: Paleoconservatism and the Ideological Struggle for the American Right', *Journal of Political Ideologies* 25:1 (2020), 28–50.

Drolet, Jean-François, and Michael C. Williams. 'From Critique to Reaction', *Journal of International Political Theory* 18:1 (2022), 23–45.

Duarte, Letícia. 'Meet the Intellectual Founder of Brazil's Far Right', *The Atlantic*, 28 December 2018.

Dugin, Alexander. *The Fourth Political Theory*. London: Arktos, 2012.

Dugin, Alexander. *Eurasian Mission*. London: Arktos, 2014.

Dugin, Alexander. *The Theory of a Multipolar World*. London: Arktos Media, 2021.

Duranton-Grabol, Anne-Marie. 'La "Nouvelle Droite" Entre Printemps et Automne, 1968–1986', *Vingtième Siècle. Revue D'Histoire* 17 (1988), 39–50.

Durocher, Guillaume. 'An Uncertain Idea of Europe', *Radix Journal*, 30 June 2016.

Eaton, George. 'Why Antonio Gramsci Is the Marxist Thinker for Our Times', *New Statesman*, 5 February 2018.

Eatwell, Roger, and Noël O'Sullivan eds. *The Nature of the Right*. London: Pinter Publishers, 1989.

Edgecliff-Johnson, Andrew. 'The War on "Woke Capitalism"', *Financial Times*, 27 May 2022.

Efstathopoulos, Charalampos. 'Southern Middle Powers and the Liberal International Order: The Options for Brazil and South Africa', *International Journal* 76:3 (2021), 384–403.

Ellmers, Glenn. '"Conservatism" Is No Longer Enough', *The American Mind*, 24 March 2021.

Encounter Books. 'About'. Available at: www.encounterbooks.com/about/ (accessed 18 July 2022).

Epstein, Charlotte, Thomas Lindemann, and Ole Jacob Sending. 'Frustrated Sovereigns: The Agency That Makes the World Go Around', *Review of International Studies* 44:5 (2018), 787–804.

Eribon, Didier. *Returning to Reims*. New York: Semiotext(e), 2013.

Essa, Asad. *Hostile Homelands: The New Alliance between India and Israel*. London: Pluto Press, 2023.

Evola, Julius. 'Spiritual and Structural Presuppositions of the European Union', reprinted in *North American New Right* 1 (2012), 14–25.

Fawcett, Edmund. *Conservatism: Fight for a Tradition*. Princeton: Princeton University Press, 2020.

Faye, Guillaume. 'Pour en finir avec la civilization occidentale', *Éléments* 34 (1980).

Faye, Guillaume. *Le système à tuer les peoples*. Paris: Copernic, 1981.

Faye, Guillaume. *Nouveau discours à la nation européene*. Paris: Albatros, 1985.

Faye, Guillaume. *Convergence of Catastrophes*. London: Arktos, 2004/2012.

Faye, Guillaume. 'The Geopolitics of Ethnopolitics: The New Concept of "Eurosiberia"', unpublished paper presented at the international conference on 'The Future of the White World', Moscow, 8–10 June 2006. Available at: counter-currents.com/2010/08/faye-on-eurosiberia/ (accessed 1 November 2023).

Faye, Guillaume. *Archeofuturism: European Visions of the Post-Catastrophic Age*. London: Arktos, 2010.

Faye, Guillaume. *Why We Fight: Manifesto of the European Resistance*. London: Artkos, 2011.

Faye, Guillaume. 'Brexit: Quake or Squib?', *Radix Journal*, 20 July 2016.

Feder, J. Lester, and Giuia Alagna. 'One of Steve Bannon's Top Allies in Italy Is under Investigation over Corruption', *BuzzFeed News*, 20 April 2019.

Field, Laura K. 'What the Hell Happened to the Claremont Institute?' *The Bulwark*, 13 July 2021.

Filc, Dani, and Sharon Pardo. 'Israel's Right-Wing Populists: The European Connection', *Survival* 63:3 (2021), 99–122.

Fleming, Thomas. 'The New Fusionism', *Chronicles*, May 1991.

Fleming, Thomas. 'America First 1941/1991', *Chronicles*, December 1991.

Fleming, Thomas, and Paul Gottfried. *The Conservative Movement*. Boston: Twayne Publisher, 1988.

Fonte, John. *Sovereignty or Submission*. New York: Encounter Books, 2012.

Fonte, John. 'What the Right Must Learn from Trump', *The American Mind*, 10 April 2019.

Francis, Samuel T. 'Beautiful Losers', *Chronicles*, May 1991.

Francis, Samuel T. 'Principalities and Power', *Chronicles*, December 1991.

Francis, Samuel T. 'Nationalism: Old and New', *Chronicles*, May 1992.

Francis, Samuel T. 'The Buchanan Revolution, Part I', *Chronicles*, July 1992.

Francis, Samuel T. 'Winning the Culture Wars', *Chronicles*, December 1993.

Francis, Samuel T. *Beautiful Losers: Essays on the Failure of American Conservatism*. Columbia: University of Missouri Press, 1994.

Francis, Samuel T. 'The New Underclass', in Sam Francis, *Revolution from the Middle*. Rockford, IL: Middle American Press, 1997, 44–57.

Francis, Samuel T. 'Beyond Conservatism', *Chronicles*, January 2000.

Francis, Samuel T. 'Paleoconservatism and Race', *Chronicles*, December 2000.

Francis, Samuel T. 'The Paleo Persuasion', *The American Conservative*, 12 December 2002.

Francis, Samuel T. *Leviathan and Its Enemies*. Arlington, VA: Radix/Washington Summit Publishers, 2016.

Freeden, Michael. *Ideologies and Political Theory: A Conceptual Approach*. Oxford: Oxford University Press, 1996.

Freistein, Katja, Frank Gadinger, and Christine Unrau. '*It Just Feels Right*: Visuality and Emotion Norms in Right-Wing Populist Storytelling', *International Political Sociology* 16:4 (2022), 1–23.

Freund, Julien. *La Décadence: Histoire sociologique et philosophique d'une catégorie d'expérience humaine*. Paris: Sirey, 1984.

Furedi, Frank. 'Brussels Needs a Hungarian Think Tank', *Politico*, 1 November 2022.

Galaup, Laura. 'El instituto de Maréchal Le Pen y Vox comparten entornos para formar a la futura élite de la extrema derecha', *El Diario*, 29 August 2021.

Ganz, John. 'The Week in Fascism: On Claremont and Tucker'. Substack, 28 March 2021. Available at: johnganz.substack.com/p/the-week-in-fascism (accessed 2 November 2023).

Geary, Daniel, Camilla Schofield, and Jennifer Sutton eds. *Global White Nationalism: From Apartheid to Trump*. Manchester: Manchester University Press, 2020.

Gennarini, Stefano. 'Best Moments of the Year for Life and Family at the United Nations', *C-Fam*, 29 December 2016.

Geoghegan, Peter. 'At NatCon London', *London Review of Books* 41:11 (June 2023).

Geoghegan, Peter. *Democracy for Sale: Dark Money and Dirty Politics*. London: Head of Zeus, 2020.

Gerfaut, Henri. 'Une certaine idée de l'Europe', *Éléments* 53 (1985).

Geva, Dorit, and Felipe G. Santos. 'Europe's Far-Right Educational Projects and Their Vision for the International Order', *International Affairs* 97:5 (2021), 1395–1414.

Gheciu, Alexandra. 'Remembering France's Glory, Securing Europe in the Age of Trump', *European Journal of International Security* 5:1 (2020), 25–45.

Gianoncelli, Eva. 'The Unification of the "New Right"? On Europe, Identity Politics and Reactionary Ideologies', *New Perspectives* 29:4 (2021), 364–375.

Gill, Stephen. 'Toward a Postmodern Prince? The Battle in Seattle as a Moment in the New Politics of Globalisation', *Millennium* 29:1 (2000), 131–140.

Glencross, Andrew. 'The EU and the Temptation to Become a Civilizational State', *European Foreign Affairs Review* 26:2 (2021), 331–350.

Go, Julian, and George Lawson eds. *Global Historical Sociology*. Cambridge: Cambridge University Press, 2017.

Goetz, Anne Marie. 'The New Competition in Multilateral Norm-Setting: Transnational Feminists and the Illiberal Backlash', *Daedalus* 149:1 (2020), 160–179.

Goldberg, Michelle. 'DeSantis Allies Plot the Hostile Takeover of a Liberal College', *New York Times*, 9 January 2023.

Goñi, Uki. 'Argentina's New Leader Is a Snake-Oil Salesman with Extreme Views on Abortion, Gay Rights and More. I Fear for My Country', *The Guardian*, 21 November 2023.

Goodhart, Michael, and Stacy Bondanella Taninchev. 'The New Sovereigntist Challenge for Global Governance: Democracy without Sovereignty', *International Studies Quarterly* 55:4 (2012), 1047–1068.

Gottfried, Paul. *After Liberalism: Mass Democracy in the Managerial State*. Princeton, NJ: Princeton University Press, 2001.

Gottfried, Paul. 'America and the West: The Multiculturalist International', *Orbis* 45 (2002), 145–161.

Gottfried, Paul. 'Some Observations from the Man Who Created the Alt-Right', *Frontpage Magazine*, 30 August 2016.

Gottfried, Paul. 'Explaining Trump', in *Revisions and Dissents: Essays*. DeKalb, IL: Northern Illinois University Press, 2017.

Gottfried, Paul, and Richard Spencer. *The Great Purge: The Deformation of the Conservative Movement*. Washington, DC: Washington Summit Publishers, 2015.

Gouldner, Alvin W. *The Future of Intellectuals and the Rise of the New Class*. London: MacMillan Press, 1979.

Gramsci, Antonio. *Selections from the Prison Notebooks*, Quintin Hoare and Geoffrey Nowell Smith trans. and ed. London: Lawrence & Wishart, 1929–1935/1971.

Graziosi, Graig. 'Japanese Cult Representative Is Speaking for the 10th Year in a Row at CPAC', *The Independent*, 9 April 2021.

GRECE Collective. *Dix Ans de Combat Culturel pour une Renaissance*. Paris: GRECE, 1977.

GRECE Collective. 'Pour un gramscisme de droite', *Éléments* 20 (1977).

Grgić, Gordana. 'The Changing Dynamics of Regionalism in Central and Eastern Europe: The Case of the Three Seas Initiative', *Geopolitics* 28:1 (2021), 216–238.

Griffin, Roger. 'Between Metapolitics and Apoliteia: The Nouvelle Droite Strategy for Conserving the Fascist Vision in the Interregnum', *Modern and Contemporary France* 8 (2000), 35–53.

Griffin, Roger. 'Interregnum or Endgame? The Radical Right in the "Post-Fascist" Era', *Journal of Political Ideologies* 5:2 (2000), 163–178.

Hall, Jeffrey J. *Japan's Nationalist Right in the Internet Age: Online Movements and Grassroots Conservative Activism*. New York: Routledge, 2021.

Hart, Gillian. 'Why Did It Take So Long? Trump-Bannonism in a Global Conjunctural Frame', *Geografiska Annaler: Series B, Human Geography* 102:3 (2020), 239–266.

Heller, Fernando. 'Far-Right Leaders Agree on "Roadmap" for Sovereign and Patriotic Europe', *Euractiv News*, 31 January 2022.

Herf, Jeffrey. *Reactionary Modernism*. Cambridge: Cambridge University Press, 1984.

Herman, Arthur. *The Idea of Decline in Western History*. New York: Free Press 2007.

Hochschild, Arlie Russell. *Strangers in Their Own Land: Anger and Mourning on the American Right*. New York: The New Press, 2016.

Hodges, Donald C. *Argentina's 'Dirty War': An Intellectual Biography*. Austin: University of Texas Press, 1991.

Honneth, Axel. 'Recognition between States: On the Moral Substrate of International Relations', in Thomas Lindemann, and Erik Ringmar eds. *The International Politics of Recognition*. Boulder: Paradigm Publishers, 2012.

Hopkins, Valerie. 'Campus in Hungary Is Flagship of Orban's Bid to Create a Conservative Elite', *New York Times*, 28 June 2021.

Hosenball, Mark. 'Steve Bannon Drafting Curriculum for Right-Wing Catholic Institute in Italy', *Reuters*, 14 September 2018.

Hungarian Conservative 2:2 (2022).

Hunter, James Davison. *Culture Wars: The Struggle to Define America*. New York: Basic Books, 1991.

Ištok, Robert, Irina Kozárová, and Anna Polačková. 'The Intermarium as a Polish Geopolitical Concept in History and in the Present', *Geopolitics* 26:1 (2018), 314–341.

ISSEP. 'Présentation'. Available at: www.issep.fr/presentation/ (accessed 6 March 2023).

Jindal, Bobby. 'Forget China: This Is America's Greatest Challenge', *Fox News*, 10 April 2023.

Johnson, Greg. 'New Right vs. Old Right', *Counter-Currents*, 11 May 2012.

Johnson, Greg. *Towards a New Nationalism*. San Francisco: Counter-Currents Publishing, 2018.

Johnson, Greg. *White Identity Politics*. San Francisco: Counter-Currents Publishing, 2020.

Joseph, Cameron. 'Trump's Favorite Extreme Think Tank Is Jumping Ship for DeSantis', *Vice News*, 27 March 2023.

Joyce, Kathryn. 'Coming to a School Near You: Stealth Religion and a Trumped-Up Version of American History', *Salon*, 16 March 2022.

Joyce, Kathryn. 'The Far Right's National Plan for Schools: Plant Charters, Defund Public Education', *Salon*, 17 March 2022.

Julien, Fréderic. *Les Etats-Unis contre l'Europe: L'impossible alliance*. Paris: Le Labyrinthe, 1987.

Kaalep, Ruuben, and August Meister. *Rebirth of Europe: The Ethnofuturist Manifesto*. London: Arktos, 2020.

Kaoma, Kapya. 'Globalizing the Culture Wars: U.S. Conservatives, African Churches, and Homophobia'. Political Research Associates, 2009.

Keck, Margaret, and Kathryn Sikkink. *Activists beyond Borders*. New York, NY: Cornell University Press, 1998.

Kelly, Jemima. 'The Reopening of the America Mind', *Financial Times*, 26 October 2023.

Kiely, Ray. *The Conservative Challenge to Globalization*. New York: Columbia University Press, 2020.

Kirk, Russell. *The Conservative Mind: From Burke to Elliot*. New York: BN Publishing, 1953/2008.

Klomegah, Kester Kenn. 'International Conference Strengthens Multifaceted Relations between Russia and Africa', *Modern Diplomacy*, 21 March 2023.

Klyszcz, Ivan U. 'Messianic Multipolarity: Russia's Resurrected Africa Doctrine', *Riddle*, 3 April 2023.

Korolczuk, Elżbieta and Agnieszka Graff. 'Gender as "Ebola from Brussels": The Anticolonial Frame and the Rise of Illiberal Populism', *Signs: Journal of Women in Culture and Society* 43:4 (2018), 797–821.

Kott, Matthew. 'A Far Right Hijack of Intermarium', *New Eastern Europe*, 26 May 2017.

Kranenberg, Rob van. 'Whose Gramsci?: Right-Wing Gramscism', *International Gramsci Society Newsletter* 9 (March 1999), 14–18.

Krastev, Ivan. 'How Donald Trump Redefined "the West"', *New York Times*, 11 July 2017.

Krein, Julius. 'James Burnham's Managerial Elite', *American Affairs* 1:1 (Spring 2017), 21–36.

Kumral, Şefika. 'Globalization, Crisis and Right-Wing Populists in the Global South: The Cases of India and Turkey', *Globalizations* 20:5 (2023), 752–781.

Kundani, Hans. *Eurowhiteness: Culture, Empire and Race in the European Project*. London: Hurst, 2023.

Laclau, Ernesto. *On Populist Reason*. London: Verso, 2005.

Laclau, Ernesto. 'Populism: What's in a Name?', in Francisco Panizza ed. *Populism and the Mirror of Democracy*. London: Verso, 2005.

Laclau, Ernesto, and Chantal Mouffe. *Hegemony and Socialist Strategy*. London: Verso 1985.

Lamour, Christian. 'The League of Leagues: Meta-Populism and the "Chain of Equivalence" in a Cross-Border Alpine Area', *Political Geography* 81 (2020), 1–11.

Lapierre, Matthew. 'Police Outnumber Bikers at "Rolling Thunder" Ceremony as Speakers Evoke Memory of "Freedom Convoy" Protests', *Ottawa Citizen*, 30 April 2022.

Laruelle, Marlène. *Russian Eurasianism: An Ideology of Empire*. Cambridge: Cambridge University Press, 2008.

Laruelle, Marlène. 'Illiberalism: A Conceptual Introduction', *East European Politics* 38:2 (2022), 303–327.
Lawson, George, and Ayşe Zarakol. 'Recognizing Injustice: The "Hypocrisy Charge" and the Future of the Liberal International Order', *International Affairs* 99:1 (2023), 201–217.
Leander, Anna, with Cristiana Gonzales, Luisa Lobato and Pedro dos Santos Maia. 'Ripples and Their Returns: Tracing the Regulatory Security State from the EU to Brazil, Back and Beyond', *Journal of European Public Policy* 30:7 (2023), 1379–1405.
Lenk, Kurt, Günter Meuter, and Henrique Ricardo Otten. *Vordenker der Neuen Rechten*. Frankfurt: Campus, 1997.
Lentin, Alana. 'Beyond Denial: "Not Racism" as Racist Violence', *Continuum* 32:4 (2018), 400–414.
Lind, Michael. *The New Class War*. New York: Penguin, 2020.
Lind, Michael. 'The Importance of James Burnham', *Tablet Magazine*, 1 September 2021.
Lipset, Seymour M. 'The Radical Right: A Problem for American Democracy', *British Journal of Sociology* 6 (1955), 176–209.
Lisicki, Paweł. 'Polski bastion wolności', *Do Rzeczy*, 4 September 2017.
Lloyd, Alice. 'The College That Wants to Take over Washington', *Politico Magazine*, 12 May 2018.
Lohausen, Jordis von. *Mut zur Macht. Denken in Kontinenten*. Berg Am See: Kurt Vowinckel, 1979.
Lowell, Norman. *Imperium Europa: The Book That Changed the World*. Baldwin, KS: Imperium Books, 2009.
Lowell, Norman. *Aristocratic Manifesto for Imperium Europa*. London: Arktos, 2019.
Luce, Edward. *The Retreat of Western Liberalism*. New York: Atlantic Monthly Press, 2017.
Ludovika University of Public Service. 'The University of a Secure Future, 2020–2025'. Available at: en.uni-nke.hu/document/en-uni-nke-hu/Institutional%20Development%20Plan%202020-2025%20UPS.pdf (accessed 6 March 2023).
Luwemba, Julius. 'Religious Leaders, African Legislators Parliamentarians Discuss Family Values', *New Vision*, 1 April 2023.
Main, Thomas J. *The Rise of the Alt-Right*. Washington, DC: Brookings Institution Press, 2018.
Mair, Peter. *Ruling the Void: The Hollowing of Democracy*. London: Verso, 2013.
Malik, Kenan. 'It's Not Just the Far Right That Should Worry Us: It's Their Ideas Seeping into the Mainstream', *The Observer*, 3 July 2022.

Mammone, Andrea. *Transnational Fascism in France and Italy*. Cambridge: Cambridge University Press, 2015.

Mannheim, Karl. *Conservatism: A Contribution to the Sociology of Knowledge*. Abingdon: Routledge, 1936/1997.

Marantz, Andrew. *Antisocial: How Online Extremists Broke America*. New York: Picador, 2019.

Marcotte, Amanda. 'How a Far-Right Think Tank Made Everything "Woke"', *Salon*, 17 March 2023.

Marini, John. 'Donald Trump and the American Crisis', *Claremont Review of Books*, 22 July 2016.

Marini, John. *Unmasking the Administrative State: The Crisis of American Politics in the Twenty-first Century*, Ken Masugi ed. New York: Encounter Books, 2019.

Masquelier, Paul. 'Le capitalisme aime habiller les jeunes', *Éléments* 115 (Winter 2004–2005), 40–44.

Matecki, Dariusz. 'Prof. Gil: Międzymorze szansą na wzmocnienie pozycji państw Europy Środkowej i Wschodniej'. Prawicowyinternet.pl, 8 July 2017.

Mayer, Nonna. 'Political Science Approaches to the Far Right', in Stephen D. Ashe, Joel Busher, Graham Macklin, and Aaron Winter eds. *Researching the Far Right: Theory, Method and Practice*. London: Routledge, 2020.

Mbembe, Achille. 'On the Power of the False', *Public Culture* 14:3 (2002), 629–641.

MCC Brussels. 'New Forum Launched to Shake Up European Debate and Discussion'. Available at: brussels.mcc.hu/news/mcc-brussels-a-new-forum-launched-to-shake-up-european-debate-and-discussion (accessed 8 May 2023).

McGlyn, Jade. 'Why Russia Markets Itself as an Anti-Colonial Power to Africans', *Foreign Policy*, 8 February 2023.

McMahon, Darren. *Enemies of the Enlightenment*. Oxford: Oxford University Press, 2001.

Meyer, Jane. *Dark Money: The Hidden History of the Billionaires Behind the Rise of the Radical Right*. New York: Free Press, 2017.

Minkenberg, Michael. 'The New Right in France and Germany: Nouvelle Droite, Neue Rechte, and the New Right Radical Right Parties', in Peter H. Merkl, and Leonard Weinberg eds. *The Revival of Right-Wing Extremism in the Nineties*. London: Frank Cass, 1997.

Mohler, Armin. *The Conservative Revolution in Germany*. Whitefish, MT: Washington Summit Publishers, 1950/2018.

Molnar, Thomas. *The Two Faces of American Foreign Policy*. Indianapolis: Bobbs-Merrill Co., 1962.

Molnar, Thomas. *The Emerging Atlantic Culture*. New Brunswick: Transaction, 1994.

Mondon, Aurelien, and Aaron Winter. 'From Demonization to Normalisation: Reflecting on Far Right Research', in Stephen D. Ashe, Joel Busher, Graham Macklin, and Aaron Winter eds. *Researching the Far Right: Theory, Method and Practice*. London: Routledge, 2020.

Morgan, Lynn. 'Anti-Abortion Strategizing and the Afterlife of the Geneva Consensus Declaration', *Developing World Bioethics* 23:2 (2023), 185-195.

Mouffe, Chantal. *Toward a Left Populism*. London: Verso, 2019.

Mudde, Cas. 'The War of Words Defining the Extreme Right Party Family', *West European Politics* 19:2 (1996), 225-248.

Mudde, Cas. 'The Populist Zeitgeist', *Government and Opposition* 39:4 (2004), 542-563.

Mudde, Cas ed. *The Populist Radical Right: A Reader*. London: Routledge, 2017.

Mudde, Cas. *The Far Right Today*. Cambridge: John Wiley & Sons, 2019.

Muller, Jerry Z. 'Carl Schmitt, Hans Freyer and the Radical Conservative Critique of Liberal Democracy in the Weimar Republic', *History of Political Thought* 12:4 (1991), 695-715.

Munster, Ben. 'The Last Stand at Steve Bannon's "Gladiator School"', *The New Yorker*, 24 May 2021.

Murray, Kyle, and Owen Worth. 'Building Consent: Hegemony, "Conceptions of the World" and the Role of Evangelicals in Global Politics', *Political Studies* 61:4 (2013), 731-747.

Murray, Michelle. *The Struggle for Recognition in International Relations*. Oxford: Oxford University Press, 2018.

Nair, Deepak. 'Populists in the Shadow of Great Power Competition: Duterte, Sukarno, and Sihanouk in Comparative Perspective', *European Journal of International Relations* 29:3 (2023), 723-750.

Narita, Karin, 'Travelling Theory and Its Consequences: José Ortega y Gasset and Radical Conservatism in Post-Cold War Japan', *Millennium* 49:3 (2023), 556-576.

Nash, George H. *The Conservative Intellectual Movement in American since 1945*, Thirtieth-Anniversary edition. Wilmington: ISI, 2006.

Ndlovu-Gatsheni, Sabelo J. 'Africa for Africans or Africa for "Natives" Only? "New Nationalism" and Nativism in Zimbabwe and South Africa', *Africa Spectrum* 44:1 (2009), 61-78.

Negria, Camilo, Rebecca Lemos Igreja, and Simone Roderigues Pinto. 'It Happened in Brazil Too: The Radical Right's Capture of Networks of Hope', *Cahiers des Amériques Latines* 92 (2019), 17-38.

Nisbet, Robert. *Conservatism*. Milton Keynes: The Open University, 1986.

Nishibe, Susumu. *Bunmei no Teki Minshushugi: Kiki no Seijitetsugaku* [Democracy's Threat to Civilization: A Political Philosophy of Crisis]. Tokyo: Jiji Press, 2011.

O'Boyle, Brendon. 'At CPAC Mexico, "Orphaned" Right Tries to Build Home as Region Tacks Left', *Reuters*, 19 November 2022.

O'Meara, James J. *Mysticism after Modernism: Crowley, Evola, Neville, Watts, Colin Wilson, and Other Populist Gurus*. Melbourne: Manticore Press, 2020.

O'Meara, Michael. *New Culture, New Right: Anti-Liberalism in Postmodern Europe*. London: Arktos, 2004.

O'Sullivan, John. 'A Moveable Feast?' *National Review*, 27 November 2020.

O'Toole, Kathleen. 'The Hillsdale 1776 Curriculum Was Made by Professors and Teachers – Not Bureaucrats, Not Activists, Not Journalists – Teachers', Hillsdale College K-12 Education Office. Available at: k12.hillsdale.edu/Curriculum/The-Hillsdale-1776-Curriculum/Dear-Teacher/ (accessed 6 March 2023).

Orbán, Victor. Speech at the CPAC. *Visegrad Post*, 19 May 2022. Available at visegradpost.com/en/2022/05/24/viktor-orbans-speech-at-the-cpac-on-19-may-2022/ (accessed 31 October 2023).

Osiel, Mark J. *Mass Atrocity, Ordinary Evil, and Hannah Arendt: Criminal Consciousness in Argentina's Dirty War*. New Haven: Yale University Press, 2001.

Ott, Haley. 'Steve Bannon Backs "Gladiator School" to Bolster Europe's Right Wing', *CBS News*, 3 March 2019.

Pestritto, Ronald J. *America Transformed: The Rise and Legacy of American Progressivism*. New York: Encounter Books, 2021.

Peterson Academy. 'Coming Soon'. Available at: petersonacademy.com (accessed 2 November 2023).

Peterson, Matthew J. 'Claremont vs. Foreign Policy Establishment', *The American Mind*, 21 January 2019.

Peunova, Marina. 'An Eastern Incarnation of the European New Right: Aleksandr Panarin and New Eurasianist Discourse in Contemporary Russia', *Journal of Contemporary European Studies* 16:3 (2008), 407–419.

Phillips, Aleks. 'Javier Milei's Ominous Warning to Americans', *Newsweek*, 20 November 2023.

Phillips-Fein, Kim. *Invisible Hands: The Businessmen's Crusade against the New Deal*. New York: W. W. Norton & Company, 2010.

Piłka, Marian. 'Wielka Strategia'. Geopolityka.net, 23 November 2018.

Pishko, Jessica. 'Here's the Secret "Sheriff Fellowship" Curriculum from the Country's Most Prominent MAGA Think Tank', *Slate*, 21 September 2022.

Pogue, James. 'Inside the New Right: Where Peter Theil Is Placing His Biggest Bets', *Vanity Fair*, 20 April 2022.

Potter, Gary. 'The New Catholic "Far" Right in France, Part II', Catholicism.org, 23 January 2019.

Preussen, Wilhelmine. 'Victor Orbán Funded Think Tank Vows to Shake up Brussels', *Politico*, 1 November 2022.

Protzer, Eric, and Paul Summerville. *Reclaiming Populism: How Economic Fairness Can Win Back Disenchanted Voters*. London: Polity, 2022.

Purcell, Mark. 'Resisting Neoliberalization: Communicative Planning or Counter-Hegemonic Movements?', *Planning Theory* 8:2 (2009), 140–165.

Quintana Paz, Miguel Ángel. '¿Qué queremos decir cuando decimos que estamos en una guerra cultural?', *The Objective*, 5 December 2019.

Rabkin, Jeremy. *Law without Nations: Why Constitutional Government Requires Sovereign States*. Princeton: Princeton University Press, 2007.

Ramaswamy, Vivek. 'The "Stakeholders" vs The People', *Wall Street Journal*, 12 February 2020.

Regnery. 'About Regnery Publishing' and 'New Releases'. Available at: www.regnery.com/our-story/ and www.regnery.com/books/new-releases/ (accessed 6 March 2023).

Ringmar, Erik. 'Introduction. The International Politics of Recognition', in Thomas Lindemann and Erik Ringmar eds. *The International Politics of Recognition*. Boulder: Paradigm Publishers, 2012.

Risen, Clay. 'Angelo Codevilla, Whose Writings Anticipated Trumpism, Dies at 78', *New York Times*, 30 October 2021.

Rizzi, Bruno. *The Bureaucratisation of the World*. New York: Free Press, 1939/1985.

Rodkiewicz, Witold. 'An Anti-Colonial Alliance with the Global South. The New "Foreign Policy Concept of the Russian Federation"'. Center for Eastern Studies, 7 April 2023.

Rodriguez, J. Luis, and Chrisy Thornton. 'The Liberal International Order and the Global South: A View from Latin America', *Cambridge Review of International Affairs* 35:5 (2022), 626–638.

Rodrik, Dani. 'Why Does Globalization Fuel Populism? Economics, Culture, and the Rise of Right-Wing Populism', *Annual Review of Economics* 13:1 (2021), 133–170.

Roger, Benjamin. 'Russia: How Yevgeny Prigozhin Funded Kemi Seba to Serve His Own African Ambitions', *The Africa Report*, 11 April 2023.

Rolland, Nadège. 'China's Vision for a New World Order'. NBR Special Report #83. Seattle: National Bureau of Asian Research, 2020.

Rose, David. 'Yoram Hazony: "In Britain and in Israel, There Is No Stopping National Conservatism"', *The Jewish Chronicle*, 18 May 2023.

Rose, Matthew. *A World after Liberalism: Philosophers of the New Right*. New Haven: Yale University Press, 2021.

Roulin, Stéphanie, Giles Scott-Smith, and Lu van Dongen eds. *Transnational Anti-Communism and the Cold War*. London: Palgrave, 2014.

Rubio, Marco. 'The Left's Civic Religion Is a Threat to National Security', *Washington Examiner*, 20 June 2023.

Rufo, Christopher. *America's Cultural Revolution: How the Radical Left Conquered Everything*. New York: Broadside Books, 2023.

Sacchi, Franco. 'The Italian New Right', *Telos* 98–99 (1993), 71–80.

Saeki, Keishi. *Gendai Nihon no Ideorogī: Gurōbarizumu to Kokka Ishiki* [Contemporary Japanese Ideology: Globalism and State Consciousness]. Tokyo: Kodansha, 1998.

Saeki, Keishi. *Rinri toshite no Nashonarizumu: Gurōbarizumu no Kyomu wo Koete* [Nationalism as Ethics: Beyond the Nihilism of Globalism]. Tokyo: NTT Publishing, 2005.

Sanbonmatsu, John. *The Postmodern Prince: Critical Theory, Left Strategy, and the Making of a New Political Subject*. New York: Monthly Review Press, 2004.

Sanders, Richard. 'Spain's Vox Sets Its Sights on Latin America', *World Politics Review*, 14 December 2021.

Santoro, Philip. 'White Environmentalism', *American Renaissance*, 29 April 2017.

Sassen, Saskia. *Territory, Authority, Rights*. Princeton: Princeton University Press, 2006.

Schmitt, Carl. 'The *Großraum* Order of International Law with a Ban on Intervention for Spatially Foreign Powers: A Contribution to the Concept of *Reich* in International Law (1939–1941)', in Timothy Nunan ed. *Carl Schmitt: Writings on War*. Cambridge: Polity Press, 2011.

Schroeder, Ralph. 'Digital Media and the Entrenchment of Right Wing Populist Agendas', *Social Media + Society* 5:4 (2019), 1–11.

Schullenberger, Geoff. 'Theorycels in Trumpworld', *Outsider Theory*, 5 January 2021.

Schultheis, Emily. 'Teaching the Holocaust in Germany as a Resurgent Far Right Questions It', *The Atlantic*, 10 April 2019.

Scotchie, Joseph. *The Paleoconservatives: New Voices of the Old Right*. New York: Transaction Publishers, 1999.

Scott-Smith, Giles. *Western Anti-Communism and the Interdoc Network: Cold War Internationale*. London: Palgrave, 2021.

Scruton, Roger. *A Dictionary of Political Thought*. London: Pan, 1982.

Scruton, Roger. *Fools, Frauds, and Firebrands*. London: Bloomsbury, 2015.

Scruton, Roger. 'The Future of European Civilization: Lessons for America', Heritage Foundation Report, 8 December 2015.

Scuola di Fomazione Politica. 'Home'. Available at: www.scuoladiformazionepolitica.it (accessed 6 March 2023).

Seba, Kemi. *Supra-négritude: Autodétermination, antivictimisation, virilité du people*. Paris: Fiat-Lux editions, 2013.

Seba, Kemi. 'Russia Is at War with Globalism', *Geopolitika*, 24 March 2022.

Sedgwick, Mark. *Against the Modern World*. Oxford: Oxford University Press, 2009.

Sedgwick, Mark ed. *Key Thinkers of the Radical Right*. Oxford: Oxford University Press, 2019.

Seidman, Michael. *The Imaginary Revolution: Parisian Students and Workers in 1968*. New York: Berghahn, 2004.

Semonsen, Robert. 'Vox's Abascal Meets Bolsonaro to Promote Transatlantic Alliance', *The European Conservative*, 15 December 2021.

Senra, Ricardo. 'O encontro entre o "mito" e o "messias": o que Bolsonaro traz na volta da Índia para Brasil', *BBC Brazil*, 28 January 2020.

Settle, Jamie E. *Frenemies: How Social Media Polarizes America*. Cambridge: Cambridge University Press, 2018.

Shatz, Marshall S. *Jan Waclaw Machajski: A Radical Critic of the Russian Intelligentsia and Socialism*. Pittsburgh, PA: University of Pittsburgh Press, 1999.

Shekthovsov, Anton. *Russia and the Western Far Right*. London: Routledge, 2018.

Shenk, Timothy. 'The Dark History of Donald Trump's Revolt', *The Guardian*, 16 August 2016.

Simpson, Patricia Ann, and Helga Druxes eds. *Digital Media Strategies of the Far Right in Europe and the United States*. Lanham: Lexington Books, 2015.

Sire, Adeline. 'Le Pen's Niece Opens Grad School to Train New Generation of French Far-Right Leaders', *Public Radio International*, 4 January 2019.

Slobodian, Quinn. *Globalists: The End of Empire and the Birth of Neoliberalism*. Cambridge, MA: Harvard University Press, 2018.

Sloen, Tinus. 'Right-Wing Gramscianism: The Hegemonic Project of Thierry Beaudet', *Digit Magazine*, 29 March 2021.

Smith, Evan. *No Platform: A History of Anti-Fascism, Universities and the Limits of Free Speech*. London: Routledge, 2020.

Snyder, Jack. 'Is There a Coherent Ideology of Illiberal Modernity, and Is It a Source of Soft Power?', in Burcu Baykurt, and Victoria de Grazia eds. *Soft-Power Internationalism*. New York: Columbia University Press, 2021.

Somaskanda, Sumi. 'A New, New Right Rises in Germany', *The Atlantic*, 22 June 2017.

Southern Poverty Law Center. 'Greg Johnson'. Available at: www.splcenter.org/fighting-hate/extremist-files/individual/greg-johnson (accessed 6 March 2023).

Southgate, Troy. *Tradition and Revolution: Collected Writings of Troy Southgate*. London: Arktos, 2011.

Sowell, Thomas. *Black Rednecks and White Liberals*. New York: Encounter Books, 2009.

Spektorowski, Alberto. 'The New Right: Ethno-Regionalism, Ethno-Pluralism and the Emergence of a Neo-Fascist "Third Way"', *Journal of Political Ideologies* 8:1 (2003), 111–130.

Spoehr, Thomas. 'The Rise of Wokeness in the Military', Heritage Foundation, 30 September 2022.

Steffek, Jens. 'Fascist Internationalism', *Millennium* 44:1 (2015), 3–22.

Steffek, Jens, and Yannick Lasshof. 'Steve Bannon on "Productive Capitalism": Investigating the Economic Ideology of the American Populist Right', *Journal of Political Ideologies* (2022), First View.

Stengel, Frank A., David B. MacDonald, and Dirk Nabers eds. *Populism and World Politics: Exploring Inter-and Transnational Dimensions*. London: Palgrave, 2019.

Sternhell, Zeev. *Neither Right, Nor Left: Fascist Ideology in France*. Princeton: Princeton University Press, 1995.

Steuckers, Robert. 'La Russie, L'Europe et L'Occident', *Orientation* 4 (1983).

Steuckers, Robert. 'Sécurité et Défense en Europe', in *Le défi de Disneyland: Actes du XXe colloque national de la revue 'Éléments'*. Paris: Le Labyrinthe, 1987.

Steuckers, Robert. 'Post-Modern Challenges: Between Faust and Narcissus', in Greg Johnson ed., *North American New Right, vol. 1*. San Francisco: Counter-Currents Publishing, 2012.

Steuckers, Robert. *Europa: De l'Eurasie aux périphéries: une géopolitique continentale, 3 vols*. Lille: Bios, 2017.

Steuckers, Robert. 'Géopolitique et avenir de l'Europe', *Geopolitika*, 8 September 2022.

Stoeckl, Kristina. 'Traditional Values, Family, Homeschooling: The Role of Russia and the Russian Orthodox Church in Transnational Moral Conservative Networks and Their Efforts at Reshaping Human Rights', *International Journal of Constitutional Law* 21:1 (2023), 224–242.

Stoeckl, Kristina, and Dmitry Uzlaner. *The Moralist International: Russia in the Global Culture Wars*. New York: Fordham University Press, 2022.

Stone, Marla, and Giuliana Chamedis. 'Naming the Enemy: Anti-Communism in Transnational Perspective', *Journal of Contemporary History* 53:1 (2018), 4–11.

Stonor Saunders, Frances. *The Cultural Cold War: The CIA and the World of Arts and Letters*. New York: New York Press, 2001.

Stroop, Krissy. 'A Right-Wing International? Russian Social Conservatism, the U.S.-Based WCF, and the Global Culture Wars in Historical Context'. Political Research Associates, 2016.

Stuenkel, Oliver, and Matthew Taylor eds. *Brazil on the Global Stage: Power, Ideas, and the Liberal International Order*. London: Palgrave, 2015.

Subotic, Jelena. 'Antisemitism in the Global Populist International', *The British Journal of Politics and International Relations* 24:3 (2022), 458–474.

Subotic, Jelena, and Srdjan Vucetic. 'Performing Solidarity: Whiteness and Status-Seeking in the Non-Aligned World', *Journal of International Relations and Development* 22:3 (2019), 722–743.

Sunić, Tomislav ed. *Against Democracy and Equality: The European New Right*. London: Arktos, 1990/2011.

Sunić, Tomislav. 'L'Union Européenne est entrain de s'autodétruire', *Éléments*, 8 May 2014.

Swyngedouw, Erik. 'Illiberalism and the Democratic Paradox: The Infernal Dialectic of Neoliberal Emancipation', *European Journal of Social Theory* 25:1 (2021), 53–74.

Szechenyi, Bence X. 'Victor Orbán's Pet University is All about Propaganda – I Know, I Was There', *The Guardian*, 11 September 2023.

Taguieff, Pierre-André. 'La stratégie culturelle de la "Nouvelle Droite" en France (1968–1983)', in Robert Badinter ed. *Vous Avez Dit Fascismes?* Paris: Montalba, 1984.

Táíwò, Olúfẹ́mi. *Against Decolonization: Taking African Agency Seriously*. London: Hurst, 2022.

Tanenhaus, Sam. 'I'm Tired of America Wasting Our Blood and Treasure: The Strange Ascent of Betsy Devos and Erik Prince', *Vanity Fair*, 6 September 2018.

Tarchi, Marco. 'Italie: Une nouvelle droite pour aller plus loin', *Totalité* 11 (1980), 39–46.

Taylor, Jared. *The Real American Dilemma: Race, Immigration and the Future of America*. Oakton, VA: New Century Books, 1998.

Teitelbaum, Benjamin. *Lions of the North: Sounds of the New Nordic Radical Nationalism*. New York: Oxford University Press, 2017.

Teitelbaum, Benjamin. 'Daniel Friberg and Metapolitics in Action', in Mark Sedgwick ed. *Key Thinkers on the Radical Right*. Oxford: Oxford University Press, 2019.

Teitelbaum, Benjamin. *War for Eternity: The Return of Traditionalism and the Rise of the Populist Right*. New York: HarperCollins, 2020.

Terraciano, Carlo. *Nel Fiume Della Storia*. Rome: Insegna del Veltro, 1986/2012.

Tharoor, Ishaan. 'The GOP Alliance with Europe's Far-Right Deepens', *The Washington Post*, 12 October 2021.

The Economist. 'The Strange Afterlife of Antonio Gramsci's "Prison Notebooks"', *The Economist*, 7 November 2017.

The Economist. 'Trumpism's New Washington Army', *The Economist*, 9 July 2022.

The Institute for Women's Health. 'Together We Are Stronger', Video for the launch of the Geneva Consensus Declaration, Institute of Women's Health. Available at: www.theiwh.org/geneva-consensus-declaration/ (accessed 2 November 2023).

Thiriart, Jean. *Europe: An Empire of 400 Millions*. London: Arktos, 1964/2021.

Thiriart, Jean. 'L'Empire Euro-Soviétique de Vladivostock à Dublin', in Christian Bouchet ed. *L'Empire Euro-Soviétique de Vladivostock à Dublin*. Nantes: Arg Magna, 1981/2018.

Tjalve, Vibeke Schou. 'Judeo-Christian Democracy and the Transatlantic Right: Travels of a Contested Civilizational Imaginary', *New Perspectives* 29:4 (2021), 332–348.

Toplin, Robert. *Radical Conservatism: The Right's Political Religion*. Lawrence: University Press of Kansas, 2006.

Tudor, Lucian. 'The Philosophy of Identity: Ethnicity, Culture, and Race in Identitarian Thought', *The Occidental Quarterly* 14:3 (2014), 83–112.

Tuğal, Cihan. 'The Counter-Revolution's Long March: The American Right's Shift from Primitive to Advanced Leninism', *Critical Sociology* 46:3 (2020), 343–358.

Ungar-Sargon, Batya. *Bad News: How Woke Media Is Undermining Democracy*. New York: Encounter Books, 2021.

Varga, Mihai, and Aron Buzogány. 'The Two Faces of the "Global Right": Revolutionary Conservatives and National-Conservatives', *Critical Sociology* 48:6 (2022), 1089–1107.

Vial, Pierre. 'Le GRECE et la Revolution du XXI Siècle', *Le Monde*, 24 August 1979.

Vial, Pierre. *Pour une Renaissance Culturelle: Le GRECE Prend la Parole*. Paris: Copernic, 1979.

Wallison, Peter J. *Judicial Fortitude: The Last Chance to Reign in the Administrative State*. New York: Encounter Books, 2018.

Weatherby, Leif. 'Politics Is Downstream from Culture, Part 2: Hegel to Obama', *The Hedgehog Review*, 18 April 2017.

Wegierski, Mark. 'The New Right in Europe', *Telos* 98/99 (1993–1994), 55–70.

Weiss, Volker. *Die Autoritäre Revolte: Die Neue Rechte und der Untergang des Abendlandes*. Stuttgart: Klett-Cotta Verlag, 2017.

Welsh, Jennifer. '"I" Is for Ideology: Conservatism in International Affairs', *Global Society* 17:2 (2003), 165–185.

Wendt, Alexander. 'Why a World State Is Inevitable', *European Journal of International Relations* 9:4 (2003), 491–542.

Williams, Ryan P., Arthur Milikh, and Matthew J. Peterson et al. 'The Fight Is Now: From the Editors', *The American Mind*, 5 November 2020.

Willinger, Markus. *Generation Identity*. London: Arktos, 2013.

Wilson, Ralph, and Isaac Kamola. *Free Speech and Koch Money: Manufacturing a Campus Culture War*. London: Pluto Press, 2021.

Wohlforth, William, Benjamin De Carvalho, Halvard Leira, and Iver Neumann. 'Moral Authority and Status in International Relations: Good States and the Social Dimension of Status Seeking', *Review of International Studies*, 44:3 (2018), 526–546.

Wójcik, Piotr. 'Międzymorze nie jest ostoją chrześcijaństwa', *Dziennik Gazeta Prawna*, 28 January 2018.

Woltermann, Chris. 'What Is Paleoconservatism?', *Telos* 97 (1993), 9–20.

Worth, Owen. 'Globalisation and the "Far-Right" Turn in International Affairs', *Irish Studies in International Affairs* 28 (2017), 19–28.

Wu, Wendy. 'Cold War Is Back: Bannon Helps Revive the U.S. Committee to Target "Aggressive Totalitarian Foe" China', *Washington Post*, 23 May 2019.

Wylie, Christopher. *Mindf*ck*. New York: Random House, 2019.

Yagi, Hidetsugu. *Han 'Jinken' Sengen* [Declaring against 'Human Rights']. Tokyo: Chikuma Shobo, 2001.

Yang, Joonseok, and Young Chui Cho. 'Subaltern South Korea's Anti-Communist Asia Cooperation in the Mid-1950s', *Asian Perspectives* 44:2 (2020), 255–277.

Young, Katharine G. 'Human Rights Originalism', *Georgetown Law Journal* 110 (2022), 1097–1169.

Zemmour, Eric. *Le Suicide Français*. Paris: Albin Michel, 2014.

Zerofsky, Elisabeth. 'France's Far Right Turn', *New York Times*, 5 April 2022.

Zhang, Chenchen. 'Right-Wing Populism with Chinese Characteristics?: Identity, Otherness, and Global Imaginaries in Debating World Politics Online', *European Journal of International Relations* 26:1 (2019), 88–115.

Zhang, Chenchen. 'Postcolonial Nationalism and the Global Right', *Geoforum* 144 (2023), 1–5.

Zúquete, José Pedro. *The Identitarians: The Movement against Globalism and Islam in Europe*. South Bend: Notre Dame University Press, 2018.

Index

Abascal, Santiago, 7
Adler-Nissen, Rebecca, 146
administrative state, 31, 48, 67–107, 113, 126
AfriForum, 7, 101
American Conservative Union (ACU), 4
American Moment, 139
anti-colonialism, 94, 162, 166
anti-communism, 6–7, 48, 71, 111, 170
antigenderism, 138, 153, 155, 177
anti-Islamist sentiment, 19, 27
anti-semitism, 27, 115, 182
Anton, Michael, 120, 126, 134, 180
Argentina, 5, 46
    Milei, Javier. *See* Milei, Javier
Arktos, 111–114, 118, 122
Arnn, Larry, 125–126
Asia-Pacific Conservative Union (APCU), 6
Australia, 5

Baltic New Right, 60
Bannon, Steve, 5–6, 48, 78, 104, 130
Batthyány Lajos Foundation, 133
Biden, Joseph, 126, 152, 168
Biggar, Nigel, 134
Bolsonaro, Eduardo, 5, 7
Bolsonaro, Jair, 4–6, 9, 45, 139–140, 153, 164
Bourdieu, Pierre, 167
Brazil, 1, 45, 139–140, 164
    2022 Election, 5
    Bolsonaro, Eduardo. *See* Bolsonaro, Eduardo
    Bolsonaro, Jair. *See* Bolsonaro, Jair
Breitbart, Andrew, 47
Brexit, 1, 88, 106
BRICS, 164
Buchanan, Pat, 52, 82, 98–99
Buckley, William F., 72, 117, 124
Burnham, James, 61, 71–72

Camus, Renaud, 91–92
cancel culture, 124, 138, 181
Carlson, Tucker, 8, 46, 134
Cato Institute, 118
Central European University, 124
chains of equivalence, 18, 20, 31, 63–66
Charlemagne Institute, 139
Chile, 5
    Kast, José Antonio. *See* Kast, José Antonio
China, 4, 33, 145, 160, 165
civilizationalism, 33, 158–162, 165, 170, 175
Claremont Institute, 78, 112, 118–119, 128, 141
class, 17, 20, 29–30, 36, 61, 66
Codevilla, Angelo, 89, 119
Collegium Intermarium, 137
colonialism, 12, 134, 146, 150–151, 155, 159, 162
conservatism, 21–24, 76
Conservative Political Action Conference (CPAC), 1, 10, 102, 109, 120, 130
    internationalisation of, 4–7
    as interstitial space, 12
Counter-Currents, 112–118, 121
cultural Marxism, 19, 44, 48, 139–140, 179
culture wars, 3, 28, 49, 52, 55, 137, 156, 172
Cupać, Jelena, 154

de Benoist, Alain, 20, 25, 40, 48, 57, 80, 97, 123, 149, 159
de Carvalho, Olavo, 45, 139
DeSantis, Ron, 119, 128, 181
DeVos, Betsy, 125
digital communication, 11, 32, 108
D'Souza, Dinesh, 117
Duda, Andrzej, 177
Dugin, Alexander, 20, 60, 95, 106, 113, 134, 158, 166

Ebetürk, Irem, 154
embedded liberalism, 144

Encounter Books, 112
Eribon, Didier, 29
essentialism, 16, 33, 65, 182
European New Right, 46, 51, 80, 87, 115
European Parliament, 1, 176
European Union, 88, 168, 172
Evola, Julius, 113
exit options, 145, 163
extreme Right, 23–25, 42

Faye, Guillaume, 25, 40, 42, 61, 88,
    91, 102, 169
Five Star Movement, 95
Fleming, Thomas, 26, 51
Formapolis, 131
France, 1, 29, 43, 123, 135
    Le Pen, Marine. *See* Le Pen, Marine
    Rassemblement National, 4, 25, 29
Francis, Samuel T., 26, 46–47, 51–53,
    61, 73, 79, 83, 98
Freedom Convoy, 2
French New Right. *See* Nouvelle Droite
Friberg, Daniel, 112
Furedi, Frank, 134–135, 180

Geneva Consensus Declaration, 152–153
Germany, 1, 166, 170
Global South, 90, 94, 144–145, 150, 156,
    163, 174. *See also* multipolarity
globalisation, 11–12, 17, 21, 25, 28, 31, 59,
    63, 66–67, 69, 81, 97, 144, 158, 161
Goodwin, Matthew, 134
Gottfried, Paul, 26, 51, 77, 113
Grabar-Kitarović, Kolinda, 177
Gramsci, Antonio, 3, 21, 30, 78, 108
    the radical Right's appropriation of, 40–48
Greece, 44
Groupement de recherche et d'études pour
    la civilization européenne (GRECE),
    26, 40, 42, 48, 114, 123

Harnwell, Benjamin, 130
Hazony, Yoram, 8, 134, 180–181
Hegel, Friedrich, 147
Heritage Foundation, 78, 118
Hillsdale College, 120, 125, 127
Hindu nationalism, 9, 12, 19
historic blocs, 37
Honneth, Alex, 147
Hoover Institution, 118
human rights originalism, 153

Hungary, 1, 4, 19, 132, 134
    Fidesz, 4, 25, 132
    Orbán, Viktor. *See* Orbán, Viktor
Huntington, Samuel, 158

Iberosphere. *See* Madrid Forum
illiberalism, 16, 153, 164
    illiberal elite, 32, 142. *See also* war of
        position
India, 4, 9, 44, 164–165
    Modi, Narendra. *See* Modi, Narendra
Institute of Social Sciences, Economics, and
    Politics (ISSEP), 135
Intermarium, 176–178
interstate defence cooperation, 171
Israel, 5
    Likud, 9
    Netanyahu, Benjamin. *See* Netanyahu,
        Benjamin
Italy, 4, 131
    Brothers of Italy, 4
    Lega Nord, 25, 131
    Meloni, Georgia. *See* Meloni, Georgia

Japan, 5–6, 93, 100
Johnson, Greg, 26, 53, 60, 93, 114–115
Judeo-Christian civilization, 19, 28, 171

Kaalep, Ruuben, 60, 177
Kast, José Antonio, 5
Kaufman, Eric, 134
Keynesian, 144
Kissinger, Henry, 82
Kristol, Irving, 117

Lavrov, Sergei, 162
Le Pen, Marine, 4, 135, 175
Lenin, Vladimir, 21, 43
LGBTQ+, 19, 152, 156
liberal international order (LIO), 4, 17, 32,
    34, 144–150, 156, 160–165, 182
liberalism, 17, 48, 61, 69–71, 73
    new liberalism, 69–81
Ludovika University of Public Service
    (UPS), 133

MacKinder, Halford, 169
Madhav, Ram, 44
Madrid Forum, 7
    Iberosphere, 7, 46
    *Madrid Charter In Defence of Democracy
        and Freedom in the Iberosphere*, 7

Madrid Summit, 175
managerialism, 31, 64, 67–68, 71, 80–96, 142, 150
　managerial elite, 2, 13, 20–21, 29, 31, 73–75, 77, 83, 141, 172, 180
Manhattan Institute, 128
Maréchal, Marion, 8, 43, 109, 134–135, 138
Marini, John, 79, 118
Marx, Karl, 34, 181
Mathias Corvinus Collegium, 133–134
Matvienko, Valentina, 163
Maurras, Charles, 41
Meister, August, 60, 177
Meloni, Georgia, 4, 7, 9
metapolitics, 30, 48–54, 110
methodological nationalism, 9, 12, 25
Milei, Javier, 5, 45
Modi, Narendra, 4, 9, 164
Modul University Vienna, 135
Molnar, Thomas, 82
Mouffe, Chantal, 63
multiculturalism, 18, 57, 85, 101
multipolarity, 33, 95, 145, 158–168, 175, 182
Museveni, Janet, 155
Museveni, Yoweri, 155

national conservatism, 18, 180
National Conservatism (NatCon) Conference, 8, 10, 178–182
NATO, 88, 95, 168–172
natural family, 32, 150, 154
neoliberalism, 13, 31, 144, 169
Netanyahu, Benjamin, 9
New Class, 3, 20, 31, 61, 71, 74, 92, 98, 101, 103, 105, 118. *See also* administrative state
New College of Florida, 128
Nishibe, Susumu, 94
non-alignment, 164–165
North American New Right, 26, 53, 93, 115
Nouvelle Droite, 20, 21, 25–26, 40–43, 48–50, 53, 60, 168–169

Old Right, 19, 27, 115
Opendi, Sarah, 155
Orbán, Viktor, 4, 8, 18, 77, 102, 120, 130, 135, 175
Ordo Iuris Institute, 137–138

paleoconservatism, 26, 46, 51–53
Peterson, Jordan, 134, 139

Piłsudski, Józef, 176
Poland, 1, 137
　Law and Justice Party (PiS), 137
Policy Exchange, 134
Pompeo, Mike, 152
populism, 3, 13–16, 21, 57, 63, 65, 69, 74, 94, 100–101
post-liberal alternatives, 165
postmodernism, 17, 54–61, 139
postmodernity, 158
post-politics, 144
Prince, Erik, 126
Putin, Vladimir, 95, 160–161, 163

QAnon, 105

race, 28, 53–54, 68, 76, 115. *See also* radical Right: identity
radical Right, 144–145, 149–150, 168, 176–177, 181–182
　affect, 21, 25, 67
　anti-Enlightenment current, 23, 48, 54–61
　conspiratorial character of, 2, 10, 91, 105
　counter-hegemonic strategy, 3, 10, 19, 21, 35–40, 52, 63, 103, 141, 145, 152, 176, 182. *See also* war of position
　globality of, 13
　identity, 1, 12, 56–58, 115
　intellectual foundations of, 21. *See also* Chapter Two
　political strategies of, 3, 9–10, 21, 30–32. *See also* administrative state; position
Ramaswamy, Vivek, 85
recognition diplomacy, 146, 162
revolutionary impulse, 3, 19, 24–25, 41, 60, 110, 129, 174
Roberts, Kevin, 180
Rolling Thunder Ottawa, 2
Rufo, Christopher, 128, 133–134
Russia, 4, 33, 95, 145, 160–162, 165–166, 176

Saeki, Keishi, 100
Salvini, Matteo, 131
Schmitt, Carl, 21, 77, 173
Scruton, Roger, 87
Seba, Kemi, 20, 95, 165–166
Siri, Armando, 131
social media, 27, 32, 108, 142
Soros, George, 102, 124

South Africa, 7, 101, 164
sovereigntism, 33, 140, 165, 182
sovereignty, 59, 89, 147, 156, 158, 174
Sowell, Thomas, 118
Spain
    Abascal, Santiago. *See* Abascal, Santiago
    Vox, 7, 46, 136, 175
Spektorowski, Alberto, 174
Spengler, Oswald, 56, 113
status recognition, 146–147, 163
Sunic, Tomislav, 113

The Left
    New Left, 26
The Netherlands, 43
    FVD, 43
    Thierry Baudet, 43
Trump, Donald, 1, 5, 9, 47, 99, 117, 120, 125–126, 152, 171–172
Trumpism, 25, 27, 119

Uganda, 155
Ukraine, 162
Ungar-Sargon, Batya, 118
United States of America, 4, 27, 46, 51–54, 78, 103

America First, 1, 52
Trump, Donald. *See* Trump, Donald
Universal Declaration of Human Rights, 151–154
universalism, 56, 82, 89, 149, 159, 168
University of Austin, Texas (UATX), 129

Venner, Dominique, 25, 40
Voridis, Makis, 44

war of attrition, 21, 143
war of movement, 141
war of position, 31, 40, 45, 52, 108–143
Weber, Max, 81
Weintraub, Abraham, 140
white nationalism, 12, 26, 28, 114–115
wokeness, 19, 44, 66, 102, 119, 141, 171, 181

Xi, Jinping, 160–161

Yockey, Francis Parker, 116
Young, Katherine, 153

Zarakol, Ayşe, 146
Zemmour, Eric, 43, 92

For EU product safety concerns, contact us at Calle de José Abascal, 56–1°, 28003 Madrid, Spain or eugpsr@cambridge.org.

www.ingramcontent.com/pod-product-compliance
Ingram Content Group UK Ltd.
Pitfield, Milton Keynes, MK11 3LW, UK
UKHW022231220226
468302UK00017B/240